The Idea of Race

Other Titles from
HACKETT READINGS

Certainty
Equality
Free Will
God
The Good Life
Justice
Life and Death
Other Selves
Reality
Time

The Idea of Race

Edited, with Introductions, by

Robert Bernasconi
and
Tommy L. Lott

Hackett Publishing Company, Inc.
Indianapolis/Cambridge

Copyright © 2000 by Hackett Publishing Company, Inc.

06 05 04 03 02 01 00   1 2 3 4 5 6 7 8 9

For further information, please address

Hackett Publishing Company, Inc.
P.O. Box 44937
Indianapolis, IN 46244-0937

www.hackettpublishing.com

Cover design by John Pershing

Library of Congress Cataloging-in-Publication Data

The idea of race / edited, with introductions, by Robert Bernasconi and
    Tommy L. Lott.
        p. cm.—(Hackett readings in philosophy)
    Includes bibliographical references.
    ISBN 0-87220-458-8 (paper)—ISBN 0-87220-459-6 (cloth)
    1. Race. I. Bernasconi, Robert. II. Lott, Tommy Lee, 1946– III. Series.

GN269 .I34 2000
599.97—dc21
                                                                99-052338

Contents

Introduction

This anthology brings together some of the texts important for a critical study of the historical formation of the concept of race. Although the attempt to understand almost any concept benefits from a study of the history of that concept, this procedure is particularly valuable in the case of the concept of race. Indeed, it is only by examining the forces, both cultural and political, that contributed to the formation of this concept, that one can begin to make sense of what would otherwise be its anomalous features. One thinks, for example, of the obsessive focus on the black race, often to the neglect of the other races, and of the unique association of the white race with racial purity. Nevertheless, the history of the concept of race is not widely known. There is as yet no reliable study of it. The present anthology presents some of the past layers of European thinking about race, before introducing a sample of the contemporary debates.

The focus of this volume is the theorizing of race, not racism, but the two cannot readily be separated. Nevertheless, and perhaps surprisingly, the development of a rigorous scientific concept of race in Europe in the late eighteenth century was motivated more by the obsession with classification and an obsession with the causes of black skin rather than by the need to justify slavery. To be sure, slavery as an institution played a part in determining how blacks were characterized. The leading theorists of race of the late eighteenth century, like Kant and Blumenbach, were dependent on the information available to them, which was mainly supplied by travelers involved in missionary activity, colonial enterprises, and trade, including, of course, the slave trade. As the debate about abolishing the slave trade became more intense at the end of the eighteenth century, natural historians sitting in their studies in Europe were fed information that not merely reflected existing prejudices but that was designed to reinforce and deepen those prejudices against blacks. By and large, it was another generation before the science that the natural historians produced was recycled into a defense of slavery and other racist practices. However, the story of how, during the Enlightenment period, European travelers contributed to the construction of both the scientific concept of race and the racial stereotypes by providing the descriptions of the physical type and moral character of non-European people has not yet been fully told.

The Concept of Race

There is, needless to say, a great deal of scholarly discussion about when and where the concept of race first arose. Some have tried to find it in the Purity of Blood Statutes of fifteenth-century Spain, which were employed against the *conversos,* Jews who had converted to Christianity but who were still not accepted because of their Jewish blood. Others have sought the origin of the concept of race in the debates of sixteenth-century Spain when the opponents of Bartolomé de Las Casas justified the mistreatment of Native Americans on the grounds that they were not human. Still others have sought it in the Atlantic slave trade. However, wherever one sees the roots of the concept, the term "race" was first used in 1684 in something like its contemporary meaning of a major division of humanity displaying a distinctive combination of physical traits transmitted through a line of descent. However, François Bernier, the first person to use the word in that way, did not address the crucial question of how these "races" were related to the human species as a whole. For this reason, it is not clear whether we should attribute a scientific concept of race to him.

The question of how the races were related to humanity as a whole was imposed on Europeans by the difficulty of reconciling the known age of the Egyptian and the Indian civilizations with the limited time span that a literal reading of the Bible allowed. A similar problem was presented by the need to explain how the diversity of human types could be reconciled with monogenesis, a problem exacerbated by the fact that according to some calculations, the Bible allowed only some six thousand years for the changes to take place. Isaac de la Peyrère took up these questions in his *Prae-Adamitae* in 1655 as the basis for arguing that Adam was not the first human being. La Peyrère revived the ancient idea of polygenesis, according to which there were a number of local creations. La Peyrère's ideas were heavily criticized, but a century later polygenesis was advocated again by Henry Home, Lord Kames, in his *Sketches for the History of Man* and by Voltaire in a number of works, including the *Philosophy of History*.

Immanuel Kant wrote his essay "Of the Different Human Races" in 1775 both to combat polygenesis and to show that the concept of race was a valuable way of organizing the flood of materials about distant peoples that was newly available to European scholars. One finds in Kant not only a clear and consistent terminological distinction between race and species that was lacking in his predecessors but also an insistence on the permanence of racial characteristics across the generations. Both features contribute to the claim that Kant, rather than, for example, Georges-Louis Leclerc de Buffon, was the first to develop a rigorous scientific concept of race. Whatever we now think of Kant's explanation, it resolved a contemporary puzzle. To many observers in the eighteenth century, it seemed that if environment accounted for the races, then whites who moved to America or Africa would, after a number of generations, take on the characteristics of Native Americans or Africans. Any evidence to the contrary was hard to reconcile with monogenesis. By arguing that the original human beings carried the seeds of all four races, that one of those seeds was actualized as a result of environmental conditions, and that there could be neither a reversion to the original stem nor a change to another race, Kant provided an alternative explanation.

If, for this reason, Kant was the first to propose a rigorous scientific concept of race, Johann Gottfried von Herder was the first to deny it. As a student, Herder had attended Kant's lectures on Physical Geography, and his main book, *Ideas on the Philosophy of the History of Humankind*, reflects many of the themes that Kant had addressed both in his lectures and in his publications on scientific issues. The fact that Herder rejected Kant's notion of race suggests that the frequent tendency to identify Herder as one of the main sources for the racial ideology of National Socialism at the same time that Kant's cosmopolitanism is proposed as the antidote needs further scrutiny. It was Herder, not Kant, who maintained that every people or every nation contributed to humanity and thereby provided the framework from which to argue that any action such as forced baptism, the imposition of an alien culture, colonialism, or the slave trade, that interfered with that people's capacity to fulfill its historical mission is destructive of humanity as a whole.

Herder was not alone in attacking the concept of race, but when in 1795, Johann Friedrich Blumenbach gave a place to the notion of "race" (*gens*) alongside the term he had previously favored, "variety" (*varietas*), it was clear that Herder had, at least for the time being, lost the argument. Because the first edition of Blumenbach's great work, *On the Natural Variety of Mankind*, was published in 1775, the same year as Kant's first essay on race, and because Blumenbach himself directly engaged in scientific research, it is sometimes suggested that Blumenbach introduced the scientific concept of race at the same time that Kant did. However, it was only in 1795 in the third edition of this work, seemingly under Kant's influence, that Blumenbach recognized that his own great innovation, the idea of formative force (*Bildungstrieb*), gave him a basis for an enriched discussion of degeneration, which joined physicomechanical and teleological forms of explanation. Blumenbach's varieties were thereby not merely a matter of description. Rather, they were part of what Kant had called "natural history." Nevertheless, Blumenbach remained insistent that his division of varieties of mankind was merely a classificatory convenience. This is a valuable corrective to the widespread idea that all of the early theorists of race as a scientific category were committed to the idea of racial essences.

Although Blumenbach had lent his considerable scientific authority to the emerging concept of race, its place within a universal philosophy of history remained unclear. G. W. F. Hegel's philosophy of history resolved some of these problems at the price of sacrificing both Kant's cosmopolitanism and his reservations about colonialism. In Hegel's Lectures on the Philosophy of History, world history proper begins only with the Caucasians. The other races had either a provisional, that is to say, merely structural, role or in the case of Africans, no role at all. Nevertheless, for Hegel, the decisive historical category was not race, but people (*Volk*). It was as peoples that the Caucasian race participated in history. Although Hegel maintained a clear distinction between races and peoples, in the second half of the nineteenth century, the various peoples were coming to be conceived of as races in their own right. The number of races consequently grew from four or five to fifty or even eighty. The main exception to this trend was those in the United States who sought to maintain an alliance of people of European descent by maintaining a specifically white identity so as to forge a new national identity that excluded blacks, Asians, and the Native-American population. Furthermore, as a consequence of laws going back to the seventeenth century that were mainly designed to control the slave population, European Americans had become accustomed to think of white identity as racially pure. Mulattos were counted as black. The issue of racial purity increasingly came to dominate the European and the European-American conception of race.

Like Hegel, Arthur de Gobineau understood the Caucasians as the producers of world civilizations, but for him race-mixing was an essential moment in the process. There was a law of repulsion that led all races to keep to themselves, but among members of the white race alone, this law was balanced by a law of attraction that led them to look outward. It was this law of attraction that brought about the spread of civilization, but, according to Gobineau, the weakening brought about by race-mixing ultimately caused the decline of that civilization. Whereas Kant had emphasized the progress in history in spite of the decline, Gobineau's focus fell on the inevitability of decline. It was a trend that continued in the twentieth century with Oswald Spengler's *Decline of the West*.

Gobineau's initial reception in English was mediated by Josiah Nott, a physician in Mobile, Alabama, who in 1856 prepared an English version of part of Gobineau's *Essay* with the help of Henry Hotz. The result was a severely doctored text designed to present Gobineau to white audiences that did not want to hear that they were attracted to the other races that were nevertheless not attracted to them. Thus in their edition, Nott and Hotz omitted the laws of attraction from Gobineau's account of race-mixing.

A number of American scientists (including Nott) who were initially opposed to Charles Darwin's transformation of biology became more accommodating when they saw how Darwinism could be reconciled with polygenesis. In the nineteenth century, polygenesis had become increasingly widespread, particularly in the United States, among those who wanted to maintain the separation of the races and to protect the alleged purity of the white race. Although Darwin himself opposed polygenesis, Social Darwinists, like Alfred Russel Wallace in England and Ernst Haeckel in Germany, had developed a revised view of it. Polygenesis no longer meant that the races were created separately but rather that each race became human separately within the evolutionary process. This is just one indication of how Social Darwinism departed from Darwin's own writings.

The most sinister development in the Social Darwinist approach to race was the idea of eugenics. In his essay "Of the Different Human Races," Kant had rejected Pierre-Louis Moreau de Maupertuis's proposal of selective breeding, but Kant had nevertheless insisted on the crucial caveat that there should be no race-mixing. In the first half of the nineteenth century, there had been widespread disagreement, which was based on the experience of breeding dogs, horses, and slaves, as to whether the product of race-mixing was somehow less than both races, intermediate between them, or perhaps even superior in some respects to both. By the end of the nineteenth century, the dominant view was that racial purity was necessary for a race or a nation to maintain its strength and vitality. It was a view that was used to provide a scientific justification both for segregation and for the racial policies of National Socialism.

Many of the worst racial programs of the twentieth century were conceived as attempts to assist nature's own tendency to destroy "inferior" races. This attitude is already reflected in Francis Galton's 1869 text, *Hereditary Genius*. In a chapter entitled "The Comparative Worth of Different Races," Galton, following Darwin's law of natural selection, acknowledged the peculiar fitness of a long-established race for the conditions under which it has lived. But Galton also recognized how the spread of civilization, by which he clearly meant Western civilization, had already destroyed many races. According to Galton, it was "civilization" and not "the pressure of a stronger race" that was responsible for the extermination of the races. In the United States, this suggestion not only was taken to lend a certain legitimacy to the way Native Americans had been treated but also seemed to offer to white supremacists the hope of a solution to what at the time was widely described as "the Negro problem."

Heredity and Culture

It was in the context of this threat to the survival of African Americans as a group that W. E. B. Du Bois wrote "The Conservation of Races." He argued that African Americans have a special obligation neither to assimilate culturally nor to be absorbed physically into the American main-stream. Frederick Douglass had proposed that African Americans seek to be simply Americans, a possibility that was inevitably more open to those who, like Du Bois, were of mixed race. Du Bois's argument in "Conservation" had a ready-made audience at a time when European Americans were reintroducing legal restrictions to assimilation. Based on anthropological and historical research not available in the nineteenth century, he aimed to vindicate the contribution of the Negro to ancient civilizations. He later published *The Negro* (1915), *Black Folk Then and Now* (1939), and *The World and Africa* (1945). In the earlier essay, however, he contests the European philosophies of history maintained by Kant, Herder, Hegel, and Trietschke, among others. Du Bois employs many of the same principles used by these European philosophers to argue that insofar as Africans had not played a prominent role in history, then this fact was evidence, not that Providence had excluded them from history, but rather that it had intended them for a role in the future.

Du Bois wanted to challenge the prevailing Social Darwinist view of race that relied on the theory of evolution to justify claims regarding the inferiority of blacks. Similar questions regarding the role of heredity and the environment in the development of biological and cultural differences between races provide the scientific backdrop for many of the issues discussed by Franz Boas, Alain Locke, and Ashley Montagu. In different ways they bring into question the idea of a hierarchical evolution of human "types" relatively fixed by heredity. The term "racial type" was often used to refer to a unique set of physical and mental characteristics that define the three main races, as well as the many ethnic groups within each race. Given the plasticity of human types, the influence of culture, and the relation between genetics and morphology, science has not established that so-called racial characteristics are hereditary.

From Kant through the nineteenth century, race was at least as much a matter of culture and history as of physical characteristics. Kant's insistence on the permanence of race had served to establish this feature of the concept. This feature came under scrutiny with Darwin and again with Franz Boas. However, Boas issued a broader challenge to the prevailing scientific concept of race. When he redefined anthropology by restricting it to culture, he separated culture from race. For example, in *The Mind of Primitive Man* (1911), he challenged the dogma that Western "Old World" civilizations provided evidence of the racial superiority of its peoples. Within this new framework, race became simply a matter of biology, leaving anthropology with little to say.

The question of whether mental ability is totally hereditary and permanent was the focus of the study that Boas takes up in "Instability of

Human Types." He presents empirical findings regarding changes in the physical characteristics of "branches of the same race" as an indication that mental characteristics may be subject to the modifying influences of the environment. Comparative studies of European-born and American-born children of European immigrants "indicate a decided plasticity of human types." Admitting that there are no observations that can prove that the mental makeup of certain "types" is influenced by the social and the geographical environments, he aimed only to shift the burden of proof onto those who claim that there is an absolute stability of mental characteristics of the same "type" under all possible conditions. Boas meant to challenge the idea of absolute stability of human types as a ground for the belief that certain types have hereditary superiority over others.

Questions regarding the relationship between race and culture are not limited to a concern with whether race is a determinant of culture. Alain Locke contested the claim that race is simply a matter of biology by posing, from the opposite perspective, the question of how race and culture are related. In place of biological "race-types," he proposed a social conception of race in which cultural heritage was a more important factor than inherited physical characteristics. He cites the slow process of cultural assimilation to support his claim that cultural traits were more resistant to historical modification than the biological paradigm granted. Furthermore, whereas previous theories of race had tended to emphasize racial purity as a condition for cultural development, Locke focused on cases where race-mixing at the physical level was accompanied by cultural fusion.

Locke begins with the assumption that "definite culture-traits" and "culture-types" are associated with certain racial, or ethnic, groups. This is a basis for his pluralistic standard of value for relative culture grading. Rather than using race-traits to explain culture types, he reverses this method. Culture-types are "racially composite and have only an artificial ethnic unity of historical derivation and manufacture." As an operative factor, race, when understood in this revisionist sense, can determine the "stressed values" that influence the creation of symbols and cultural traditions. These values account primarily for the persistence and resistance of culture-traits, which are the dominant patterns that establish the type. For example, many of the distinctive elements in African-American culture have developed in the historical context of mainstream influences, including biological intermingling, yet, because of the isolation imposed by law and custom, the "racial" element has persisted through long-standing cultural traditions in dance, music, and folklore. Locke draws in question the culture stages view of social evolutionists in which "primitive cultures are used as stock illustration and argument for evolution." He presents an alternative model based on what he calls an "organic" interpretation of so-called "primitive" cultures.

The attempt by Boas and others to make race strictly a biological concept paved the way to the argument found in Ashley Montagu and Anthony Appiah that race is a fiction. Montagu argues that, from the standpoint of modern experimental genetics, the anthropological conception of race as a biological unit is not only erroneous but also meaningless and thus should be discarded. He cites an important genealogical shift during the nineteenth century, from Buffon's and Blumenbach's earlier recognition of race as "an arbitrary convenience in classification" to George Cuvier's classification of all animals on the basis of possessing "an aggregate of common physical characters" that, varying only under conditions of natural selection, remain relatively unchanged. Montagu points out that it is not possible to classify people in terms of phenotypical physical characteristics because such gross aggregates are not genetically transmitted as relatively fixed complexes. Although science can fruitfully study the frequency distribution of the genes that characterize various geographic populations, Appiah and Montagu are in agreement that the anthropological concept of race has no meaningful role to play in such studies.

The definition of race that Boas employed in his study of immigrant children assumed a correlation between the physical and the mental characteristics of various European "types." Locke's cultural alternative to so-called "racial types" does not deny the biological aspects of race. Instead, Locke sought to replace the biological concept of race with the cultural concept by incorporating different "race-types" into a "civilization-type." Montagu goes a step further to reject altogether, as biological fiction, the use of racial "types." Despite attempts to discredit the biological view, what seems to hold the concept of typological races together is the idea of inheritable physical characteristics that constitute criteria for identifying and classifying people. The highly contested issue of whether race is entirely a social construction underlies this shift in twentieth-century thought toward dislodging the concept of race from its biological moorings.

Racial Identity

Du Bois proposed a definition of race based on sociohistorical criteria. He argued that because of a history of racial intermingling, scientific definitions of race based on biological criteria are inadequate. He maintained that a study of history will show that, although based on the physical, the identity of a racial group "infinitely transcends" biological difference.

Race in this sense refers to a subtle cultural bond that is more spiritual, or psychic, than physical. In his reflections on Du Bois's concern with the question of whether racial difference is a species of biological difference, Appiah emphasizes an important implication of Du Bois's point regarding intermingling, namely, that there is no strict correlation between human races as defined by scientists and the degree of morphological differentiation. According to the biological view, the mental and physical characteristics that define races are determined by a pattern of genes in interaction with the environment. Appiah argues that even if we grant that moral character, among other mental and physical characteristics, may be genetically determined, it remains that "race is a poor indicator of capacity." He takes Du Bois (and science) to task for not repudiating race altogether. As a term of difference, race "stands in, metonymically, for the Other." He insists that race refers only to a structure of relations of concepts that reflect a structure of oppositions, but not reality. The concept of race attempts to correlate gross morphological differences with subtle cultural differences. Race exists in a social world of hermeneutic understanding and not in the province of biology, for "there is nothing in the world that can do all we ask 'race' to do for us."

Appiah criticizes Du Bois for not adhering to his own recommendation that the term "civilizations" be used instead of the term "races." Du Bois, along with Locke and Leopold Senghor, understood that if culture is to replace race, then there should be no biological restriction on cultural assimilation. According to Appiah, "Talk of 'race' is particularly distressing for those of us who take culture seriously." However, Senghor points out in his essay on negritude that, in the case of the French policy of assimilation, "we could never strip off our black skins nor root out our black souls." Race in the biological sense may be largely a scientific myth but has provided the basis on which social relations governed by a European perspective have been globally structured. As a "*complex of civilised values . . . which characterise the black peoples,*" negritude was constructed in opposition to a European claim to racial superiority. Following Jean-Paul Sartre, Senghor describes his use of the mythology of race as an "anti-racial racialism." He points to negritude's humanistic use of this myth in support of what Pierre Teilhard de Chardin called "the Civilisation of the Universal." The pluralism that this use implies is reminiscent of Du Bois's earlier claim of a Negro message that would give to the world a unique cultural gift.

The negritude movement, organized in Paris in the 1930s by Leopold Senghor, from Senegal, and Aimé Cesaire, from Martinique, is well-known for its refusal to separate race and culture. The idea of negritude was developed as a counter to antiblack racism but adopted many of its characteristics. Senghor even proclaimed in a provocative formula, that "Emotion is Negro as reason is Greek." This treatment led Sartre, in a controversial essay, "Black Orpheus," to characterize the negritude movement as "an anti-racist racism" and to locate it as the antithesis in a dialectic that led beyond race. However, even if Senghor acknowledged the influence of Gobineau on the early formulations of the concept of negritude, there were already in the 1930s decisive differences between the negritude movement and other racial ideologies, over and beyond the fact that the movement was a response to oppression. Senghor, for example, proposed "cultural miscegenation" as the basis for a true humanism to replace Europe's and North America's cultural imperialism. He thereby issued a powerful challenge to those who, knowingly or not, used "humanism" as a surrogate term for Western civilization.

Michael Omi and Howard Winant argue that the concept of race is best understood in relation to a political project that it aims to engage. In the light of racial projects such as Gobineau's and Galton's, it is not difficult to understand why Du Bois and Senghor wanted to maintain for political purposes a biologized concept of race. The use of racial classifications based on physical characteristics to justify hierarchies of social privilege has been a source of social injustice. Nonetheless, a biologized notion of race is required to contest institutionalized discrimination and oppressive practices that are based on biological racial classification. For example, Du Bois and Senghor employed a biological notion of race to pursue an antiracist political agenda. Racial identity in the sense that they advocate involves issues of justice and recognition.

Social Classification and Hegemony

In the postcolonial era of the late twentieth century, the social and political implications of definitions and classifications of race are an inescapable feature of everyday experience. Reflections on this experience reveal a subjective dimension of a wide range of social transactions that commonly occur in a racialized public sphere. Linda Alcoff notes that the view of the self presented in public discourse has been influenced by race-conscious public policies. She points out that mixed-race people are more aware than others of the extent to which race is a social construction predicated on a notion of purity, wholeness, and coherence. But if the self is constituted in relationship to racially constructed communities, what happens when there are multiple conflicting communities through which a self is constituted? Alcoff appeals to her experience as a mixed-race person to propose a notion of the self without purity and coherence, and she draws from the views of Leopold Zea and Felix Guattari to present "a postmodern notion of the indeterminate self." In opposition to the prevailing concept employed in public discourse, which implicitly invokes selves that have specific racial identities, she proposes a "nomad subjectivity" that is defined by negation and resistance to racial categories. This subjectivity stands for an absence of identity bounded by no community. Alcoff presents the idea of a Mestiza race as a normative reconstruction of social identity applicable to mixed-race people.

The "nomad subjectivity" that allows mixed-race people to function as "mediators" between Anglo and Latino communities in the United States presupposes that a mixed-race person has the physical characteristics of a white person. Michael Hanchard discusses a Latin American case in which a person with a mixed-race identity (mulatta) experiences antiblack racism. His reflections suggest that racial identity is more than a matter of mere subjectivity—especially in the context of antiblack racial violence. The Ana Flávia incident shows that, with regard to blacks, a racialized public sphere similar to that in the United States exists also in Brazil. Although legally citizens, black people in Brazil, through historical practice, were denied a social status that guaranteed their constitutional rights and access to public institutions. Hanchard points out that "the apparent fluidity historically associated with racial categorization in Brazil needs to be qualified." He draws attention to the fact that, with antiblack racism as a guide, Brazilian racial categories are subjectively interpreted. Ana Flávia could be a mulatta or a Negra, depending on the attitude toward blacks of the person who judges.

What if someone who has lived her whole life thinking of herself as white and who has all the physical characteristics of a white person suddenly discovers that she is legally a black person? The extent to which race is a social construction is highlighted in legal cases regarding racial identity—cases in which the state determines the racial status of a person! Michael Omi and Howard Winant discuss just such a case to set up two opposing views of race. The essentialist view maintains that race is a fixed, concrete, and objective set of biological characteristics, whereas the antiessentialist insists that race is a mere illusion, an ideological construction designed to serve the interests of racists. Omi and Winant propose a definition that "*signifies and symbolizes social conflicts and interests by referring to different types of human bodies.*" The classification of human bodies, of course, is imprecise and, as in the case of Susie Phipps, is compeletely arbitrary. In the light of problems with defining race, these authors prefer to conceptualize race in terms of the sociohistorical process of racial formation.

Omi and Winant maintain that race is to be understood in terms of the historically situated project of organizing and representing human bodies and social structures aimed to establish the hegemony of one group over another. Racial formation is the process "by which racial categories are created, inhabited, transformed, and destroyed." This definition implies that politically motivated conservative and liberal racial projects are always multiply determined. These projects occur not only at the macrolevel of social policy and state activity but also at the microlevel of everyday experience. "Everybody learns some combination, some version, of the rules of racial classification, and of her own racial identity, often without obvious teaching or conscious inculcation." Race functions as a "common sense" way of "comprehending, explaining, and acting in the world." The process of racial formation has constantly changed over time. The present racial order is the outcome of this evolution and, for this reason, the meaning of race remains transient.

1

François Bernier, "A New Division of the Earth"

"A new division of the earth according to the different species or races of men" was published anonymously in 1684. The author has since been identified as François Bernier, who was born in Anjou in 1620 and died in Paris in 1688. Bernier traveled extensively. In 1656 he set out on a twelve-year journey that took him to Egypt, India, and Persia. The record of this journey was published in 1670 as Voyages de François Bernier *and is known in English as* Travels in the Mogul Empire. *Although many European travelers before Bernier noted the different physical characteristics of the various peoples they encountered, especially their skin color, he was the first to group those peoples specifically into "races" on that basis. For this reason, "A New Division of the Earth" can be described as the first text in which the term "race" is used in something like its modern sense to refer to discrete human groups organized on the basis of skin color and other physical attributes. Later writers, including Gottfried Wilhelm Leibniz and Johann Friedrich Blumenbach, acknowledged Bernier's contribution to the classification of humanity along biological lines.*

A new division of the earth, according to the different species or races of men who inhabit it, sent by a famous traveller to Mons. * * * * *, nearly in these terms.

Geographers up to this time have only divided the earth according to its different countries or regions. The remarks which I have made upon men during all my long and numerous travels, have given me the idea of dividing it in a different way. Although in the exterior form of their bodies, and especially in their faces, men are almost all different one from the other, according to the different districts of the earth which they inhabit, so that those who have been great travellers are often never mistaken in distinguishing each nation in that way; still I have remarked that there are four or five species or races of men in particular whose difference is so

From *Journal des Scavans*, April 24, 1684. Translated by T. Bendyshe in *Memoirs Read Before the Anthropological Society of London*, vol. 1, 1863–64, pp. 360–64.

remarkable that it may be properly made use of as the foundation for a new division of the earth.

I comprehend under the first species France, Spain, England, Denmark, Sweden, Germany, Poland, and generally all Europe, except a part of Muscovy. To this may be added a small part of Africa, that is, from the kingdoms of Fez, Morocco, Algiers, Tunis, and Tripoli up to the Nile; and also a good part of Asia, as the empire of the Grand Seignior with the three Arabias, the whole of Persia, the states of the Grand Mogul, the kingdom of Golconda, that of Visapore, the Maldivias, and a part of the kingdoms of Araucan, Pegu, Siam, Sumatra, Bantan and Borneo. For although the Egyptians, for instance, and the Indians are very black, or rather copper-coloured, that colour is only an accident in them, and comes because they are constantly exposed to the sun; for those individuals who take care of themselves, and who are not obliged to expose themselves so often as the lower class, are not darker than many Spaniards. It is true that most Indians have something very different from us in the shape of their face, and in their colour which often comes very near to yellow; but that does not seem enough to make them a species apart, or else it would be necessary to make one of the Spaniards, another of the Germans, and so on with several other nations of Europe.

Under the second species I put the whole of Africa, except the coasts I have spoken of. What induces me to make a different species of the Africans, are, 1. Their thick lips and squab noses, their being very few among them who have aquiline noses or lips of moderate thickness. 2. The blackness which is peculiar to them, and which is not caused by the sun, as many think; for if a black African pair be transported to a cold country, their children are just as black, and so are all their descendants until they come to marry with white women. The cause must be sought for in the peculiar texture of their bodies, or in the seed, or in the blood—which last are, however, of the same colour as everywhere else. 3. Their skin, which is oily, smooth, and polished, excepting the places which are burnt with the sun. 4. The three or four hairs of beard. 5. Their hair, which is not properly hair, but rather a species of wool, which comes near the hairs of some of our dogs; and, finally, their teeth whiter than the finest ivory, their tongue and all the interior of their mouth and their lips as red as coral.

The third species comprehends a part of the kingdoms of Aracan and Siam, the islands of Sumatra and Borneo, the Philippines, Japan, the kingdom of Pegu, Tonkin, Cochin-China, China, Chinese Tartary, Georgia and Muscovy, the Usbek, Turkistan, Zaquetay, a small part of Muscovy, the little Tartars and Turcomans who live along the Euphrates towards Aleppo. The people of all those countries are truly white; but they have broad shoulders, a flat face, a small squab nose, little pig's-eyes long and deep set, and three hairs of beard.

The Lapps make the fourth species. They are little stunted creatures with thick legs, large shoulders, short neck, and a face elongated immensely; very ugly and partaking much of the bear. I have only seen two of them at Dantzic; but, judging from the pictures I have seen, and the account which I have received of them from many persons who have been in the country, they are wretched animals.

As to the Americans, they are in truth most of them olive-coloured, and have their faces modelled in a different way from ours. Still I do not find the difference sufficiently great to make of them a peculiar species different from ours. Besides, as in our Europe, the stature, the turn of the face, the colour and the hair are generally very different, as we have said, so it is the same in other parts of the world; as for example, the blacks of the Cape of Good Hope seem to be of a different species to those from the rest of Africa. They are small, thin, dry, ugly, quick in running, passionately fond of carrion which they eat quite raw, and whose entrails they twine round their arms and neck, as one sees here sometimes with our butchers' dogs, that they may eat them when they want; drinking seawater when they can get no other, and speaking a language altogether strange, and almost inimitable by Europeans. Some of the Dutch say they speak *turkey.*

The remarks I have made also on the beauty of women are not less peculiar. It is certain that beautiful and ugly ones are found everywhere. I have some very handsome ones in Egypt, who recalled to my memory the beautiful and famous Cleopatra. I have also seen some very handsome ones among the blacks of Africa, who had not those thick lips and that squab nose. Seven or eight of them whom I met in different places were of a beauty so surprising, that in my opinion they eclipsed the Venus of the Farnese palace at Rome. The aquiline nose, the little mouth, the coral lips, the ivory teeth, the large and ardent eyes, that softness of expression, the bosom and all the rest, is sometimes of the last perfection. I have seen at Moka many quite naked for sale, and I may say that I have never seen anything more beautiful; but they were very dear, for they wanted to sell them three times dearer than the others.

I have also seen very handsome women in the Indies, and may say that they are beautiful brunettes. Amongst others some are coloured of ever so little a yellow, who are very much prized, and whom I found also very much to my taste; for that shade of yellow is vivid and brilliant, and has none of that ugly and livid paleness of jaundice. Imagine to yourself a beautiful and young French girl, who is only just beginning to have the jaundice, and instead of that sick, pale visage, and those yellowish eyes, dull and languishing, give her a healthy face, soft, laughing, and beautiful brilliant and very amorous eyes, and you will have as near an idea of them as I can give you.

The Indians are quite right in saying that you do not find handsome women in the countries where the water is bad, or where the soil is not vigorous and fertile. In fact, the goodness of the water, and that of the diet, doubtless, have a great deal to do with beauty. It is not, however, generally true, that wherever these two things are found, there the women are always handsome. In my opinion, that depends upon some other conditions, which make beauty more scarce and more dispersed about. It arises not only from the water, the diet, the soil, and the air, but also from the seed which must be peculiar to certain races and species.

The women who live in the Ganges at Benares, and downwards towards Bengal, are generally esteemed. Those of the kingdom of Cashmere are still more so; for besides being as white as those of Europe, they have a soft face, and are a beautiful height; so it is from there that all those come who are to be found at the Ottoman Court, and that all the Grand Seigniors keep by them. I recollect that as we were coming back from that country, we saw nothing else but little girls in the sort of cabins which the men carried on their shoulders over the mountains. But although the women of Lahore are brown like the rest of the Indian women, still they seemed to me more charming than all the others; their beautiful figure, small and easy, with the softness of their faces, quite surpassed by a great deal that of the Cashmerians.

It cannot be said that the native and aboriginal women of Persia are beautiful; but this does not prevent the city of Isfahan from being filled with an infinity of very handsome women, as well as very handsome men, in consequence of the great number of handsome slaves who are brought there from Georgia and Circassia.

The Turks have also a great number of very handsome women; besides those of the country, who are by no means ugly, they have those Greek beauties of whom you have heard so much said, and besides that an immense quantity of slaves who come to them from Mingrelia, Georgia, and Circassia, where, according to all the Levantines and all the travellers, the handsomest women of the world are to be found.

Thus the Christians and Jews are not allowed to buy a Circassian slave at Constantinople. They are reserved for the Turks alone. When our friend speaks of them he is in raptures, and declares he has seen nothing so handsome in Europe. I shall say nothing of European beauties, you doubtless know as much of them as I do.

2

François-Marie Voltaire,
"Of the Different Races of Men"
from *The Philosophy of History*

François-Marie Arouet de Voltaire (1694–1778) first published The Philosophy of History *in 1765 using the religious pseudonym of the Abbé Bazin as protection. In 1769, when preparing a collection of his works, Voltaire made of it a "Preliminary Discourse" when he added it to a work that he had initially published in 1756 under the title* Essay on General History and on the Customs and Spirit of Nations since Charlemagne until Our Times. *In its new form, the whole was given the now familiar name* Essay on Customs and the Spirit of Nations. *In 1655, Isaac de la Peyrère published* Prae-Adamitae, *a work that argued that Adam and Eve were not the first human beings. His ideas were heavily criticized, but a century later, polygenesis was again being advocated by Voltaire in various works, including* The Philosophy of History *from which the following extract is taken.*

What is the most interesting to us, is the sensible difference in the species of men, who inhabit the four known quarters of the world.

None but the blind can doubt that the whites, the negroes, the Albinoes, the Hottentots, the Laplanders, the Chinese, the Americans, are races entirely different.

No curious traveller ever passed through Leyden, without seeing part of the *reticulum mucosum* of a negro dissected by the celebrated Ruish. The remainder of this membrane is in the cabinet of curiosities at Petersburg. This membrane is black, and communicates to negroes that inherent blackness, which they do not lose, but in such disorders as may destroy this texture, and allow the grease to issue from its cells, and form white spots under the skin.

Their round eyes, squat noses, and invariable thick lips, the different configuration of their ears, their woolly heads, and the measure of their intellects, make a prodigious difference between them and other species of men; and what demonstrates, that they are not indebted for this difference to their climates, is that negro men and women, being transported into the

From *Traité de Métaphysique*, 1734. Translated in Voltaire, *The Philosophy of History*, 1766.

coldest countries, constantly produce animals of their own species; and that mulattoes are only a bastard race of black men and white women, or white men and black women, as asses, specifically different from horses, produce mules by copulating with mares.

The Albinoes are, indeed, a very small and scarce nation; they inhabit the center of Africa. Their weakness does not allow them to make excursions far from the caverns which they inhabit; the negroes, nevertheless, catch some of them at times, and these we purchase of them as curiosities. I have seen two of them, a thousand other Europeans have seen some. To say that they are dwarf negroes, whose skin has been blanched by a kind of leprosy, is like saying that the blacks themselves are whites blackened by the leprosy. An Albino no more resembles a Guinea negro, than he does an Englishman or a Spaniard. Their whiteness is not like ours, it does not appear like flesh, it has no mixture of white and brown; it is the color of linen, or rather of bleached wax; their hair and eye-brows are like the finest and softest silk; their eyes have no sort of similitude with those of other men, but they come very near partridge's eyes. Their shape resembles that of the Laplanders, but their head that of no other nation whatever; as their hair, their eyes, their ears, are all different, and they have nothing that seems to belong to man but the stature of their bodies, with the faculty of speaking and thinking, but in a degree very different from ours.

The apron, which nature has given to the Caffres, and whose flabby and lank skin falls from their navel half way down their thighs; the black breasts of the Samoiedes women, the beard of the males of our continent, and the beardless chins of the Americans, are such striking distinctions, that it is scarce possible to imagine that they are not each of them of different races.

But now, if it should be asked, from whence came the Americans, it should be asked from whence came the inhabitants of the Terra Australis; and it has been already answered, that the same providence which placed men in Norway, planted some also in America and under the antarctic circle, in the same manner as it planted trees and made grass to grow there.

Several of the learned have surmised, that some races of men, or animals approximating to men, have perished: the Albinoes are so few in number, so weak, and so ill used by the negroes, that there is reason to apprehend this species will not long subsist.

Satyrs are mentioned by all the ancient writers. I do not see why their existence should be impossible: monsters brought forth by women are still stifled in Calabria. It is not improbable that in hot countries, monkeys may have enslaved girls. Herodotus in his second book, says, that in his Voyage into Egypt, there was a woman in the province of Mendes, who publicly copulated with a he-goat; and he calls all Egypt to witness the truth of it. It is forbidden in Leviticus, chapter eighteen to commit abominations with he and she-goats. These copulations must then have been common, and till such time as we are better informed, it is to be presumed that a monstrous species must have arisen from these abominable amours; but if such did exist, they could have no influence over the human kind; and like the mules, who do not engender, they could not interrupt the course of nature in the other races.

With respect to the duration of the life of man (if you abstract that line of Adam's descendants, consecrated by the Jewish books) it is probable that all the races of man have enjoyed a life nearly as short as our own; as animals, trees and all productions of nature, have ever had the same duration.

But it should be observed, that commerce not having always introduced among mankind the productions and disorders of other climates, and men being more robust and laborious in the simplicity of a country life, for which they are born, they must have enjoyed a more equal health, and a life somewhat longer than in effeminacy, or in the unhealthy works of great cities; that is to say, that if in Constantinople, Paris, or London, one man in 20,000 attains the age of an hundred years, it is probable that twenty men in twenty years arrived formerly at that age. This is seen in several parts of America, where mankind have preserved a pure state of nature.

The plague and the small pox, which the Arabian caravans communicated in a course of years to the people of Asia and Europe, were for a long time unknown. Thus mankind in Asia and the fine climates of Europe multiplied more easily than elsewhere. Accidental disorders, and some wounds were not, indeed, cured, as they are at present; but the advantage of never being afflicted with the plague or smallpox, compensated all the dangers attendant on our nature; so that, every thing considered, it is to be believed that human kind formerly enjoyed in the favorable climates a more healthy and happy life, than since the foundation of great empires.

3

Immanuel Kant,
"Of the Different Human Races"

Immanuel Kant's (1724–1804) "Of the Different Human Races" is widely recognized as the first attempt to give a scientific definition of race based on a clear distinction between race and species. The translation that follows is the first complete rendering in English of the 1777 version of Kant's essay, which is a revised and an expanded version of the original 1775 essay. The only previous translation omitted a number of passages and corresponds to neither version of Kant's text. The importance to Kant of the concept of race is reflected in the fact that he defended it in two further essays, in 1785 and 1787. The second of these, "Of the Use of Teleological Principles in Philosophy," prepares for the second part of the Critique of Judgment, *thereby suggesting a possible link between Kant's writings on race and his critical project that is currently being debated by scholars.*

1. Of the diversity of races in general

In the animal kingdom, the natural division into genera and species is based on the law of common propagation and the unity of the genera is nothing other than the unity of the reproductive power that is consistently operative within a specific collection of animals. For this reason, Buffon's rule, that animals that produce fertile young with one another belong to one and the same physical genus (no matter how dissimilar in form they may be), must properly be regarded only as a definition of a natural genus of animals in general. A natural genus may, however, be distinguished from every artificial division. An artificial division is based upon classes and divides things up according to similarities, but a natural division is based upon identifying distinct lines of descent that divide according to reproductive relations. The first of these creates an artificial system for memorization, the second a natural system for the understanding. The first has only the intent of bringing creatures under headings; the second has the intent of bringing them under laws.

Immanuel Kant, "Von der verschiedenen Rassen der Menschen," 1777, translated by Jon Mark Mikkelsen, 1999, Hackett Publishing Company, Inc. All rights reserved.

According to this second way of thinking, all human beings anywhere on earth belong to the same natural genus, because they always produce fertile children with one another even if we find great dissimilarities in their form. The unity of such a natural genus is, in other words, tantamount to the unity of its common effective reproductive power. To account for such unity, we can introduce only a single natural cause. More specifically, we must, to account for the unity of the natural genus, assume that all human beings belong to the one line of descent from which— regardless of their dissimilarities—they emerged, or from which they might at least possibly have emerged. In the first case, human beings belong not merely to one and the same genus, but also to one family. Alternatively, differing human beings might be viewed as similar to one another, but not related, and we would have to assume that there were many different local creations. This alternative is, however, a view that needlessly multiplies the number of causes. An animal genus, which at the same time has a common line of descent, is not comprised of different species (since being comprised of different species just indicates dissimilarities of descent), but their divergences from one another are called deviations when they are inheritable. Similarly, the hereditary marks of descent are called resemblances when they agree with their origin. However, if the deviation can no longer produce the original formation of the line, it would be called a degeneration.

Among the deviations, that is, among the hereditary dissimilarities that we find in animals that belong to a single line of descent, are those called races. Races are deviations that are constantly preserved over many generations and come about as a consequence of migration (dislocation to other regions) or through interbreeding with other deviations of the same line of descent, which always produces half-breed off-spring. Those deviate forms that always preserve the distinction of their deviation are called variations. Variations resemble each other, but they do not necessarily produce half-breeds when they mix with others. Those deviations which often, but not always, resemble one another may, on the other hand, be called varieties. Conversely, the deviation which produces half-breed off-spring with others, but which gradually dies out through migration, may be called a special stock.

Proceeding in this way, Negroes and whites are clearly not different species of human beings (since they presumably belong to one line of descent), but they do comprise two different races. This is because each of them perpetuate themselves in all regions of the earth and because they both, when they interbreed, necessarily produce half-breed children, or blends (Mulattoes). Blonds and brunettes are not, by contrast, different races of whites, because a blond man who is the child of a brunette woman can also have distinctly blond children, although each of these deviations is always preserved, even when migration occurs frequently over many generations. For this reason, they are only variations of whites. At long last, then, the condition of the earth (dampness or dryness), along with the food that a people commonly eat, eventually produces one hereditary distinction or stock among animals of a single line of descent and race, especially with regard to their size, the proportion of their limbs (plump or slim), and their natural disposition. This stock will surely produce half-breed resemblances when it mixes with hereditary stocks foreign to it. Such half-breed resemblances disappear, however, in only a few generations when members of the stock live in other places and change their diet (even when there is no change in climate). We take pleasure in becoming aware of how we can account for the origin of the different stock of human beings according to the variety of causes that account for these differences. Thus someone from the same region is recognizable simply according to the features characteristic of any one from that province. The Boeotians, who live in a region with damp soil, are, for example, distinguishable from the Athenians, who live in a region with dry soil. Such dissimilarity is of course often easily recognizable only to a keen observer, while others find it laughable. Those features that belong to varieties—which are, therefore, by themselves hereditary (even if not always)—can, through marriages that always take place within the same families, even produce, in time, something that I call the family stock. These features ultimately become rooted in the reproductive power so characteristically that they come near to forming a variation in the way that they perpetuate themselves. Indeed, this development has presumably been observed in the old Venetian nobility, particularly in the women. At any rate, all of the noble women on the recently discovered island of Tahiti do have longer noses than is common.—Maupertuis believes that we might cultivate a noble stock of human beings in any province, a stock in whom understanding, diligence, and probity were hereditary. His view rests on the possibility that an enduring family stock might eventually be established through the careful selection of the degenerate from the normal births. I think, however, that even though such a scheme is, strictly speaking, certainly practicable, nature, in its wisdom, acts to hinder it rather well. This is because major driving forces lie even within the mixing of evil with good that set the sleeping powers of humanity into play. These forces require that human beings develop all of their talents and approach the perfection of their calling. If nature, when undisturbed (without the effects of migration or foreign interbreeding) can effect procreation everywhere, she can eventually produce an enduring stock at any time. The people of this stock would always be recognizable and might even be called a race, if their characteristic feature does not seem too insignificant and so difficult to describe that we are unable to use it to establish a special division.

2. Division of the human genus into its different races

I believe that we only need to assume four races in order to be able to derive all of the enduring distinctions immediately recognizable within the human genus. They are: (1) the white race; (2) the Negro race; (3) the Hun race (Mongol or Kalmuck); and (4) the Hindu or Hindustani race. I also count among the first of these, which we find primarily in Europe, the Moors (Mauritanians from Africa), the Arabs (following Niebuhr), the Turkish-Tatars, and the Persians, including all the other peoples of Asia who are not specifically excepted from them in the other divisions. The Negro race of the northern hemisphere is native (indigenous) only in Africa; that of the southern hemisphere (except Africa) is native only to New Guinea and is to be found on several neighboring islands only because of migration. The Kalmuck race seems to be purest among the Khoshuts, to be mixed a little with Tatar blood among the Torguts, and to be mixed more with Tatar blood among the Zingari. This is the same race which in the oldest times carried the name Huns, later that of Mongols (in the wider sense), and currently that of Oliuts. The Hindustani race is, in the land of the same name, very pure and ancient, but is to be distinguished from the people who live on the other half of the Indian peninsula. I believe that it is possible to derive all of the other hereditary characters of peoples from these four races either as mixed races or as races that originate from them. The first of these two alternatives occurs when different races interbreed; the second occurs when a people has not yet lived long enough in a specific climate to take on fully the character of the race peculiar to that climate. Thus, the mixing of Tatar and Hunnish blood in the Kara-Kalpaks, the Nagas, and others, has produced half-races. Similarly, the inhabitants of the other side of the Indian peninsula, the Tonkinese and Chinese, were possibly produced as mixed races when Hindustani blood was mixed with that of the ancient Scyths (in and around Tibet) and with either more or less of that of the Huns. The inhabitants of the northern arctic coast of Asia are, on the other hand, an example of a race that has not yet taken on fully the characteristics of the Huns. This claim is based on the observation that these people already display uniformly black hair, beardless chins, flat faces, and eyes placed within long slits that seem to be barely opened. These features indicate the effect of the arctic climate on a people that were only recently driven into this region from a milder climate. This is the same sort of development that the sea Lapplander, a lineage deriving from the Hungarians, seem to have undergone. If the sea Lapplander did indeed originate from a well-developed people that previously lived in the temperate zone, then they have already, in only a few centuries, acclimated themselves quite well to the peculiarities of a cold climate. Finally, the native Americans appear to be a Hunnish race that is still not fully acclimated. For in the extreme northwest region of America, on the northern coast of Hudson Bay, the inhabitants are quite similar to the Kalmucks (a likely explanation for this is that the inhabitants of this part of the world might have originated in northeastern Asia, since the kinds of animals found in both of these regions are in agreement). Further south, the face is indeed more open and higher, but the beardless chin, the uniformly black hair, the red-brown facial color, together with the coldness and insensitivity of the natural disposition—genuine remnants of the effect of a long residence in a cold region of the world, as we will soon see—continue from the far north of this part of the world to Staten Island. The long residence of the lineal ancestors of the native Americans in northeastern Asia and the neighboring northwestern region of America brought about the perfection of the Kalmuck form, but the speedy dispersal of their descendants toward the south of this region fostered the perfection of the form now characteristic of the native American. Outside of America, there is no further resettlement of this people. This is shown by the fact that all inhabitants of the Pacific islands, except for a few Negroes, have beards. Furthermore, these people show some signs of originating from Malaysians, the same as do the inhabitants of the Sunda islands. This supposition is indeed confirmed by the kind of feudalism that we find on the island of Tahiti, since this sort of political system is also common in Malaysia.

The reason for assuming that Negroes and whites are the base races is self-evident. As for the Hindustani and Kalmuck races, the olive-yellow skin color of the first of these races—which accounts for the lighter or darker brown skin color that we find in peoples living in hot lands—is no more to be derived from some other known national character as is the original face of the Kalmucks. Both leave their mark inevitably in mixed matings. Exactly the same circumstances explain the origin of the closely-related native American race. This race was first struck in the Kalmuck form, but developed through the effects of the same causes. We may also assume, then, that the yellow Mestizo arose from the interbreeding of east Indians with whites, just as red-skinned peoples arose from the interbreeding of native Americans with whites. Similarly, Mulattoes arose from the interbreeding of whites with Negroes, and the Kabugl, or black Caribs, arose from the interbreeding of native Americans with Negroes.

These other peoples may, therefore, be viewed as recognizably marked blends with origins derivable from genuine races.

3. Of the immediate causes of the origin of these different races

The causes lying in the nature of an organic body (plant or animal) that account for a specific development are called seeds when this development concerns a particular part of the plant or animal. When, however, such development only concerns the size or the relationship of the parts to one another, I call them natural predispositions. For example, in birds of the same species which can nevertheless live in different climates, there are seeds for the development of a new layer of feathers. These feathers appear when such birds live in cold climates, but they are held back when they live in temperate climates. Similarly, the wheat kernel must be more protected against damp cold in a cold climate than in a dry or warm climate. Therefore, a previously determined capacity or natural predisposition lies in it to produce, within a certain period of time, a thicker skin. This solicitude of nature to equip her creatures through hidden inner measures for all possible future circumstances is certainly admirable and enables these creatures to preserve themselves and to be fit for different climates and lands. These hidden measures also make possible the migration and transplantation of animals and plants. Such migration and transplantation may even lead us to believe that new species of animals and plants have arisen, but these apparent new species are really nothing other than deviations and races of the same genus whose seeds and natural predispositions have only occasionally developed in different ways in the long course of time.[1]

1. We commonly make no distinction between the expressions "the description of nature" and "natural history." However, it is obvious that knowledge of the things of nature as they now are will always leave us wishing for knowledge of how they once were and by what series of changes they went through to come to their present place and condition. Natural history, of which we presently have very little, would teach us about the changes in the earth's form, including the changes that the earth's creatures (plants and animals) have sustained as a result of natural migrations, and about the deviations from the prototype of the lineal root genus that have originated as a consequence of these migrations. Natural history would presumably lead us back from the great number of seemingly different species to races of the same genus and transform the presently overly detailed artificial system for the description of nature into a physical system for the understanding.

Neither chance nor general mechanistic laws could produce such matches. For this reason, we must view this sort of chance development as preformed. The mere ability to reproduce a specific acquired character in just those cases where nothing purposive presents itself is already proof enough that a special seed or natural predisposition is to be found in organic creation. For external factors might well be occasional but not productive causes of those creatures that necessarily pass on the same characteristic features that they have inherited. It is just as unlikely that chance or physical-mechanical causes could produce an organic body as that they might add something to the reproductive power of such a body, that is, as that they might effect the particular form or relationship among the various parts of a thing that can reproduce itself.[2] Air, sun, and diet can modify the growth of the body of an animal. Factors such as these cannot, however, produce this change together with a reproductive power capable of producing such change without these causes. Any possible change with the potential for replicating itself must instead have already been present in the reproductive power so that chance development appropriate to the circumstances might take place according to a previously determined plan. Such development makes it possible for things to turn out well for the creature and for it to preserve itself continually. For nothing can become a part of an animal's reproductive power that is foreign to it, since this would make it possible for the creature to distance itself gradually from its original and essential determination and produce true degenerate forms that might perpetuate themselves.

Human beings were created in such a way that they might live in every climate and endure each and every condition of the land. Consequently, numerous seeds and natural predispositions must lie ready in human beings either to be developed or held back in such a way that we might become fitted to a particular place in the world. These seeds and natural predispositions appear to be inborn and made for these conditions through the on-going process of reproduction. Making use of these ideas, we wish to examine the entire human genus as it can be found all over the earth and to specify purposive causes to account for the appearance of deviations in those cases where natural causes are not readily discernible. However, we also wish to specify natural causes in those cases where we cannot become aware of any purposes. I note here only that air and sun

---

2. Diseases are, at times, hereditary. For this to occur, however, no special organization is needed. There needs instead only to be a ferment of harmful juices that are passed on through infection. Diseases are also not necessarily passed on to the next generation.

appear to be the sort of causes that influence most intimately the reproductive power. They also seem to produce a long-lasting development on the seeds and predispositions. This is to say that they could be the factors responsible for establishing a race. My reason for saying this is that a specific diet can surely produce a stock of humans, but the distinctions that identify such a stock as distinct quickly disappear when this stock is transplanted to another place. The reproductive power ought not be responsible for the maintenance of life, but instead for its source, i.e., it ought to affect the first principles of its animal organization and movement.

Displaced into an arctic region, human beings had gradually to take on a smaller build. This is because with a smaller build the power of the heart remains the same but blood circulation takes place in a shorter time. Consequently, the pulse is more rapid and the blood warmer. In fact, Cranz found the Greenlanders not only far smaller in stature than Europeans, he also found the natural heat of their bodies to be noticeably greater. The disproportion between the full body height and the short legs of northern peoples is itself very appropriate for their climate, since this part of the body suffers more danger from the cold due to its distance from the heart. All the same, most of the currently known inhabitants of this region seem to be newcomers. For example, the Lapplanders, who are of the same line of descent as the Finns, that is to say, who emerged from the Hungarian line, have occupied their present place of residence only since the migration of the Hungarians (from east Asia). They are nevertheless already to a certain degree acclimated to this climate.

However, when a northern people is compelled to withstand the influence of the cold of this region for a long time, even greater changes must take place. All development which causes the body only to squander its juices must eventually be impeded in so dry a region as this. For this reason, the seeds for hair growth are suppressed over the course of time so that only so much hair remains as is needed for the necessary covering of the head. By means of a natural predisposition the protruding part of the face, which is the part of the face that is least capable of being covered by hair, gradually becomes flatter. This happens through the intervention of a solicitous nature, in order that this people might better survive, since this part of the face also suffers the most from the effect of the cold. The bulging, raised area under the eyes and the half-closed and squinting eyes themselves seem to guard this same part of the face partly against the parching cold of the air and partly against the light of the snow (against which even the Eskimo need snow goggles). This part of the face seems indeed to be so well arranged that it could just as well be viewed as the natural effect of the climate, since these features are to be found only infrequently in milder regions of the earth. Thus, the Kalmuck facial form, marked by its beardless chin, snarled nose, thin lips, squinting eyes, flat face, and the red-brown color with black hair, emerged only gradually. Indeed, this development of an enduring race took root only after an extended period of reproductive activity in the same climate. These features would, therefore, be preserved even if such a people were to migrate immediately to a more temperate climate.

Doubtlessly, someone might ask how I can justify deriving the Kalmuck form from a people that has lived primarily in the far north or northeast when we can presently find them in their most complete development in a mild climatic zone. I would explain this possibility in the following way. Herodotus reported already in his time that the Argippeans, inhabitants of a land situated at the feet of high mountains in a region that we can assume to be the Urals, were bald and that they covered their trees with a white covering (he was presumably thinking of felt tents). We now find this form, in greater or smaller numbers, in northeastern Asia, but even more prominently in the American northwest, which can be explored outward from Hudson Bay. In fact, according to many reports the inhabitants of this region look like true Kalmucks. If we bear in mind then that both animals and humans must have passed back and forth in this region between Asia and America in the most ancient time, that we find the same animals in the cold parts of both of these regions, that this human race first showed itself to the Chinese in a region beyond the Amur river approximately 1,000 years before the Christian era (according to de Guignes), and that it gradually drove other people of Tatar, Hungarian and other lines of descent out of their places of residence, then this account of the origin of this people from out of the cold regions of the world will not seem completely forced.

However, the foremost case, namely, the derivation of the native Americans as a people that has inhabited the northern most part of the earth for a long time but which has not yet fully acclimated itself to this region as would a distinct race, is confirmed completely by the suppressed growth of hair on all parts of their body except the head and by the reddish, iron rust color that marks this people when they live in the colder regions of this part of the world and the dark copper color that marks them when they live in the hotter regions. For the red-brown skin color (as an effect of the acidic air) seems to be just as suited to the cold climate as the olive-brown skin color (as an effect of briny bile of the juices) is suited to the hot regions of the earth. We can, in fact, come to this conclusion without even taking into account the natural disposition of the native American, which reveals a half-extinguished life power.[3] This diminishment of life power can, however, also be seen as entirely natural for the effect of a cold region of the world.

The extreme, humid heat of the warm climate must, on the other hand, show quite opposite effects on a people that has lived under such conditions long enough to have become fully acclimated. Conditions such as these will produce exactly the reverse of the Kalmuck form. The growth of the spongy parts of the body had to increase in a hot and humid climate. This growth produced a thick, turned up nose and thick, fatty lips. The skin had to be oily, not only to lessen the too heavy perspiration, but also to ward off the harmful absorption of the foul, humid air. The profusion of iron particles, which are otherwise found in the blood of every human being, and, in this case, are precipitated in the net-shaped substance through the evaporation of the phosphoric acid (which explains why all Negroes stink), is the cause of the blackness that shines through the epidermis. The heavy iron content in the blood also seems to be necessary in order to prevent the enervation of all the parts of the body. The oily skin, which weakens the nourishing mucus necessary for the growth of hair, hardly even allows for the production of the wool that covers the head. Besides all this, humid warmth generally promotes the strong growth of animals. In short, all of these factors account for the origin of the Negro, who is well-suited to his climate, namely, strong, fleshy, and agile. However, because he is so amply supplied by his motherland, he is also lazy, indolent, and dawdling.

The indigenous peoples of Hindustan may be viewed as a race that has sprouted from one of the oldest human races. Their land, which is protected to the north by a high mountain range, is cut through from north to south, to the tip of the peninsula, by a long row of mountains. (I am still including, in the northern part of this region, Tibet, which was, perhaps, the common place of refuge for humankind during the earth's last great geological revolution, and, in the period following that revolution, a plant nursery for the re-vegetation of the entire earth.) This land is also fortunate to have the most perfect drainage system (draining toward two different oceans) of any of the regions lying in the similarly fortunate climatic zones of mainland Asia. This land could, therefore, have been dry

3. To cite just one example, red slaves (native-Americans) are used only for domestic work in Surinam, because they are too weak to work in the fields. Negroes are thus needed for fieldwork. The difficulties in this case are not the result of a lack of coercive measures, but the natives in this part of the world lack ability and durability.

and inhabitable in ancient times, since not only the eastern Indian peninsula, but also China (because its rivers run parallel instead of diverging
from one another) must have been uninhabitable in those times of floods.
A fixed human race could, therefore, have established itself in this region
over a long period of time. The olive-yellow skin of the Asian-Indians, the
true gypsy color that is the basis for the more or less dark brown skin color
of the Asian peoples, is equally characteristic of these people and does not
vary in the successive generations. This characteristic skin color and the
fact that it is passed on to successive generations is, in fact, just as fixed for
this people as is the black skin color of the Negro, and seems, together
with other well-developed features and distinct natural dispositions, just
as much to be the effect of a dry heat as the well-developed features of the
Negro seem to be the effect of a humid heat. According to Ives, the
common illnesses of Asian-Indians are clogged gall bladders and swollen
livers. However, their inborn skin color is virtually jaundiced and seems to
manifest a continuous separation of the bile that enters the blood. This
continual separating process also has a cleansing effect that quite possibly
loosens up and volatilizes the thickened juices and, by this means, cools off
the blood in the outer part of the body, even if it does nothing else. The
cold hands of the Asian-Indians might well also be explained by a self-
defense mechanism based-upon this process, or a similar one, that continually eliminates whatever it is that, through a certain organization (that
shows itself in the skin), stimulates the blood.[4] This natural self-defense
mechanism may even be the cause of a generally lower blood temperature
(although we have not yet observed this) that makes it possible to bear the
heat of the climate without its negative consequence.

4. I have indeed previously read that these Asian-Indians have the peculiarity of
having even colder hands when it becomes very hot and that this could be a fruit of
their sobriety and self-control. However, I once had the pleasure of talking with a
certain Mr. Eaton, an attentive and reasonable well-traveled man who had served
for many years as the Dutch consul and head of their establishments in Basra, etc.
He was passing through Königsberg and informed me that as he was once dancing
with the wife of a European consul in Surat he was taken aback when he became
aware of her sweaty and cold hands (the habit of shaking hands is not yet accepted
there). Since he told others about his surprise, he was told, by way of explanation,
that this woman's mother had been an Asian-Indian and that she had inherited this
peculiarity from her mother. Eaton also reported that the difference between the
races is immediately apparent when the children of Parsees are seen together there
with the children of Asian-Indians, since the children of the Parsees are white and
the children of Asian-Indians are gold-brown. Similarly, he said that the build of
Asian-Indians still possesses the distinguishing characteristic of this race, namely,
thighs of a length that exceed the proportion to which we are accustomed.

We now have some ideas about these matters that at least provide us with reasons enough to counter the ideas of others who find the differences among the human genera so irreconcilable that they prefer instead to assume that there must have been numerous local creations of human beings. As Voltaire says: God—who created the reindeer in Lapland to eat the moss of this cold region, and who also created the Lapplander to eat the reindeer—is a pretty good inspiration for the poet, but he does not provide much assistance to the philosopher, who is not permitted to abandon the chain of natural causes except in those cases where he clearly sees these causes connected to his immediate fate.

We now justifiably account for the different colors of plants by noting that the iron content of certain identifiably distinct plant juices varies. Similarly, since the blood of all animals contains iron, there is nothing to prevent us from accounting for the different colors of the human races by referring to exactly the same causes. Perhaps the hydrochloric acid, or the phosphoric acid, or the volatile alkaline content of the exporting vessels of the skin, were, in this way, reflected red, or black, or yellow, in the iron particles in the reticulum. Among whites, however, these acids and the volatile alkaline content are not reflected at all because the iron in the bodily juices has been dissolved, thereby demonstrating both the perfect mixing of these juices and the strength of this human stock in comparison to the others. I must also say, however, that my opinions in these matters are only preliminary, and I offer them only for the purpose of stimulating further investigation in a field with which I am too unfamiliar to do anything more than venture, but with some confidence, some ideas of my own.

We have identified four human races. We can understand all the diversity of this genus on the basis of these four races. However, all deviations surely require a lineal root genus. We must either conclude that this lineal root genus is already extinct or that we can find evidence of it among the existing stock, from which we can generally construct a comparative account of the lineal root genus. To be sure, we cannot hope now to find anywhere in the world an unchanged example of the original human form. However, it is only because of this natural propensity to take on the characteristics of any natural setting over many successive generations that the human form must now everywhere be subject to local modifications. The only part of the earth that we can justifiably think to have the most fortunate combination of influences of both the cold and hot regions is the area between 31 and 52 degrees latitude in the old world (which also seems to deserve the name old world because of the peoples that inhabit it). The greatest riches of earth's creation are found in this region and this is also where human beings must diverge least from their original form, since the human beings living in this region were already well-prepared to be transplanted into every other region of the earth. We certainly find in this region white, indeed, brunette inhabitants. We want, therefore, to assume that this form is that of the lineal root genus. The nearest northern deviation to develop from this original form appears to be the noble blond form. This form is characterized by its tender white skin, reddish hair, and pale blue eyes. This form inhabited the northern regions of Germany and, if we believe other available evidence, the region that stretches further to the east up to the Altai mountains, a cold region filled with vast wooded areas. At this time the influence of cold and humid air, which drew the bodily juices toward a tendency for scurvy, produced a certain stock of human beings. This stock would have gotten on well enough to persist as a race if the further development of this deviation had not been so frequently interrupted by interbreeding with alien stocks. We can, therefore, at least take all this as a tentative account of the origins of the real races. If so, the four presently existing races and the natural causes that account for their origins can be illustrated by means of the following summary:

Lineal root genus
White of brownish color

First race
Noble blond (northern Europe)
from humid cold

Second race
Copper red (America)
from dry cold

Third race
Black (Senegambia)
from humid heat

Fourth race
Olive-yellow (Asian-Indians)
from dry heat

4. Of the occasional causes of the establishment of the different races

No matter what explanation one might accept, the greatest difficulty presented by the diversity of races on the surface of the earth is this: the same race is not to be found in similar regions of land at similar latitudes. We do not, for example, find east-Asian Indians in the hottest climatic regions of America and there are even fewer indigenous peoples in America that exhibit the form of the Negro. Similarly, there are no peoples native to Arabia or Persia that have the same olive-yellow skin color of the Asian-Indians, even though these lands are very much in agreement in climate and air quality, etc. The first of these difficulties can be resolved easily enough by examining the type of people who inhabit this climatic zone. For once a race has established itself as the result of a long residency of its ancestral people in northeast Asia, or in the neighboring land of America, as has now happened, no further climatic influences could cause it to change into another race. For only the original lineal formation can turn into a race. However, in those regions where a race has become deeply rooted and stifled the other seeds, it resists further transformation, because the character of the race has become predominant in the reproductive powers.

How, then, are we to explain the particular location of the Negro race?[5] This race is peculiar to Africa (and in its most completely developed form to Senegambia). It is, therefore, similar to the Asian-Indian race, which is also confined to its own land (except to the east, where it also appears in half-breed form). I believe that the cause of these peculiarities is to be found in an ancient inland sea which kept Hindustan, as well as Africa, separated from other lands that are in close proximity. For the strip of land that stretches in an only slightly broken continuous land mass from the Baikalia border to Mongolia, lesser Bokhara, Persia, Arabia, Nubia, and the Sahara to Cape Blanc, looks, for the most part, like the bottom of an ancient sea. Bauche calls the lands of this region plate formations. They are high and comprised of numerous horizontally placed flat regions. The mountains that we find in this region have been placed upon these flat regions and nowhere do the slopes of these mountains extend very far. The base of these mountains is also buried under horizontal layers of sand. For these reasons, the few rivers that we find in this region only flow a short distance and then dry up in the sand. They are similar to the basins of ancient seas, because they are surrounded by regions of high altitude and in their interiors, considered in their entirety, they hold whatever water that drains into them. For these reasons, rivers neither flow into nor out of these regions. For the most part, these regions are also covered with sand that might have been left behind from an ancient, calm sea. Taking into account all these factors, it becomes comprehensible how the Asian-Indian character was not able to take root in Persia and Arabia, since these regions

---

5. There is also a small strain of Negroes in the hot southern part of the world that has spread out to neighboring islands. Of this strain, we should almost believe— because of the mixing with Asian-Indian half-breeds—that they are not native to these regions but were instead brought over a long time ago by Malaysians who had contact with Africa.

still served as the basin of a sea when Hindustan had presumably already been inhabited for a long time. Further, these factors also explain how the Negro, as well as the Asian-Indian race, could survive without mixing with northern blood for such a long time. This occurred because the Negro race was cut off by this same sea. We see, then, that the description of nature (i.e., the condition of nature at the present time) does not suffice to explain the diversity of human deviations. We must, therefore, venture to offer a history of nature, even if we are also—and rightfully so—hostile to the impudence of mere opinion. This kind of history is, however, a separate special science and it could well serve to move us gradually from opinions to true insights.

4

Johann Gottfried von Herder, *Ideas on the Philosophy of the History of Humankind*

Johann Gottfried von Herder (1744–1803) is best known as the author of Ideas on the Philosophy of the History of Humankind *(Ideen zur Philosophie der Geschichte der Menschheit), the first volume of which appeared in 1784. The first half of Herder's* Ideas *located human diversity within the system of nature, and it is in that portion of the book (Book VII, section one) that Herder rejected the differentiation of humanity into races and insisted that a division into peoples is more appropriate. The second half of the* Ideas *was a broad survey of the history of the world, together with a reflection on how human diversity contributes to the idea of humanity. As a student, Herder had attended Kant's lectures on* Physical Geography, *and his interests as expressed in the* Ideas *reflect some of the themes that Kant had explored in those lectures. Herder's rejection of the concept of race is directed against Kant and represents an important moment in their dispute during the second half of the 1780s.*

NO MATTER HOW DIFFERENT THE FORMS
IN WHICH HUMANKIND APPEARS ON EARTH:
IT IS STILL EVERYWHERE ONE AND THE SAME HUMAN SPECIES

Just as in nature no two leaves of a tree are the same, even less so are two human faces and two human organizations. What an infinite diversity is possible for our skillfully crafted construction! Its solid particles dissolve into such fine, numerously interwoven fibers that no eye can follow them: these are held together by a glue whose fragile mixture escapes all calculative skills, and yet these particles are the least significant things that we have about us. They are nothing other than containers, shells, and holders of the manifold and diversely animated juices that are present in much greater amounts, the juices through which we enjoy and live. "No human being," says Haller, "is completely similar to another in his inner con-

From Johann Gottfried von Herder, *Ideen zur Philosophie der Geschichte der Menschheit,* third edition, 1828. Translated by Thomas Nenon, 1999. Reprinted by permission of the translator.

struction: he is differentiated in the path of his nerves and veins into millions and millions of cases so that it is almost impossible to discover, in the face of these differences between these fine particles, wherein they coincide." If the mere eye of the anatomist can discover this incalculable differentiation, how much greater differentiation must dwell in the invisible forces of such a skillful organization! so that each human being in the end becomes a world, that may have a similar appearance from the outside; but on the inside has a nature of its own that cannot be measured against any other.

And since human beings are not independent substances, but rather are connected to all the elements of nature, they live from the breath of the air as well as from the most diverse children of the earth, from different foods and drinks: they work with fire, just as they soak up light and foul the air: awake and asleep, moving and resting, they contribute to change in the universe. And should they not be changed by it? It is greatly understated to compare humans to an absorbent sponge, a glowing fuse; they are each an innumerable harmony, a living self that has an effect on all of the forces that surround them.

The whole course of a human being's life is transformation; all of the stages of his life are fables on it and hence the whole of humankind is engaged in a continuing metamorphosis. Blossoms fall off and wilt; others bloom and send out shoots: the giant tree bears all of the seasons on its crown at once. So if, according to the calculation of excretions alone, an eighty-year old man has renewed his entire body at least twenty-four times, who can follow the change in matter and its forces throughout the whole human realm on earth in all of the causes of its changing? For no point on our diverse sphere, no wave in the stream of time, is the same as another. The inhabitants of Germany were Patagonians a few centuries ago and are no longer so; the inhabitants of future climates will not resemble us. If we then return to those times where everything on earth seems to have been so different, to the time, for example, when elephants lived in Siberia and North America, when those larger animals existed whose skeletons are found next to the Ohio River, etc.; if humans lived in these areas at that time, how different they were from those that live there now! And so human history becomes a theater of transformations that only He can survey who animates all of these constructs and who enjoys and feels Himself in all of them. He stages and destroys, refines the figures and revises them after He has transformed the world around them. The pilgrim on earth, the quickly disappearing ephemeron, can do nothing but wonder at the miracle of this great spirit in a small spectrum, enjoy the form that he has become among the choir of others, worship it and disappear with this form. "I too was in Arcadia!" is the gravestone inscription for all the living in ever transforming, ever aborning creation.

Since however the human intellect seeks unity through all of this differentiation, and its model, the divine intellect, has married unity with the innumerable diversity on earth, we can therefore return here once again from the colossal domain of changes back to the simplest statement: only *One and the same species is humankind on earth.*

How many ancient fables about human monsters and deformities have already been lost through the light of history! And wherever a tale still repeats remnants of such fables, I am certain that the brighter light of examination will allow this to be enlightened into a more pleasant truth. We are now familiar with the Orang-Outang and know that they have no right to humanity or language; with more careful reports about the Orang-Cooboo and the Orang-Googoo on Borneo, Sumatra, and the Nicobar Islands, the forest people with tails will also be lost. The humans with the backward feet on Malacca, the probably rickets-diseased nation of pygmies on Madagascar, the men dressed as women in Florida, etc., deserve the same correction that the Albinos, the Dondos, the Patagonians, and the aprons of the female Hottentots have received. Men who succeed in banishing mistakes from creation, lies from our memory, and insults from our nature are to the realm of truth just what the heroes in the fables were to the first world; they reduce the number of monsters on earth.

Nor would I ever like the comparison of humans to the apes to be taken so far that one seeks a ladder of things, but overlooks the real rungs and spaces between them without which there cannot be any ladder. What for example could the certainly rickets-stricken satyr in the form of a Kamchadal explain, the little sylvan in the size of a Greenlander or the pongo among the Patagonians? And if one took the matter further and derived certain deformities in our kind genetically from the apes: it seems to me that this supposition would be just as improbable as it is insulting. Most of these apparent similarities to apes occur in countries where there have never been any apes, as the receding skull of the Kalmucks and the Malakulans, the protruding ears of the Yagua and the Amicuans, the small hands of some of the savages in Carolina, etc., demonstrate. Besides, these are things that, once one goes beyond the initial visual deception, bear so little resemblance to apes that the Calmucks and the Negroes remain completely humans even in the construction of their heads and the Malakulans demonstrate abilities that some other nations do not possess. Indeed apes and humans have never been one and the same species, and I would like to see every little bit of the tale refuted that they have ever lived together anywhere on earth in normal fertile community. Nature has provided for each kind and given each one its own inheritance. She has distributed the apes in as many species and varieties and spread them out as far as she could spread them; you human, however, should honor yourself. Neither the pongo nor the gibbon is your brother, whereas the American and the Negro certainly are. You should not oppress him, nor murder him, nor steal from him: for he is a human being just as you are; you may not enter into fraternity with the apes.

Finally, I would not like the distinctions that have been interjected into humankind out of a laudable zeal for a comprehensive science, to be extended beyond their legitimate boundaries. Some have for example ventured to call four or five divisions among humans, which were originally constructed according to regions or even according to colors, *races;* I see no reason for this name. Race derives from a difference in ancestry that either does not occur here or that includes the most diverse races within each of these regions in each of these colors. For each people is a people: it has its national culture and its language; the zone in which each of them is placed has sometimes put its stamp, sometimes only a thin veil, on each of them, but it has not destroyed the original ancestral core construction of the nation. This extends itself even into families, and the transitions are as malleable as they are imperceptible. In short, there are neither four nor five races, nor are there exclusive varieties on earth. The colors run into one another; the cultures serve the genetic character; and overall and in the end everything is only a shade of one and the same great portrait that extends across all the spaces and times of the earth. It belongs less to the systematic history of nature than to the physical-geographic history of humanity.

5

Johann Friedrich Blumenbach,
On the Natural Variety of Mankind

Johann Friedrich Blumenbach (1752–1840) published On the Natural
Variety of Mankind, *his doctoral dissertation, in 1775. He was only
twenty-three years old. It was reprinted unchanged the following year, revised in 1781, and rewritten in 1795. In the first edition of the* De generis
humane varietate nativa, *Blumenbach enumerated only four varieties, but
in 1781 he extended these to five to accommodate reports of "the new
Southern world" provided by such authors as J. R. Forster, who accompanied Captain Cook. It was only in the third edition in 1795 that
Blumenbach named the varieties and, in the course of doing so, introduced
the term "Caucasian." The following selection is from a nineteenth-century
translation of the 1795 edition.*

Five Principal Varieties
of Mankind, One Species.

80. *Innumerable varieties of mankind run into one another by insensible
degrees.* We have now completed a universal survey of the genuine varieties
of mankind. And as, on the one hand, we have not found a single one
which does not (as is shown in the last section but one) even among other
warm-blooded animals, especially the domestic ones, very plainly, and in a
very remarkable way, take place as it were under our eyes, and deduce its
origin from manifest causes of degeneration; so, on the other hand . . . ,
no variety exists, whether of colour, countenance, or stature, &c., so singular as not to be connected with others of the same kind by such an
imperceptible transition, that it is very clear they are all related, or only
differ from each other in degree.

81. *Five principal varieties of mankind may be reckoned.* As, however, even
among these arbitrary kinds of divisions, one is said to be better and
preferable to another; after a long and attentive consideration, all mankind, as far as it is at present known to us, seems to me as if it may best,
according to natural truth, be divided into the five following varieties;
which may be designated and distinguished from each other by the names
Caucasian, Mongolian, Ethiopian, American, and *Malay.* I have allotted the

From Johann Friedrich Blumenbach, *The anthropological treatises of Johann
Friedrich Blumenbach,* translated by Thomas Bendyshe, 1865.

first place to the Caucasian, for the reasons given below, which make me esteem it the primeval one. This diverges in both directions into two, most remote and very different from each other; on the one side, namely, into the Ethiopian, and on the other into the Mongolian. The remaining two occupy the intermediate positions between that primeval one and these two extreme varieties; that is, the American between the Caucasian and Mongolian; the Malay between the same Caucasian and Ethiopian.

82. *Characters and limits of these varieties.* In the following notes and descriptions these five varieties must be generally defined. To this enumeration, however, I must prefix a double warning; first, that on account of the multifarious diversity of the characters, according to their degrees, one or two alone are not sufficient, but we must take several joined together; and then that this union of characters is not so constant but what it is liable to innumerable exceptions in all and singular of these varieties. Still this enumeration is so conceived as to give a sufficiently plain and perspicuous notion of them in general.

Caucasian variety. Colour white, cheeks rosy . . . ; hair brown or chestnut-coloured . . . ; head subglobular . . . ; face oval, straight, its parts moderately defined, forehead smooth, nose narrow, slightly hooked, mouth small. . . . The primary teeth placed perpendicularly to each jaw . . . ; the lips (especially the lower one) moderately open, the chin full and rounded. . . . In general, that kind of appearance which, according to our opinion of symmetry, we consider most handsome and becoming. To this first variety belong the inhabitants of Europe (except the Lapps and the remaining descendants of the Finns) and those of Eastern Asia, as far as the river Obi, the Caspian Sea and the Ganges; and lastly, those of Northern Africa.

Mongolian variety. Colour yellow . . . ; hair black, stiff, straight and scanty . . . ; head almost square . . . ; face broad, at the same time flat and depressed, the parts therefore less distinct, as it were running into one another; glabella flat, very broad; nose small, apish; cheeks usually globular, prominent outwardly; the opening of the eyelids narrow, linear; chin slightly prominent. . . . This variety comprehends the remaining inhabitants of Asia (except the Malays on the extremity of the trans-Gangetic peninsula) and the Finnish populations of the cold part of Europe, the Lapps, &c. and the race of Esquimaux, so widely diffused over North America, from Behring's straits to the inhabited extremity of Greenland.

Ethiopian variety. Colour black . . . ; hair black and curly . . . ; head narrow, compressed at the sides . . . ; forehead knotty, uneven; malar bones protruding outwards; eyes very prominent; nose thick, mixed up as it were with the wide jaws . . . ; alveolar edge narrow, elongated in front;

the upper primaries obliquely prominent . . . ; the lips (especially the upper) very puffy; chin retreating. . . . Many are bandy-legged. . . . To this variety belong all the Africans, except those of the north.

American variety. Copper-coloured . . . ; hair black, stiff, straight and scanty . . . ; forehead short; eyes set very deep; nose somewhat apish, but prominent; the face invariably broad, with cheeks prominent, but not flat or depressed; its parts, if seen in profile, very distinct, and as it were deeply chiselled . . . ; the shape of the forehead and head in many artificially distorted. This variety comprehends the inhabitants of America except the Esquimaux.

Malay variety. Tawny-coloured . . . ; hair black, soft, curly, thick and plentiful . . . ; head moderately narrowed; forehead slightly swelling. . . ; nose full, rather wide, as it were diffuse, end thick; mouth large . . . , upper jaw somewhat prominent with the parts of the face when seen in profile, sufficiently prominent and distinct from each other. . . . This last variety includes the islanders of the Pacific Ocean, together with the inhabitants of the Marianne, the Philippine, the Molucca and the Sunda Islands, and of the Malayan peninsula.

83. *Divisions of the varieties of mankind by other authors.* It seems but fair to give briefly the opinions of other authors also, who have divided mankind into varieties, so that the reader may compare them more easily together, and weigh them, and choose which of them he likes best. The first person, as far as I know, who made an attempt of this kind was a certain anonymous writer who towards the end of the last century divided mankind into four races; that is, first, one of all Europe, Lapland alone excepted, and Southern Asia, Northern Africa, and the whole of America; secondly, that of the rest of Africa; thirdly, that of the rest of Asia with the islands towards the east; fourthly, the Lapps.[1] Leibnitz divided the men of our continent into four classes. Two extremes, the Laplanders and the Ethiopians; and as many intermediates, one eastern (Mongolian), one western (as the European).[2]

Linnæus, following common geography, divided men into (1) the red American, (2) the white European, (3) the dark Asiatic, and (4) the black Negro.[3] Buffon distinguished six varieties of man: (1) Lapp or polar, (2)

---

1. *Journal des Scavans,* a. 1684, p. 133. [Translated as "A New Division of the Earth," pp. 2–3 above.] Comp. Rob. de Vaugondy, fil. *Nouvel Atlas portatif,* Paris, 1778, 4to, Pl. 4.

2. In Feller in *Otium Hanoveranum,* p. 159.

3. After the year 1735, in all the editions of his immortal work. Gmelin has added to the last edition, brought out by himself, my division, T. I. p. 23.

Tartar (by which name according to ordinary language he meant the Mongolian), (3) south Asian, (4) European, (5) Ethiopian, (6) American.[4] Amongst those who reckoned three primitive nations of mankind answering to the number of the sons of Noah, Governor Pownall is first entitled to praise, who, as far as I know, was also the first to pay attention to the racial form of skull as connected with this subject. He divided these stocks into white, red and black. In the middle one he comprised both the Mongolians and Americans, as agreeing, besides other characters, in the configuration of their skulls and the appearance of their hair.[5] Abbé de la Croix divides man into white and black. The former again into white, properly so called, brown (*bruns*), yellow (*jaunâtres*), and olive-coloured.[6]

Kant derives four varieties from dark-brown Autochthones: the white one of northern Europe, the copper-coloured American, the black one of Senegambia, the olive-coloured Indian.[7] John Hunter reckons seven varieties: (1) of black men, that is, Ethiopians, Papuans, &c.; (2) the blackish inhabitants of Mauritania and the Cape of Good Hope; (3) the copper-coloured of eastern India; (4) the red Americans; (5) the tawny, as Tartars, Arabs, Persians, Chinese, &c.; (6) brownish, as the southern Europeans, Spaniards, &c., Turks, Abyssinians, Samoiedes and Lapps; (7) white, as the remaining Europeans, the Georgians, Mingrelians and Kabardinski.[8]

Zimmermann is amongst those who place the aborigines of mankind in the elevated Scythico-Asiatic plain, near the sources of the Indus, Ganges and Obi rivers; and thence deduces the varieties of Europe (1), northern Asia, and the great part of North America (2), Arabia, India, and the Indian Archipelago (3), Asia to the north-east, China, Corea, &c. (4). He is of opinion that the Ethiopians deduce their origin from either the first or the third of these varieties.[9]

Meiners refers all nations to two stocks: (1) handsome, (2) ugly; the first white, the latter dark. He includes in the handsome stock the Celts, Sarmatians, and oriental nations. The ugly stock embraces all the rest of mankind.[10] Klügel distinguishes four stocks: (1) the primitive, auto-

4. These six varieties have been beautifully described, and in fact painted as it were by the glowing brush of Haller, in his classical work, *Ideen zur philosophie der geschichte der menschheit*, T. II. p. m. 4—68.

5. Comp. *A New Collection of Voyages*, &c. Lond. 1767, 8vo, Vol. II. p. 273.

6. See *Geographie moderne*, T. I. p. 62, ed. 5, and Vaugondy, *l. c.* Pl. 3.

7. Both in Engel, *Philosoph. für die Welt*. T. II. [translated as "Of the Different Human Races," pp. 8–22 above] and in *Berliner monatsschrift*, 1785, T. VI.

8. *Disput. de hominum varietatibus*, Edinb. 1775, p. 9.

9. In that very copious work *Geographische geschichte des Menschen*, &c. T. I.

10. See his *Grundriss der Geschichte der menschheit*, ed. 2. Lemgov. 1793, 8vo.

chthones of that elevated Asiatic plain we were speaking of, from which he derives the inhabitants of all the rest of Asia, the whole of Europe, the extreme north of America, and northern Africa; (2) the Negroes; (3) the Americans, except those of the extreme north; (4) the Islanders of the southern ocean.[11] Metzger makes two principal varieties as extremes: (1) the white man native of Europe, of the northern parts of Asia, America and Africa; (2) the black, or Ethiopian, of the rest of Africa. The transition between the two is made by the rest of the Asiatics, the inhabitants of South America, and the Islanders of the southern ocean.[12]

84. *Notes on the five varieties of Mankind.* But we must return to our pentad of the varieties of mankind. I have indicated separately all and each of the characters which I attribute to them in the sections above. Now, I will string together, at the end of my little work, as a finish, some scattered notes which belong to each of them in general.

85. *Caucasian variety.* I have taken the name of this variety from Mount Caucasus, both because its neighbourhood, and especially its southern slope, produces the most beautiful race of men, I mean the Georgian;[13] and because all physiological reasons converge to this, that in that region, if anywhere, it seems we ought with the greatest probability to place the autochthones of mankind. For in the first place, that stock displays, as we have seen . . . , the most beautiful form of the skull, from which, as from a mean and primeval type, the others diverge by most easy gradations on both sides to the two ultimate extremes (that is, on the one side the Mongolian, on the other the Ethiopian). Besides, it is white in colour, which we may fairly assume to have been the primitive colour of mankind, since, as we have shown above . . . , it is very easy for that to degenerate into brown, but very much more difficult for dark to become white, when the secretion and precipitation of this carbonaceous pigment . . . has once deeply struck root.

86. *Mongolian variety.* This is the same as what was formerly called, though in a vague and ambiguous way, the Tartar variety;[14] which

---

11. See his *Encyclopädie,* T. I. p. 523, ed. 2.

12. See his *Physiologie in Aphorismen,* p. 5.

13. From a cloud of eye-witnesses it is enough to quote one classical one, Jo. Chardin, T. I. p. m. 171. "The blood of Georgia is the best of the East, and perhaps in the world. I have not observed a single ugly face in that country, in either sex; but I have seen angelical ones. Nature has there lavished upon the women beauties which are not to be seen elsewhere. I consider it to be impossible to look at them without loving them. It would be impossible to paint more charming visages, or better figures, than those of the Georgians."

14. On the origin of this erroneous confusion, by which the name of Tartars began

denomination has given rise to wonderful mistakes in the study of the
varieties of mankind which we are now busy about. So that Buffon and his
followers, seduced by that title, have erroneously transferred to the genuine Tartars, who beyond a doubt belong to our first variety, the racial
characters of the Mongols, borrowed from ancient authors,[15] who
described them under the name of Tartars.

But the Tartars shade away through the Kirghis and the neighbouring
races into the Mongols, in the same way as these may be said to pass
through the Tibetans[16] to the Indians, through the Esquimaux to the
Americans, and also in a sort of way through the Philippine Islanders[17] to
the men of the Malay variety.

87. *Ethiopian variety.* This variety, principally because it is so different
in colour from our own, has induced many to consider it, with the witty,
but badly instructed in physiology, Voltaire, as a peculiar species of mankind. But it is not necessary for me to spend any time here upon refuting
this opinion, when it has so clearly been shown above that there is no
single character so peculiar and so universal among the Ethiopians, but
what it may be observed on the one hand everywhere in other varieties of

---

to be transferred to the Mongolian nations, compare J. Eberh. Fischer, *Conjecturæ
de gente et nomine Tatarorum* in his *Quæstiones Petropolitanæ,* p. 46, and his *Sib-
irische Geschichte,* T. I. p. 28, 142.

15. The original source, from which the description of the Mongols which has
been so often repeated, and which has been copied as if that of Tartars by so many
authors on natural history, I have found in the letter of a certain Yvo, a churchman
of Narbonne, dated at Vienna in 1243, and sent to Giraldus, archbishop of Bor-
deaux, and inserted by his contemporary Matthew Paris, the English monk of St
Albans, in what is called his *Historia Major,* p. 530, ed. Lond. 1686, fol. This letter
of Yvo is about the terrible devastations of that inhuman nation called the Tartars,
and he speaks of them in the following words: "The Tartars have hard and strong
breasts, thin and pale faces, stiff and upright cheekbones, short and twisted noses,
chins prominent and sharp, the upper jaw low and deep, the teeth long and few, the
eyebrows reaching from the hair of the head to the nose, the eyes black and
unsettled, the countenance one-sided and fierce, the extremities bony and nervous,
the legs also big, but the calf-bones short, the stature however the same as our own;
for what is wanting in the legs, is made up for in the upper part of the body."

16. Thus, at least, I consider myself entitled to conclude from the pictures of the
Tibetans, painted from nature by the great artist Kettle, and shown me by Warren
Hastings.

17. The Indian from the Philippine Islands, whom I saw alive in London at Alex.
Dalrymple's, was in appearance exactly this sort of middle man.

men;[18] and on the other that many Negroes are seen to be without each. And besides there is no character which does not shade away by insensible gradation from this variety of mankind to its neighbours, which is clear to every one who has carefully considered the difference between a few stocks of this variety, such as the Foulahs, the Wolufs, and Mandingos, and how by these shades of difference they pass away into the Moors and Arabs.

The assertion that is made about the Ethiopians, that they come nearer the apes than other men, I willingly allow so far as this, that it is in the same way that the solid-hoofed . . . variety of the domestic sow may be said to come nearer to the horse than other sows. But how little weight is for the most part to be attached to this sort of comparison is clear from this, that there is scarcely any other out of the principal varieties of mankind, of which one nation or other, and that too by careful observers, has not been compared, as far as the face goes, with the apes; as we find said in express words of the Lapps,[19] the Esquimaux,[20] the Caaiguas of South America,[21] and the inhabitants of the Island Mallicollo.[22]

18. There is only one thing I should like to add to what has been more copiously discussed about this point in the section above, that the sort of powder-like soot which can be distinguished in the skin of black men, can by no means, as some authors think, be peculiar to the Malpighian mucus of the Ethiopians, because I have perfectly observed the same thing, although more scattered and less equally distributed, in so many of those Indian sailors who are called Lascars. In one Indian woman, a native of Bombay, who is a servant in my household, I can see as time goes on, the same blackness in the face and arms gradually vanish, though in other respects the precipitated carbon remains unaltered, of a chestnut colour, effused under the epidermis.

19. Thus Regnard concludes his description of the Lapps in these words: "Such is the description of that little man they call the Laplander, and I may say that there is no animal, after the ape, which so nearly approaches the man." *Oeuvres*, T. I. p. 71.

20. When the Esquimaux Attuioch, whose picture taken from the life I owe to Sir Joseph Banks, saw an ape in London for the first time, he asked his companion Cartwright in astonishment, "Is that an Esquimaux?" and he adds in his account, "I must confess, that both the colour and contour of the countenance had considerable resemblance to the people of their nation."

21. "As like apes as men," says Nic. del Techo of them, *Relatione de Caaiguarum gente*, p. m. 34.

22. Of these, J. R. Forster says in his *Bemerkungen*, p. 217, "The inhabitants of the island Mallicollo appear to have a nearer relationship to the apes than any I have ever seen."

88. *American variety.* It is astonishing and humiliating what quantities
of fables were formerly spread about the racial characters of this variety.
Some have denied beards to the men,[23] others menstruation to the
women.[24] Some have attributed one and the same colour[25] to each and all
the Americans; others a perfectly similar countenance to all of them.[26] It
has been so clearly demonstrated now by the unanimous consent of accu-
rate and truthful observers, that the Americans are not naturally beardless,
that I am almost ashamed of the unnecessary trouble I formerly took to get
together a heap of testimony,[27] by which it is proved that not only
throughout the whole of America, from the Esquimaux downwards to the
inhabitants of Tierra del Fuego, are there groups of inhabitants who
cherish a beard; but also it is quite undeniable as to the other beardless
ones that they eradicate and pluck out their own by artifice and on purpose, in the same way as has been customary among so many other nations,
the Mongolians[28] for example, and the Malays.[29] We all know that the
beard of the Americans is thin and scanty, as is also the case with so many
Mongolian nations. They ought therefore no more to be called beardless,
than men with scanty hair to be called bald. Those therefore who thought
the Americans were naturally beardless fell into the same error as that
which induced the ancients to suppose and persuade others, that the birds
of paradise, from whose corpses the feet are often cut off, were naturally
destitute of feet.

The fabulous report that the American women have no menstruation,
seems to have had its origin in this, that the Europeans when they
discovered the new world, although they saw numbers of the female
inhabitants almost entirely naked, never seem to have observed in them
the stains of that excretion.[30] For this it seems likely that there were two

---

23. See De Pauw in *Recherches philosophiques sur les Americains,* T. I. p. 37.

24. See Schurigius, *Parthenologia,* p. 200.

25. See Home in *Sketches of the History of Man,* Vol. I. p. 13.

26. Comp. Robertson's *History of America,* Vol. II. p. m. 404.

27. I cited a few out of many others some years ago in *Gottingisch. Magazin,* 2d
year, P. VI. p. 419.

28. See besides many others J. G. Gmelin, *Reise durch Sibirien,* T. II. p. 125. "It is
very difficult to find amongst the Tungus, or any of these people, a beard. For as
soon as one appears, they pull the hair out, and at last bring it to this that there is
nothing more spring up."

29. Comp. on the Sumatrans, Marsden; on the Magindans, Forrest; on the Pelew
Islanders, Wilson; on the Papuans, Carteret; on the inhabitants of the Navigator's
group, Bougainville, &c.

30. Lery, *Voyage faict en le terre du Bresil,* p. m. 270.

reasons; first, that amongst those nations of America, the women during menstruation are, by a fortunate prejudice, considered as poisonous, and are prohibited from social intercourse, and for so long enjoy a beneficial repose in the more secluded huts far from the view of men;[31] secondly, because, as has been noticed,[32] they are so commendably clean in their bodies, and the commissure of their legs so conduces to modesty, that no vestiges of the catamenia ever strike the eye.

As to the colour of the skin of this variety, on the one hand it has been observed above, that it is by no means so constant as not in many cases to shade away into black . . . ; and on the other, that it is easily seen, from the nature of the American climate,[33] and the laws of degeneration when applied to the extremely probable origin of the Americans from northern Asia,[34] why they are not liable to such great diversities of colour, as the other descendants of Asiatic autochthones, who peopled the ancient world. The same reason holds good as to the appearance of the Americans. Careful eye-witnesses long ago laughed at the foolish, or possibly facetious hyperbole of some, who asserted that the inhabitants of the new world were so exactly alike, that when a man had seen one, he could say that he had seen all,[35] &c. It is, on the contrary, proved by the finished drawings of Americans by the best artists, and by the testimony of the most trustworthy eye-witnesses, that in this variety of mankind, as in others, countenances of all sorts occur;[36] although in general that sort of racial confor-

31. Comp. Sagard, *Voyage du pays des Hurons*, p. 78.

32. Van Berkel's *Reisen nach R. de Berbice und Surinam*, p. 46.

33. Zimmermann, *Geographische geschichte des menschen*, T. I. p. 87.

34. Kant, in *Teutschen Mercur*, a. 1788, T. I. p. 119.

35. See Molina, *Sulla storia naturale del Chili*, p. 336. "I laugh in my sleeve when I read in certain modern writers, supposed to be diligent observers, that all the Americans have the same appearance, and that when a man has seen one, he may say that he has seen them all. Such authors allow themselves to be too easily deceived by certain vague appearances of similarity which have to do for the most part with colour, and which vanish as soon as ever the individuals of one nation are confronted with those of another. A Chilian does not differ less in aspect from a Peruvian, than an Italian from a German. I have seen myself Paraguayanos, Cujanos, and Magellanos, all of whom have their peculiar lineaments which are easily distinguished from those of the others."

36. Thus, to bring a few examples from South America alone, Nic. del Techo describes the Caaiguas with apish nostrils: Mart. Dobrizhoffer says that the neighbouring Abipones, on the contrary, are often remarkable for aquiline noses: Ulloa attributes a narrow and hooked nose to the Peruvians; Molina, one somewhat broad to the Chilians; G. Forster, one very depressed to the islanders of Tierra del Fuego.

mation may be considered as properly belonging to them which we attributed to them above. . . . It was justly observed by the first Europeans[37] who visited the new continent, that the Americans came very near to the Mongolians, which adds fresh weight to the very probable opinion that the Americans came from northern Asia, and derived their origin from the Mongolian nation. It is probable that migrations of that kind took place at different times, after considerable intervals, according as various physical, geological, or political catastrophes gave occasion to them; and hence, if any place is allowed for conjecture in these investigations, the reason may probably be derived, why the Esquimaux have still much more of the Mongolian appearance[38] about them than the rest of the Americans: partly, because the catastrophe which drove them from northern Asia must be much more recent, and so they are a much later arrival;[39] and partly because the climate of the new country, which they now inhabit, is much more homogeneous with that of their original country. In fact, unless I am much mistaken, we must attribute to the same influence I mentioned above . . . , which the climate has in preserving or restoring the racial appearance, the fact that the inhabitants of the cold southern extremity of South America, as the barbarous inhabitants of the Straits of Magellan, seem to come nearer, and as it were fall back, to the original Mongolian countenance.[40]

89. *The Malay variety.* As the Americans in respect of racial appearance hold as it were a place between the medial variety of mankind, which we called the Caucasian, and one of the two extremes, that is the Mongolian; so the Malay variety makes the transition from that medial variety to the other extreme, namely, the Ethiopian. I wish to call it the Malay, because the majority of the men of this variety, especially those who inhabit the Indian islands close to the Malacca peninsula, as well as the Sandwich, the

37. *Lettere di Amer. Vespucci*, p. 9, ed. Bandini. "They are not very handsome, because their faces are wide, which makes them like Tartars."

38. This I see most clearly both in two Esquimaux skulls from Nain, a colony of Labrador, which adorn my collection, and in the pictures of these barbarians taken from the life by good artists, which I owe to the liberality of Sir J. Banks.

39. The paradox of Robertson, who derived the Esquimaux from the Normans, in his *History of America*, Vol. II. p. 40, scarcely deserves a refutation at this time.

40. Thus that classical Argonaut and capital eye-witness and observer, Linschot, compares the inhabitants of the strait of Magellan whom he saw, in physiognomy, appearance, colour, hair and beard, to the Samoiedes, with whom he was very well acquainted through his famous journey to the strait of Nassovitch, in his notes to *Acosta*, p. 46 *b*.

Society, and the Friendly Islanders, and also the Malambi of Madagascar down to the inhabitants of Easter Island, use the Malay idiom.[41]

Meanwhile even these differ so much between themselves through various degrees of beauty and other corporeal attributes, that there are some who divide the Otaheitans themselves into two distinct races;[42] the first paler in colour, of lofty stature, with face which can scarcely be distinguished from that of the European; the second, on the other hand, of moderate stature, colour and face little different from that of Mulattos, curly hair, &c.[43] This last race then comes very near those men who inhabit the islands more to the south in the Pacific Ocean, of whom the inhabitants of the New Hebrides in particular come sensibly near the Papuans and New Hollanders, who finally on their part graduate away so insensibly towards the Ethiopian variety, that, if it was thought convenient, they might not unfairly be classed with them, in that distribution of the varieties we were talking about.

90. *Conclusion.* Thus too there is with this that insensible transition by which as we saw the other varieties also run together, and which, compared with what was discussed in the earlier sections of the book, about the causes and ways of degeneration, and the analogous phenomena of degeneration in the other domestic animals, brings us to that conclusion, which seems to flow spontaneously from physiological principles applied by the aid of critical zoology to the natural history of mankind; which is, *That no doubt can any longer remain but that we are with great probability right in referring all and singular as many varieties of man as are at present known to one and the same species.*

41. Sir J. Banks first of all showed this in Hawkesworth's *Collection*, Vol. III. p. 373, then after him Bryant in Cook's *Voyage to the Northern Hemisphere*, Vol. III. App. No. 2, p. 528, and Marsden in *Archæologia*, Vol. VI. p. 154.

42. See Bougainville in *Voyage autour du Monde*, p. 213.

43. Thus long ago the immortal De Quiros, who first discovered the Society Islands, accurately distinguished these varieties among the inhabitants of the islands in the Pacific Ocean, when he called some white, and compared some to the Mulattos, and some to the Ethiopians. See Dalrymple, *Collection of Voyages to the South Pacific Ocean*, Vol. I. p. 164.

6

G. W. F. Hegel,
"Anthropology,"
from the *Encyclopaedia of the*
Philosophical Sciences

Georg Wilhelm Friedrich Hegel (1770–1831) was Professor of Philosophy in Berlin. The following sketch of Hegel's account of the races is taken from the 1830 text of Hegel's Encyclopaedia of the Philosophical Sciences *and includes the Additions* (Zusätze). *The* Zusätze *were compiled from a variety of sources, mainly the lecture notes of Hegel's students, by Ludwig Boumann when in 1845 he edited Hegel's text for republication. Although Hegel's readers have found the* Zusätze *helpful as a way into Hegel's thought, they must always be used with some caution, and there is no exception in this case. Nevertheless, the impact of Hegel's thought on race, as reflected in some of his followers like Michelet, and in particular in his scandalous caricature of Africa, that is set out in more detail in the various editions of Hegel's* Lectures on the Philosophy of History, *give these passages a historical importance that transcends any doubts that one might entertain about their authenticity.*

§393

According to the concrete differences of the terrestrial globe, the general planetary life of the nature-governed mind specializes itself and breaks up into the several nature-governed minds which, on the whole, give expression to the nature of the geographical continents and constitute the diversities of *race*.

The contrast between the earth's poles, the land towards the north pole being more aggregated and preponderant over sea, whereas in the southern hemisphere it runs out in sharp points, widely distant from each other, introduces into the differences of continents a further modification which Treviranus (*Biology*, Part II) has exhibited in the case of the flora and fauna.

Zusatz. With respect to the diversity of races of mankind it must be remembered first of all that the purely historical question, whether all these races sprang from a single pair of human beings or from several, is of no concern whatever to us in philosophy. Importance was attached to this question because it was believed that by assuming descent from several couples, the mental or spiritual superiority of one race over another could be explained, indeed, it was hoped to prove that human beings are by nature so differently endowed with mental or spiritual capacities that some can be dominated like animals. But descent affords no ground for granting or denying freedom and dominion to human beings. Man is implicitly rational; herein lies the possibility of equal justice for all men and the futility of a rigid distinction between races which have rights and those which have none. The difference between the races of mankind is still a natural difference, that is, a difference which, in the first instance, concerns the natural soul. As such, the difference is connected with the geographical differences of those parts of the world where human beings are gathered together in masses. These different parts are what we call continents. In these organic divisions of the Earth's individuality there is an element of necessity, the detailed exposition of which belongs to geography

The basic division of the Earth is into the Old and the New World. In the first instance, this distinction relates to the earlier or later knowledge of the continents in world history. Here, this distinction is for us a matter of indifference. What we are concerned with is the determinateness which constitutes the distinctive character of the continents. In this respect, it must be said that America has a younger appearance than the Old World and in its historical development is inferior to the latter. America exhibits only the general difference of north and south with a quite narrow middle between the two extremes. The indigenous races of this continent are dying out; the Old World is refashioning itself in the New. The Old World is distinguished from America by the fact that it is sundered into specific differences, into three continents, of which one, Africa, taken as a whole, appears as a land mass belonging to a compact unity, as a lofty mountain range shutting off the coast; the second, Asia, presents the antithesis of highlands and great valleys irrigated by broad rivers; while the third, Europe, reveals the unity of the undifferentiated unity of Africa and the unmediated antithesis of Asia, since in it mountain and valley are not juxtaposed as two great halves of the continent as in Asia, but everywhere penetrate each other. These three continents which are circumjacent to the Mediterranean are not separated but linked together by it. North Africa up to the boundary of the sandy desert already by its character belongs to Europe; the inhabitants of this part of Africa are not strictly

Africans, that is, negroes, but are akin to Europeans. Similarly the whole of Western Asia is European in character; the Asiatic race proper, the Mongols, inhabit the Far East.

After having thus attempted to show that the differences between the continents are not contingent but necessary, we shall now characterize the racial diversities of humanity in their physical and mental or spiritual bearings which go together with these differences. As regards physical characteristics, physiology distinguishes the Caucasian, Ethiopian, and Mongolian races, with which must also be reckoned the races of Malay and America which, however, form an aggregate of infinitely various particularities rather than a sharply distinct race. Now the physical difference between all these races is shown mainly in the formation of the skull and the face. The formation of the skull is defined by a horizontal and a vertical line, the former running from the outer ear-ducts to the root of the nose, the latter from the frontal bone to the upper jaw-bone. It is by the angle formed by these two lines that the head of the animal is distinguished from the human head; in animals this angle is extremely acute. Another important factor, noted by Blumenbach, concerns the greater or less prominence of the cheek-bones. The arching and width of the forehead is also a determining factor.

Now in the Caucasian race this angle is almost or entirely a right-angle. This applies particularly to the Italian, Georgian, and Circassian physiognomy. In this race the skull is spherical on top, the forehead gently arched, the cheek-bones pushed back, the front teeth in both jaws perpendicular, the skin white with red cheeks and the hair long and soft.

The characteristic of the Mongol race is revealed in the prominence of the cheek-bones, in the eyes which are not round but narrow-slit, in the compressed nose, in the yellow colour of the skin and in the short stiff black hair.

Negroes have narrower skulls than Mongols and Caucasians, their foreheads are arched but bulging, their jaw-bones are prominent and the teeth slope, their lower jaw juts well out, their skin is more or less black, their hair is woolly and black.

The Malayan and American Indian races are less sharply distinguished in their physical formation than the races just described; the skin of the Malays is brown and that of the American Indian copper-coloured.

The mental and spiritual characteristics of these races are as follows.

Negroes are to be regarded as a race of children who remain immersed in their state of uninterested *naïveté*. They are sold, and let themselves be sold, without any reflection on the rights or wrongs of the matter. The Higher which they feel they do not hold fast to, it is only a fugitive thought. This Higher they transfer to the first stone they come across, thus making it their fetish and they throw this fetish away if it fails to help them. Good-natured and harmless when at peace, they can become suddenly enraged and then commit the most frightful cruelties. They cannot be denied a capacity for education; not only have they, here and there, adopted Christianity with the greatest gratitude and spoken movingly of the freedom they have acquired through Christianity after a long spiritual servitude, but in Haiti they have even formed a State on Christian principles. But they do not show an inherent striving for culture. In their native country the most shocking despotism prevails. There they do not attain to the feeling of human personality, their mentality is quite dormant, remaining sunk within itself and making no progress, and thus corresponding to the compact, differenceless mass of the African continent.

The Mongols, on the other hand, rise above this childish *naïveté;* they reveal as their characteristic feature a restless mobility which comes to no fixed result and impels them to spread like monstrous locust swarms over other countries and then to sink back again into the thoughtless indifference and dull inertia which preceded this outburst. Similarly, the Mongols display in themselves an acute contrast between the sublime and monstrous, on the one hand, and the most trivial, pettiest pedantry, on the other. Their religion already contains the conception of a universal which they venerate as God. But they cannot as yet endure this God as invisible; he is present in human shape, or at least announces himself through some human being or other. This occurs with the Tibetans, where often a child is chosen to be the present, visible god, and when such a god dies, the monks seek another one among the people; but all this succession of gods enjoys the profoundest veneration. The essential feature of this religion reaches as far as India where the Hindus likewise regard a human being, the Brahmin, as god, and the withdrawal of the human spirit into its indeterminate universality is held to be divine, to be the immediate identity with God. In the Asiatic race, therefore, mind is already beginning to awake, to separate itself from the life of Nature. But this separation is not yet clear-cut, not yet absolute. Mind does not as yet grasp itself in its absolute freedom, does not as yet know itself as the concrete universal which is for itself, has not as yet made its Notion into an object for itself in the form of thought. For this reason it still exists as an immediate individual, a form which contradicts the nature of mind. God does indeed become objective, but not in the form of absolutely free thought, but in that of an immediately existent finite mind or spirit. With this is connected the worship of the dead, for in these the life of Nature has perished; the remembrance of them holds fast only to the universal manifested in them and rises, therefore, above the individuality of the manifestation. But the universal is always, on the one hand, held fast only as a quite abstract universal, and on the other hand, is perceived only in an out-and-out contingent, immediate existence. The Hindus, for example, contemplate the universal God as present in the whole of Nature, in rivers and mountains just as in men. Asia represents, therefore, both in a physical and a spiritual reference the moment of opposition, but of unmediated opposition, the mediationless collapse of the opposed determinations. Here, on the one hand, mind separates itself from Nature, and on the other hand, falls back again into the life of Nature, since it attains actuality not within itself but only in the natural sphere. In this identity of mind with Nature true freedom is impossible. Here man cannot as yet attain to consciousness of his personality and in his individuality has neither value nor rights, neither with the Hindus nor the Chinese; the latter have no compunction in exposing or simply destroying their infants.

It is in the Caucasian race that mind first attains to absolute unity with itself. Here for the first time mind enters into complete opposition to the life of Nature, apprehends itself in its absolute self-dependence, wrests itself free from the fluctuation between one extreme and the other, achieves *self*-determination, *self*-development, and in doing so creates world-history. The Mongols, as we have already mentioned, are characterized by an impetuosity which impels them outwards beyond their borders, but it dies away as quickly as it came, acts not constructively but only destructively, and produces no advance in world-history. This advance is first brought about by the Caucasian race.

In this, however, we have to distinguish two sides, the Western Asiatics and the Europeans; this distinction now coincides with that of Mohammedans and Christians.

In Mohammedanism the limited principle of the Jews is expanded into universality and thereby overcome. Here, God is no longer, as with the Asiatics, contemplated as existent in immediately sensuous mode but is apprehended as the one infinite sublime Power beyond all the multiplicity of the world. Mohammedanism is, therefore, in the strictest sense of the word, the religion of sublimity. The character of the western Asiatics, especially the Arabs, is completely in accord with this religion. This race, in its aspiration to the One God, is indifferent to everything finite, to all misery, and gives generously of its life and its wealth; even today its courage and liberality earns our recognition. But the western Asiatic mind which clings to the abstract One does not get as far as the determination, the particularization, of the universal and consequently does not attain to a concrete formation. Here, it is true, this mind destroys the caste system and all its works which prevail in India, and every Mohammedan is free; despotism in the strict meaning of the word does not exist among them. Political life, however, does not yet achieve the form of a rationally organized whole, of a differentiation into special governmental powers. And as regards individuals these, on the one hand, certainly hold themselves sublimely aloof from subjective, finite aims but again, on the other hand, they also hurl themselves with unbridled instincts into the pursuit of such aims which, with them, lack all trace of the universal because here the universal has so far not attained to an immanent self-differentiation. So it is that here, along with the noblest sentiments, there exists the greatest vindictiveness and guile.

Europeans, on the contrary, have for their principle and character the concrete universal, self-determining Thought. The Christian God is not merely the differenceless One, but the triune God who contains difference within himself, who has become man and who reveals himself. In this religious conception the opposition of universal and particular, of Thought and Being, is present in its most developed form and yet has also been brought back again to unity. Here, then, the particular is not left so quiescent in its immediacy as in Mohammedanism; on the contrary, it is determined by thought, just as, conversely, the universal here develops itself to particularization. The principle of the European mind is, therefore, self-conscious Reason which is confident that for it there can be no insuperable barrier and which therefore takes an interest in everything in order to become present to itself therein. The European mind opposes the world to itself, makes itself free of it, but in turn annuls this opposition, takes its Other, the manifold, back into itself, into its unitary nature. In Europe, therefore, there prevails this infinite thirst for knowledge which is alien to other races. The European is interested in the world, he wants to know it, to make this Other confronting him his own, to bring to view the genus, law, universal, thought, the inner rationality, in the particular forms of the world. As in the theoretical, so too in the practical sphere, the European mind strives to make manifest the unity between itself and the outer world. It subdues the outer world to its ends with an energy which has ensured for it the mastery of the world. The individual here, in his particular actions proceeds from fixed general principles; and in Europe the State, by its rational institutions, exhibits more or less the development and realization of freedom unimpeded by the caprice of a despot.

But finally, with regard to the original inhabitants of America, we have to remark that they are a vanishing, feeble race. It is true that in some parts of America at the time of its discovery, a pretty considerable civilization was to be found; this, however, was not comparable with European culture and disappeared with the original inhabitants. In addition, the dullest savages dwell there, e.g. the Pecherais and Eskimos. The Caribs of earlier times are almost completely extinct. When brought into contact with brandy and guns, these savages become extinct. In South America, it is the

Creoles who have made themselves independent of Spain; the native Indians were incapable of doing so. In Paraguay, they were just like small children and were even treated as such by the Jesuits. The natives of America are, therefore, clearly not in a position to maintain themselves in face of the Europeans. The latter will begin a new culture over there on the soil they have conquered from the natives.

7

Arthur de Gobineau,
The Inequality of Human Races

Arthur de Gobineau (1816–1882) is remembered both for his literary works and his racist philosophy of history. The latter is most clearly expounded in his Essay on the Inequality of Human Races. *Although Gobineau placed race at the very center of history, he never offered a clear definition of what he meant by race. Indeed, his division of the races into White (Caucasians, Semitic, or Juphetic), Black, and Yellow (Altaic, Mongol, Finnish, and Tartar) was somewhat crude for its time. The first two books of Gobineau's* Essay *were published in 1853. By 1856, Josiah Nott of Mobile, Alabama, prepared an English version with the help of Henry Hotz. The result was a seriously doctored text. Nott added an Appendix of his own, and Hotz supplied numerous notes. From the chapter printed here, Nott and Hotz omitted the laws of repulsion and attraction, which were at the heart of Gobineau's account of the role of race-mixing in the rise and fall of civilizations.*

The word *degenerate*, when applied to a people, means (as it ought to mean) that the people has no longer the same intrinsic value as it had before, because it has no longer the same blood in its veins, continual adulterations having gradually affected the quality of that blood. In other words, though the nation bears the name given by its founders, the name no longer connotes the same race; in fact, the man of a decadent time, the *degenerate* man properly so called, is a different being, from the racial point of view, from the heroes of the great ages. I agree that he still keeps something of their essence; but the more he degenerates the more attenuated does this "something" become. The heterogeneous elements that henceforth prevail in him give him quite a different nationality—a very original one, no doubt, but such originality is not to be envied. He is only a very distant kinsman of those he still calls his ancestors. He, and his civilization with him, will certainly die on the day when the primordial race-unit is so broken up and swamped by the influx of foreign elements, that its effective qualities have no longer a sufficient freedom of action. It will not, of course, absolutely disappear, but it will in practice be so beaten

From Arthur de Gobineau, *The Inequality of Human Races, [1853–55]*. Translated by A. Collins, 1915.

down and enfeebled, that its power will be felt less and less as time goes on. It is at this point that all the results of degeneration will appear, and the process may be considered complete.

If I manage to prove this proposition, I shall have given a meaning to the word "degeneration." By showing how the essential quality of a nation gradually alters, I shift the responsibility for its decadence, which thus becomes, in a way, less shameful, for it weighs no longer on the sons, but on the nephews, then on the cousins, then on collaterals more or less removed. And when I have shown by examples that great peoples, at the moment of their death, have only a very small and insignificant share in the blood of the founders, into whose inheritance they come, I shall thereby have explained clearly enough how it is possible for civilizations to fall—the reason being that they are no longer in the same hands. At the same time I shall be touching on a problem which is much more dangerous than that which I have tried to solve in the preceding chapters. This problem is: "Are there serious and ultimate differences of value between human races; and can these differences be estimated?"

I will begin at once to develop the series of arguments that touch the first point; they will indirectly settle the second also.

To put my ideas into a clearer and more easily intelligible form I may compare a nation to a human body, which, according to the physiologists, is constantly renewing all its parts; the work of transformation that goes on is incessant, and after a certain number of years the body retains hardly any of its former elements. Thus, in the old man, there are no traces of the man of middle age, in the adult no traces of the youth, nor in the youth of the child; the personal identity in all these stages is kept purely by the succession of inner and outer forms, each an imperfect copy of the last. Yet I will admit one difference between a nation and a human body; in the former there is no question of the "forms" being preserved, for these are destroyed and disappear with enormous rapidity. I will take a people, or better, a tribe, at the moment when, yielding to a definite vital instinct, it provides itself with laws and begins to play a part in the world. By the mere fact of its wants and powers increasing, it inevitably finds itself in contact with other similar associations, and by war or peaceful measures succeeds in incorporating them with itself.

Not all human families can reach this first step; but it is a step that every tribe must take if it is to rank one day as a nation. Even if a certain number of races, themselves perhaps not very far advanced on the ladder of civilization, have passed through this stage, we cannot properly regard this as a general rule.

Indeed, the human species seems to have a very great difficulty in raising itself above a rudimentary type of organization; the transition to a more complex state is made only by those groups of tribes, that are eminently gifted. I may cite, in support of this, the actual condition of a large number of communities spread throughout the world. These backward tribes, especially the Polynesian negroes, the Samoyedes and others in the far north, and the majority of the African races, have never been able to shake themselves free from their impotence; they live side by side in complete independence of each other. The stronger massacre the weaker, the weaker try to move as far away as possible from the stronger. This sums up the political ideas of these embryo societies, which have lived on in their imperfect state, without possibility of improvement, as long as the human race itself. It may be said that these miserable savages are a very small part of the earth's population. Granted; but we must take account of all the similar peoples who have lived and disappeared. Their number is incalculable, and certainly includes the vast majority of the pure-blooded yellow and black races.

If then we are driven to admit that for a very large number of human beings it has been, and always will be, impossible to take even the first step towards civilization; if, again, we consider that these peoples are scattered over the whole face of the earth under the most varying conditions of climate and environment, that they live indifferently in the tropics, in the temperate zones, and in the Arctic circle, by sea, lake, and river, in the depths of the forest, in the grassy plains, in the arid deserts, we must conclude that a part of mankind, is in its own nature stricken with a paralysis, which makes it for ever unable to take even the first step towards civilization, since it cannot overcome the natural repugnance, felt by men and animals alike, to a crossing of blood.

Leaving these tribes, that are incapable of civilization, on one side, we come, in our journey upwards, to those which understand that if they wish to increase their power and prosperity, they are absolutely compelled, either by war or peaceful measures, to draw their neighbours within their sphere of influence. War is undoubtedly the simpler way of doing this. Accordingly, they go to war. But when the campaign is finished, and the craving for destruction is satisfied, some prisoners are left over; these prisoners become slaves, and as slaves, work for their masters. We have class distinctions at once, and an industrial system: the tribe has become a little people. This is a higher rung on the ladder of civilization, and is not necessarily passed by all the tribes which have been able to reach it; many remain at this stage in cheerful stagnation.

But there are others, more imaginative and energetic, whose ideas soar beyond mere brigandage. They manage to conquer a great territory, and assume rights of ownership not only over the inhabitants, but also over their land. From this moment a real nation has been formed. The two races often continue for a time to live side by side without mingling; and yet, as they become indispensable to each other, as a community of work and interest is gradually built up, as the pride and rancour of conquest begin to ebb away, as those below naturally tend to rise to the level of their masters, while the masters have a thousand reasons for allowing, or even for promoting, such a tendency, the mixture of blood finally takes place, the two races cease to be associated with distinct tribes, and become more and more fused into a single whole.

The spirit of isolation is, however, so innate in the human race, that even those who have reached this advanced stage of crossing refuse in many cases to take a step further. There are some peoples who are, as we know positively, of mixed origin, but who keep their feeling for the clan to an extraordinary degree. The Arabs, for example, do more than merely spring from different branches of the Semitic stock; they belong at one and the same time to the so-called families of Shem and Ham, not to speak of a vast number of local strains that are intermingled with these. Nevertheless, their attachment to the tribe, as a separate unit, is one of the most striking features of their national character and their political history. In fact, it has been thought possible to attribute their expulsion from Spain not only to the actual breaking up of their power there, but also, to a large extent, to their being continually divided into smaller and mutually antagonistic groups, in the struggles for promotion among the Arab families at the petty courts of Valentia, Toledo, Cordova, and Grenada.[1]

We may say the same about the majority of such peoples. Further, where the tribal separation has broken down, a national feeling takes its place, and acts with a similar vigour, which a community of religion is not enough to destroy. This is the case among the Arabs and the Turks, the Persians and the Jews, the Parsees and the Hindus, the Nestorians of Syria and the Kurds. We find it also in European Turkey, and can trace its course in Hungary, among the Magyars, the Saxons, the Wallachians, and the Croats. I know, from what I have seen with my own eyes, that in certain parts of France, the country where races are mingled more than perhaps anywhere else, there are little communities to be found to this day, who feel a repugnance to marrying outside their own village.

---

1. This attachment of the Arab tribes to their racial unity shows itself sometimes in a very curious manner. A traveller (M. Fulgence Fresnel, I think) says that at Djiddah, where morals are very lax, the same Bedouin girl who will sell her favours for the smallest piece of money would think herself dishonoured if she contracted a legal marriage with the Turk or European to whom she contemptuously lends herself.

I think I am right in concluding from these examples, which cover all countries and ages, including our own, that the human race in all its branches has a secret repulsion from the crossing of blood, a repulsion which in many of the branches is invincible, and in others is only conquered to a slight extent. Even those who most completely shake off the yoke of this idea cannot get rid of the few last traces of it; yet such peoples are the only members of our species who can be civilized at all.

Thus mankind lives in obedience to two laws, one of repulsion, the other of attraction; these act with different force on different peoples. The first is fully respected only by those races which can never raise themselves above the elementary completeness of the tribal life, while the power of the second, on the contrary, is the more absolute, as the racial units on which it is exercised are more capable of development.

Here especially I must be concrete. I have just taken the example of a people in embryo, whose state is like that of a single family. I have given them the qualities which will allow them to pass into the state of a nation. Well, suppose they have become a nation. History does not tell me what the elements were that constituted the original group; all I know is that these elements fitted it for the transformation which I have made it undergo. Now that it has grown, it has only two possibilities. One or other of two destinies is inevitable. It will either conquer or be conquered.

I will give it the better part, and assume that it will conquer. It will at the same time rule, administer, and civilize. It will not go through its provinces, sowing a useless harvest of fire and massacre. Monuments, customs, and institutions will be alike sacred. It will change what it can usefully modify, and replace it by something better. Weakness in its hands will become strength. It will behave in such a way that, in the words of Scripture, it will be magnified in the sight of men.

I do not know if the same thought has already struck the reader; but in the picture which I am presenting—and which in certain features is that of the Hindus, the Egyptians, the Persians and the Macedonians—two facts appear to me to stand out. The first is that a nation, which itself lacks vigour and power, is suddenly called upon to share a new and a better destiny—that of the strong masters into whose hands it has fallen; this was the case with the Anglo-Saxons, when they had been subdued by the Normans. The second fact is that a picked race of men, a sovereign people, with the usual strong propensities of such a people to cross its blood with another's, finds itself henceforth in close contact with a race whose inferiority is shown, not only by defeat, but also by the lack of the attributes that may be seen in the conquerors. From the very day when the conquest is accomplished and the fusion begins, there appears a noticeable change of quality in the blood of the masters. If there were no other modifying influence at work, then—at the end of a number of years, which would vary according to the number of peoples that composed the original stock—we should be confronted with a new race, less powerful certainly than the better of its two ancestors, but still of considerable strength. It would have developed special qualities resulting from the actual mixture, and unknown to the communities from which it sprang. But the case is not generally so simple as this, and the intermingling of blood is not confined for long to the two constituent peoples.

The empire I have just been imagining is a powerful one, and its power is used to control its neighbours. I assume that there will be new conquests; and, every time, a current of fresh blood will be mingled with the main stream. Henceforth, as the nation grows, whether by war or treaty, its racial character changes more and more. It is rich, commercial, and civilized. The needs and the pleasures of other peoples find ample satisfaction in its capitals, its great towns, and its ports; while its myriad attractions cause many foreigners to make it their home. After a short time, we might truly say that a distinction of castes takes the place of the original distinction of races.

I am willing to grant that the people of whom I am speaking is strengthened in its exclusive notions by the most formal commands of religion, and that some dreadful penalty lurks in the background, to awe the disobedient. But since the people is civilized, its character is soft and tolerant, even to the contempt of its faith. Its oracles will speak in vain; there will be births outside the caste-limits. Every day new distinctions will have to be drawn, new classifications invented; the number of social grades will be increased, and it will be almost impossible to know where one is, amid the infinite variety of the subdivisions, that change from province to province, from canton to canton, from village to village. In fact, the condition will be that of the Hindu countries. It is only, however, the Brahman who has shown himself so tenacious of his ideas of separation; the foreign peoples he civilized have never fastened these cramping fetters on their shoulders, or any rate have long since shaken them off. In all the States that have made any advance in intellectual culture, the process has not been checked for a single moment by those desperate shifts to which the law-givers of the Aryavarta were put, in their desire to reconcile the prescriptions of the Code of Manu with the irresistible march of events. In every other place where there were really any castes at all, they ceased to exist at the moment when the chance of making a fortune, and of becoming famous by useful discoveries or social talents, became open to the whole world, without distinction of origin. But also, from that same day, the nation that was originally the active, conquering, and civilizing power began to disappear; its blood became merged in that of all the tributaries which it had attracted to its own stream.

Generally the dominating peoples begin by being far fewer in number than those they conquer; while, on the other hand, certain races that form the basis of the population in immense districts are extremely prolific—the Celts, for example, and the Slavs. This is yet another reason for the rapid disappearance of the conquering races. Again, their greater activity and the more personal part they take in the affairs of the State make them the chief mark for attack after a disastrous battle, a proscription, or a revolution. Thus, while by their very genius for civilization they collect round them the different elements in which they are to be absorbed, they are the victims, first of their original smallness of number, and then of a host of secondary causes which combine together for their destruction.

It is fairly obvious that the time when the disappearance takes place will vary considerably, according to circumstances. Yet it does finally come to pass, and is everywhere quite complete, long before the end of the civilization which the victorious race is supposed to be animating. A people may often go on living and working, and even growing in power, after the active, generating force of its life and glory has ceased to exist. Does this contradict what I have said above? Not at all; for while the blood of the civilizing race is gradually drained away by being parcelled out among the peoples that are conquered or annexed, the impulse originally given to these peoples still persists. The institutions which the dead master had invented, the laws he had prescribed, the customs he had initiated—all these live after him. No doubt the customs, laws, and institutions have quite forgotten the spirit that informed their youth; they survive in dishonoured old age, every day more sapless and rotten. But so long as even their shadows remain, the building stands, the body seems to have a soul, the pale ghost walks. When the original impulse has worked itself out, the last word has been said. Nothing remains; the civilization is dead.

I think I now have all the data necessary for grappling with the problem of the life and death of nations; and I can say positively that a people will never die, if it remains eternally composed of the same national elements. If the empire of Darius had, at the battle of Arbela, been able to fill its ranks with Persians, that is to say with real Aryans; if the Romans of the later Empire had had a Senate and an army of the same stock as that which existed at the time of the Fabii, their dominion would never have come to an end. So long as they kept the same purity of blood, the Persians and Romans would have lived and reigned. In the long run, it might be said, a conqueror, more irresistible than they, would have appeared on the scene; and they would have fallen under a well-directed attack, or a long siege, or simply by the fortune of a single battle. Yes, a State might be overthrown in this way, but not a civilization or a social organism. Invasion and defeat are but the dark clouds that for a time blot out the day, and then pass over. Many examples might be brought forward in proof of this.

In modern times the Chinese have been twice conquered. They have always forced their conquerors to become assimilated to them, and to respect their customs; they gave much, and took hardly anything in return. They drove out the first invaders, and in time will do the same with the second.

The English are the masters of India, and yet their moral hold over their subjects is almost non-existent. They are themselves influenced in many ways by the local civilization, and cannot succeed in stamping their ideas on a people that fears its conquerors, but is only physically dominated by them. It keeps its soul erect, and its thoughts apart from theirs. The Hindu race has become a stranger to the race that governs it to-day, and its civilization does not obey the law that gives the battle to the strong. External forms, kingdoms, and empires have changed, and will change again; but the foundations on which they rest, and from which they spring, do not necessarily change with them. Though Hyderabad, Lahore, and Delhi are no longer capital cities, Hindu society none the less persists. A moment will come, in one way or another, when India will again live publicly, as she already does privately, under her own laws; and, by the help either of the races actually existing or of a hybrid proceeding from them, will assume again, in the full sense of the word, a political personality.

The hazard of war cannot destroy the life of a people. At most, it suspends its animation for a time, and in some ways shears it of its outward pomp. So long as the blood and institutions of a nation keep to a sufficient degree the impress of the original race, that nation exists. Whether, as in the case of the Chinese, its conqueror has, in a purely material sense, greater energy than itself; whether, like the Hindu, it is matched, in a long and arduous trial of patience, against a nation, such as the English, in all points its superior; in either case the thought of its certain destiny should bring consolation—one day it will be free. But if, like the Greeks, and the Romans of the later Empire, the people has been absolutely drained of its original blood, and the qualities conferred by the blood, then the day of its defeat will be the day of its death. It has used up the time that heaven granted at its birth, for it has completely changed its race, and with its race its nature. It is therefore degenerate.

In view of the preceding paragraph, we may regard as settled the vexed question as to what would have happened if the Carthaginians, instead of falling before the fortunes of Rome, had become masters of Italy. Inasmuch as they belonged to the Phœnician stock, a stock inferior in the citizen-virtues to the races that produced the soldiers of Scipio, a different issue of the battle of Zama could not have made any change in their destiny. If they had been lucky on one day, the next would have seen their luck recoil on their heads; or they might have been merged in the Italian race by victory, as they were by defeat. In any case the final result would have been exactly the same. The destiny of civilizations is not a matter of chance; it does not depend on the toss of a coin. It is only men who are killed by the sword; and when the most redoubtable, warlike, and successful nations have nothing but valour in their hearts, military science in their heads, and the laurels of victory in their hands, without any thought that rises above mere conquest, they always end merely by learning, and learning badly, from those they have conquered, how to live in time of peace. The annals of the Celts and the Nomadic hordes of Asia tell no other tale than this.

I have now given a meaning to the word *degeneration;* and so have been able to attack the problem of a nation's vitality. I must next proceed to prove what for the sake of clearness I have had to put forward as a mere hypothesis; namely, that there are real differences in the relative value of human races. The consequences of proving this will be considerable, and cover a wide field. But first I must lay a foundation of fact and argument capable of holding up such a vast building; and the foundation cannot be too complete. The question with which I have just been dealing was only the gateway of the temple.

8

Charles Darwin,
"On the Races of Man,"
from *The Descent of Man*

Charles Darwin (1809–1882) is best known as the author of The Origin
of Species by Means of Natural Selection or the Preservation of
Favoured Races in the Struggle for Life, *which he published in 1859. The
full title employs the term "race" only in the broad biological use of the
word, which refers to varieties throughout organic life; however, speculation
about the implications of his views specifically for the question of the human
races began almost as soon as the book was published. Darwin's fullest statement on racial issues can be found in "On the Races of Man," the seventh
chapter of* The Descent of Man, *published in 1871 and reprinted here.*

It is not my intention here to describe the several so-called races of men;
but to inquire what is the value of the differences between them under a
classificatory point of view, and how they have originated. In determining
whether two or more allied forms ought to be ranked as species or varieties, naturalists are practically guided by the following considerations:
namely, the amount of difference between them, and whether such
differences relate to few or many points of structure, and whether they are
of physiological importance; but more especially whether they are constant. Constancy of character is what is chiefly valued and sought for by
naturalists. Whenever it can be shown, or rendered probable, that the
forms in question have remained distinct for a long period, this becomes
an argument of much weight in favor of treating them as species. Even a
slight degree of sterility between any two forms when first crossed, or in
their offspring, is generally considered as a decisive test of their specific
distinctness; and their continued persistence without blending within the
same area, is usually accepted as sufficient evidence, either of some degree
of mutual sterility, or in the case of animals of some repugnance to mutual
pairing.

Independently of blending from intercrossing, the complete absence, in
a well-investigated region, of varieties linking together any two closely-
allied forms, is probably the most important of all the criterions of their

From Charles Darwin, *The Descent of Man and Selection in Relation to Sex*, ch. 7,
1871.

specific distinctness; and this is a somewhat different consideration from mere constancy of character, for two forms may be highly variable and yet not yield intermediate varieties. Geographical distribution is often unconsciously and sometimes consciously brought into play; so that forms living in two widely-separated areas, in which most of the other inhabitants are specifically distinct, are themselves usually looked at as distinct; but in truth this affords no aid in distinguishing geographical races from so-called good or true species.

Now let us apply these generally-admitted principles to the races of man, viewing him in the same spirit as a naturalist would any other animal. In regard to the amount of difference between the races, we must make some allowance for our nice powers of discrimination gained by the long habit of observing ourselves. In India, as Elphinstone remarks,[1] although a newly-arrived European cannot at first distinguish the various native races, yet they soon appear to him extremely dissimilar; and the Hindoo cannot at first perceive any difference between the several European nations. Even the most distinct races of man, with the exception of certain negro tribes, are much more like each other in form than would at first be supposed. This is well shown by the French photographs in the Collection Anthropologique du Muséum of the men belonging to various races, the greater number of which, as many persons to whom I have shown them have remarked, might pass for Europeans. Nevertheless, these men if seen alive would undoubtedly appear very distinct, so that we are clearly much influenced in our judgment by the mere color of the skin and hair, by slight differences in the features, and by expression.

There is, however, no doubt that the various races, when carefully compared and measured, differ much from each other—as in the texture of the hair, the relative proportions of all parts of the body,[2] the capacity of the lungs, the form and capacity of the skull, and even in the convolutions of the brain.[3] But it would be an endless task to specify the numerous points of structural difference. The races differ also in constitution, in

1. "History of India," 1841, vol. i. p. 323. Father Ripa makes exactly the same remark with respect to the Chinese.

2. A vast number of measurements of Whites, Blacks, and Indians, are given in the "Investigations in the Military and Anthropology. Statistics of American Soldiers," by B. A. Gould, 1869, pp. 298–358; on the capacity of the lungs, p. 471. See also the numerous and valuable tables, by Dr. Weisbach, from the observations of Dr. Scherzer and Dr. Schwarz, in the "Reise der Novara: Anthropolog. Theil," 1867.

3. See, for instance, Mr. Marshall's account of the brain of a Bushwoman in "Phil. Transact." 1864, p. 519.

acclimatization, and in liability to certain diseases. Their mental characteristics are likewise very distinct; chiefly as it would appear in their emotional, but partly in their intellectual, faculties. Every one who has had the opportunity of comparison, must have been struck with the contrast between the taciturn, even morose, aborigines of South America and the light hearted, talkative negroes. There is a nearly similar contrast between the Malays and the Papuans,[4] who live under the same physical conditions, and are separated from each other only by a narrow space of sea.

We will first consider the arguments which may be advanced in favor of classing the races of man as distinct species, and then those on the other side. If a naturalist, who had never before seen such beings, were to compare a Negro, Hottentot, Australian, or Mongolian, he would at once perceive that they differed in a multitude of characters, some of slight and some of considerable importance. On inquiry he would find that they were adapted to live under widely-different climates, and that they differed somewhat in bodily constitution and mental disposition. If he were then told that hundreds of similar specimens could be brought from the same countries, he would assuredly declare that they were as good species as many to which he had been in the habit of affixing specific names. This conclusion would be greatly strengthened as soon as he had ascertained that these forms had all retained the same character for many centuries; and that negroes, apparently identical with existing negroes, had lived at least 4,000 years ago.[5] He would also hear from an excellent observer, Dr. Lund,[6] that the human skulls found in the caves of Brazil, entombed with

4. Wallace, "The Malay Archipelago," vol. ii. 1869, p. 178.

5. With respect to the figures of the famous Egyptian caves of Abou-Simbel, M. Pouchet says ("The Plurality of the Human Races," English translat. 1864, p. 50), that he was far from finding recognizable representations of the dozen or more nations which some authors believe that they can recognize. Even some of the most strongly-marked races cannot be identified with that degree of unanimity which might have been expected from what has been written on the subject. Thus Messrs. Nott and Gliddon ("Types of Mankind," p. 148) state that Rameses II., or the Great, has features superbly European; whereas Knox, another firm believer in the specific distinction of the races of man ("Races of Man," 1850, p. 201), speaking of young Memnon (the same person with Rameses II., as I am informed by Mr. Birch) insists in the strongest manner that he is identical in character with the Jews of Antwerp. Again, while looking in the British Museum with two competent judges, officers of the establishment, at the statue of Amunoph III., we agreed that he had a strongly negro cast of features; but Messrs. Nott and Gliddon (ibid. p. 146, fig. 53) describe him as "a hybrid, but not of negro intermixture."

6. As quoted by Nott and Gliddon, "Types of Mankind," 1854, p. 439. They give

many extinct mammals, belonged to the same type as that now prevailing throughout the American Continent.

Our naturalist would then, perhaps, turn to geographical distribution, and he would probably declare that forms differing not only in appearance, but fitted for the hottest and dampest or driest countries, as well as for the Arctic regions, must be distinct species. He might appeal to the fact that no one species in the group next to man, namely, the Quadrumana, can resist a low temperature or any considerable change of climate; and that those species which come nearest to man have never been reared to maturity, even under the temperate climate of Europe. He would be deeply impressed with the fact, first noticed by Agassiz,[7] that the different races of man are distributed over the world in the same zoological provinces, as those inhabited by undoubtedly distinct species and genera of mammals. This is manifestly the case with the Australian, Mongolian, and Negro races of man; in a less well-marked manner with the Hottentots; but plainly with the Papuans and Malays, who are separated, as Mr. Wallace has shown, by nearly the same line which divides the great Malayan and Australian zoological provinces. The aborigines of America range throughout the continent; and this at first appears opposed to the above rule, for most of the productions of the Southern and Northern halves differ widely; yet some few living forms, as the opossum, range from the one into the other, as did formerly some of the gigantic Edentata. The Esquimaux, like other Arctic animals, extend round the whole polar regions. It should be observed that the mammalian forms which inhabit the several zoological provinces, do not differ from each other in the same degree; so that it can hardly be considered as an anomaly that the Negro differs more, and the American much less, from the other races of man than do the mammals of the same continents from those of the other provinces. Man, it may be added, does not appear to have aboriginally inhabited any oceanic island; and in this respect he resembles the other members of his class.

In determining whether the varieties of the same kind of domestic animal should be ranked as specifically distinct, that is, whether any of them are descended from distinct wild species, every naturalist would lay much stress on the fact, if established, of their external parasites being specifically distinct. All the more stress would be laid on this fact, as it

---

also corroborative evidence; but C. Vogt thinks that the subject requires further investigation.

7. "Diversity of Origin of the Human Races," in the "Christian Examiner," July, 1850.

would be an exceptional one, for I am informed by Mr. Denny that the most different kinds of dogs, fowls, and pigeons, in England, are infested by the same species of Pediculi or lice. Now Mr. A. Murray has carefully examined the Pediculi collected in different countries from the different races of man;[8] and he finds that they differ, not only in color, but in the structure of their claws and limbs. In every case in which numerous specimens were obtained the differences were constant. The surgeon of a whaling-ship in the Pacific assured me that when the Pediculi, with which some Sandwich Islanders on board swarmed, strayed on to the bodies of the English sailors, they died in the course of three or four days. These Pediculi were darker colored and appeared different from those proper to the natives of Chiloe in South America, of which he gave me specimens. These, again, appeared larger and much softer than European lice. Mr. Murray procured four kinds from Africa, namely from the Negroes of the Eastern and Western coasts, from the Hottentots and Caffres; two kinds from the natives of Australia; two from North, and two from South America. In these latter cases it may be presumed that the Pediculi came from natives inhabiting different districts. With insects slight structural differences, if constant, are generally esteemed of specific value: and the fact of the races of man being infested by parasites, which appear to be specifically distinct, might fairly be urged as an argument that the races themselves ought to be classed as distinct species.

Our supposed naturalist, having proceeded thus far in his investigation, would next inquire whether the races of men, when crossed, were in any degree sterile. He might consult the work[9] of a cautious and philosophical observer, Prof. Broca; and in this he would find good evidence that some races were quite fertile together; but evidence of an opposite nature in regard to other races. Thus it has been asserted that the native women of Australia and Tasmania rarely produce children to European men; the evidence, however, on this head has now been shown to be almost value-less. The half-castes are killed by the pure blacks; and an account has lately been published of eleven half-caste youths murdered and burnt at the same time, whose remains were found by the police.[10] Again, it has often

8. "Transact. R. Soc. of Edinburgh," vol. xxii. 1861, p. 567.

9. "On the Phenomena of Hybridity in the Genus Homo," Eng. translation, 1864.

10. See the interesting letter by Mr. T. A. Murray, in the "Anthropolog. Review," April, 1868, p. liii. In this letter Count Strzelecki's statement, that Australian women who have borne children to a white man are afterward sterile with their own race, is disproved. M. A. de Quatrefages has also collected ("Revue des Cours Scientifiques," March, 1869, p. 239) much evidence that Australians and Euro-peans are not sterile when crossed.

been said that when mulattoes intermarry they produce few children; on the other hand, Dr. Bachman of Charleston[11] positively asserts that he has known mulatto families which have intermarried for several generations, and have continued on an average as fertile as either pure whites or pure blacks. Inquiries formerly made by Sir C. Lyell on this subject led him, as he informs me, to the same conclusion. In the United States the census for the year 1854 included, according to Dr. Bachman, 405,751 mulattoes; and this number, considering all the circumstances of the case, seems small; but it may partly be accounted for by the degraded and anomalous position of the class, and by the profligacy of the women. A certain amount of absorption of mulattoes into negroes must always be in progress; and this would lead to an apparent diminution of the former. The inferior vitality of mulattoes is spoken of in a trustworthy work[12] as a well-known phenomenon; but this is a different consideration from their lessened fertility; and can hardly be advanced as a proof of the specific distinctness of the parent races. No doubt both animal and vegetable hybrids, when produced from extremely distinct species, are liable to premature death; but the parents of mulattoes cannot be put under the category of extremely distinct species. The common Mule, so notorious for long life and vigor, and yet so sterile, shows how little necessary connection there is in hybrids between lessened fertility and vitality: other analogous cases could be added.

Even if it should hereafter be proved that all the races of men were perfectly fertile together, he who was inclined from other reasons to rank them as distinct species, might with justice argue that fertility and sterility are not safe criterions of specific distinctness. We know that these qualities are easily affected by changed conditions of life or by close inter-breeding, and that they are governed by highly complex laws, for instance that of the unequal fertility of reciprocal crosses between the same two species. With forms which must be ranked as undoubted species, a perfect series exists from those which are absolutely sterile when crossed, to those which are almost or quite fertile. The degrees of sterility do not coincide strictly with the degrees of difference in external structure or habits of life. Man in many respects may be compared with those animals which have long been domesticated, and a large body of evidence can be advanced in favor of the Pallasian doctrine,[13] that domestication tends to eliminate the ster-

11. "An Examination of Prof. Agassiz's Sketch of the Nat. Provinces of the Animal World," Charleston, 1855, p. 44.
12. "Military and Anthropolog. Statistics of American Soldiers," by B. A. Gould, 1869, p. 319.
13. "The Variation of Animals and Plants under Domestication," vol. ii. p. 109. I

ility which is so general a result of the crossing of species in a state of nature. From these several considerations, it may be justly urged that the perfect fertility of the intercrossed races of man, if established, would not absolutely preclude us from ranking them as distinct species.

Independently of fertility, the character of the offspring from a cross has sometimes been thought to afford evidence whether the parent-forms ought to be ranked as species or varieties; but after carefully studying the evidence, I have come to the conclusion that no general rules of this kind can be trusted. Thus with mankind the offspring of distinct races resemble in all respects the offspring of true species and of varieties. This is shown, for instance, by the manner in which the characters of both parents are blended, and by one form absorbing another through repeated crosses. In this latter case the progeny both of crossed species and varieties retain for a long period a tendency to revert to their ancestors, especially to that one which is prepotent in transmission. When any character has suddenly appeared in a race or species as the result of a single act of variation, as is

---

may here remind the reader that the sterility of species when crossed is not a specially-acquired quality; but, like the incapacity of certain trees to be grafted together, is incidental on other acquired differences. The nature of these differences is unknown, but they relate more especially to the reproductive system, and much less to external structure or to ordinary differences in constitution. One important element in the sterility of crossed species apparently lies in one or both having been long habituated to fixed conditions; for we know that changed conditions have a special influence on the reproductive system, and we have good reason to believe (as before remarked) that the fluctuating conditions of domestication tend to eliminate that sterility which is so general with species in a natural state when crossed. It has elsewhere been shown by me (ibid. vol. ii. p. 185, and "Origin of Species," 5th edit. p. 317) that the sterility of crossed species has not been acquired through natural selection: we can see that when two forms have already been rendered very sterile, it is scarcely possible that their sterility should be augmented by the preservation or survival of the more and more sterile individuals; for as the sterility increases fewer and fewer offspring will be produced from which to breed, and at last only single individuals will be produced, at the rarest intervals. But there is even a higher grade of sterility than this. Both Gärtner and Kölreuter have proved that in genera of plants including numerous species, a series can be formed from species which when crossed yield fewer and fewer seeds, to species which never produce a single seed, but yet are affected by the pollen of the other species, for the germen swells. It is here manifestly impossible to select the more sterile individuals, which have already ceased to yield seeds; so that the acme of sterility, when the germen alone is affected, cannot be gained through selection. This acme, and no doubt the other grades of sterility, are the incidental results of certain unknown differences in the constitution of the reproductive system of the species which are crossed.

general with monstrosities,[14] and this race is crossed with another not thus characterized, the characters in question do not commonly appear in a blended condition in the young, but are transmitted to them either perfectly developed or not at all. As with the crossed races of man cases of this kind rarely or never occur, this may be used as an argument against the view suggested by some ethnologists, namely, that certain characters, for instance the blackness of the negro, first appeared as a sudden variation or sport. Had this occurred, it is probable that mulattoes would often have been born either completely black or completely white.

We have now seen that a naturalist might feel himself fully justified in ranking the races of man as distinct species; for he has found that they are distinguished by many differences in structure and constitution, some being of importance. These differences have, also, remained nearly constant for very long periods of time. He will have been in some degree influenced by the enormous range of man, which is a great anomaly in the class of mammals, if mankind be viewed as a single species. He will have been struck with the distribution of the several so-called races, in accordance with that of other undoubtedly distinct species of mammals. Finally, he might urge that the mutual fertility of all the races has not yet been fully proved; and even if proved would not be an absolute proof of their specific identity.

On the other side of the question, if our supposed naturalist were to inquire whether the forms of man kept distinct like ordinary species, when mingled together in large numbers in the same country, he would immediately discover that this was by no means the case. In Brazil he would behold an immense mongrel population of Negroes and Portuguese; in Chiloe and other parts of South America he would behold the whole population consisting of Indians and Spaniards blended in various degrees.[15] In many parts of the same continent he would meet with the most complex crosses between Negroes, Indians, and Europeans; and such triple crosses afford the severest test, judging from the vegetable kingdom, of the mutual fertility of the parent-forms. In one island of the Pacific he would find a small population of mingled Polynesian and English blood; and in the Viti Archipelago a population of Polynesians and Negritos crossed in all degrees. Many analogous cases could be added, for instance,

14. "The Variation of Animals," etc., vol. ii. p. 92.
15. M. de Quatrefages has given ("Anthropolog. Review," Jan. 1869, p. 22) an interesting account of the success and energy of the Paulistas in Brazil, who are a much crossed race of Portuguese and Indians, with a mixture of the blood of other races.

in South Africa. Hence the races of man are not sufficiently distinct to coexist without fusion; and this it is which, in all ordinary cases, affords the usual test of specific distinctness.

Our naturalist would likewise be much disturbed as soon as he perceived that the distinctive characters of every race of man were highly variable. This strikes every one when he first beholds the negro-slaves in Brazil, who have been imported from all parts of Africa. The same remark holds good with the Polynesians, and with many other races. It may be doubted whether any character can be named which is distinctive of a race and is constant. Savages, even within the limits of the same tribe, are not nearly so uniform in character as has often been said. Hottentot women offer certain peculiarities, more strongly marked than those occurring in any other race, but these are known not to be of constant occurrence. In the several American tribes, color and hairiness differ considerably; as does color to a certain degree, and the shape of the features greatly, in the Negroes of Africa. The shape of the skull varies much in some races;[16] and so it is with every other character. Now all naturalists have learned, by dearly-bought experience, how rash it is to attempt to define species by the aid of inconstant characters.

But the most weighty of all the arguments against treating the races of man as distinct species, is that they graduate into each other, independently in many cases, as far as we can judge, of their having intercrossed. Man has been studied more carefully than any other organic being, and yet there is the greatest possible diversity among capable judges whether he should be classed as a single species or race, or as two (Virey), as three (Jacquinot), as four (Kant), five (Blumenbach), six (Buffon), seven (Hunter), eight (Agassiz), eleven (Pickering), fifteen (Bory St. Vincent), sixteen (Desmoulins), twenty-two (Morton), sixty (Crawfurd), or as sixty-three, according to Burke.[17] This diversity of judgment does not prove that the races ought not to be ranked as species, but it shows that they graduate into each other, and that it is hardly possible to discover clear distinctive characters between them.

Every naturalist who has had the misfortune to undertake the description of a group of highly-varying organisms, has encountered cases (I

16. For instance with the aborigines of America and Australia. Prof. Huxley says ("Transact. Internat. Congress of Prehist. Arch." 1868, p. 105) that the skulls of many South Germans and Swiss are "as short and as broad as those of the Tartars," etc.

17. See a good discussion on this subject in Waitz, "Introduct. to Anthropology," Eng. translat. 1863, pp. 198–208, 227. I have taken some of the above statements from H. Tuttle's "Origin and Antiquity of Physical Man," Boston, 1866, p. 35.

speak after experience) precisely like that of man; and if of a cautious disposition, he will end by uniting all the forms which graduate into each other as a single species; for he will say to himself that he has no right to give names to objects which he cannot define. Cases of this kind occur in the Order which includes man, namely, in certain genera of monkeys; while in other genera, as in Cercopithecus, most of the species can be determined with certainty. In the American genus Cebus, the various forms are ranked by some naturalists as species, by others as mere geographical races. Now, if numerous specimens of Cebus were collected from all parts of South America, and those forms which at present appear to be specifically distinct, were found to graduate into each other by close steps, they would be ranked by most naturalists as mere varieties or races; and thus the greater number of naturalists have acted with respect to the races of man. Nevertheless it must be confessed that there are forms, at least in the vegetable kingdom,[18] which we cannot avoid naming as species, but which are connected together, independently of intercrossing, by numberless gradations.

Some naturalists have lately employed the term "subspecies" to designate forms which possess many of the characteristics of true species, but which hardly deserve so high a rank. Now, if we reflect on the weighty arguments, above given, for raising the races of man to the dignity of species, and the insuperable difficulties on the other side in defining them, the term "sub-species" might here be used with much propriety. But from long habit the term "race" will perhaps always be employed. The choice of terms is only so far important as it is highly desirable to use, as far as that may be possible, the same terms for the same degrees of difference. Unfortunately, this is rarely possible; for within the same family the larger genera generally include closely-allied forms, which can be distinguished only with much difficulty, while the smaller genera include forms that are perfectly distinct; yet all must equally be ranked as species. So again the species within the same large genus by no means resemble each other to the same degree: on the contrary, in most cases some of them can be arranged in little groups round other species, like satellites round planets.[19]

The question whether mankind consists of one or several species has of late years been much agitated by anthropologists, who are divided into two

---

18. Prof. Nägeli has carefully described several striking cases in his "Botanische Mittheilungen," B. ii. 1866, s. 294–369. Prof. Asa Gray has made analogous remarks on some intermediate forms in the Compositæ of North America.

19. "Origin of Species," 5th edit. p. 68.

schools of monogenists and polygenists. Those who do not admit the principle of evolution, must look at species either as separate creations or as in some manner distinct entities; and they must decide what forms to rank as species by the analogy of other organic beings which are commonly thus received. But it is a hopeless endeavor to decide this point on sound grounds, until some definition of the term "species" is generally accepted; and the definition must not include an element which cannot possibly be ascertained, such as an act of creation. We might as well attempt without any definition to decide whether a certain number of houses should be called a village, or town, or city. We have a practical illustration of the difficulty in the never-ending doubts whether many closely-allied mammals, birds, insects, and plants, which represent each other in North America and Europe, should be ranked species or geographical races; and so it is with the productions of many islands situated at some little distance from the nearest continent.

Those naturalists, on the other hand, who admit the principle of evolution, and this is now admitted by the greater number of rising men, will feel no doubt that all the races of man are descended from a single primitive stock; whether or not they think fit to designate them as distinct species, for the sake of expressing their amount of difference.[20] With our domestic animals the question whether the various races have arisen from one or more species is different. Although all such races, as well as all the natural species within the same genus, have undoubtedly sprung from the same primitive stock, yet it is a fit subject for discussion, whether, for instance, all the domestic races of the dog have acquired their present differences since some one species was first domesticated and bred by man; or whether they owe some of their characters to inheritance from distinct species, which had already been modified in a state of nature. With mankind no such question can arise, for he cannot be said to have been domesticated at any particular period.

When the races of man diverged at an extremely remote epoch from their common progenitor, they will have differed but little from each other, and been few in number; consequently they will then, as far as their distinguishing characters are concerned, have had less claim to rank as distinct species, than the existing so-called races. Nevertheless such early races would perhaps have been ranked by some naturalists as distinct species, so arbitrary is the term, if their differences, although extremely slight, had been more constant than at present, and had not graduated into each other.

20. See Prof. Huxley to this effect in the "Fortnightly Review," 1865, p. 275.

It is, however, possible, though far from probable, that the early progenitors of man might at first have diverged much in character, until they became more unlike each other than are any existing races; but that subsequently, as suggested by Vogt,[21] they converged in character. When man selects for the same object the offspring of two distinct species, he sometimes induces, as far as general appearance is concerned, a considerable amount of convergence. This is the case, as shown by Von Nathusius,[22] with the improved breeds of pigs, which are descended from two distinct species; and in a less well-marked manner with the improved breeds of cattle. A great anatomist, Gratiolet, maintains that the anthropomorphous apes do not form a natural sub-group; but that the orang is a highly-developed gibbon or semnopithecus; the chimpanzee a highly-developed macacus; and the gorilla a highly-developed mandrill. If this conclusion, which rests almost exclusively on brain-characters, be admitted, we should have a case of convergence at least in external characters, for the anthropomorphous apes are certainly more like each other in many points than they are to other apes. All analogical resemblances, as of a whale to a fish, may indeed be said to be cases of convergence; but this term has never been applied to superficial and adaptive resemblances. It would be extremely rash in most cases to attribute to convergence close similarity in many points of structure in beings which had once been widely different. The form of a crystal is determined solely by the molecular forces, and it is not surprising that dissimilar substances should sometimes assume the same form; but with organic beings we should bear in mind that the form of each depends on an infinitude of complex relations, namely, on the variations which have arisen, these being due to causes far too intricate to be followed out—on the nature of the variations which have been preserved, and this depends on the surrounding physical conditions, and in a still higher degree on the surrounding organisms with which each has come into competition—and lastly, on inheritance (in itself a fluctuating element) from innumerable progenitors, all of which have had their forms determined through equally complex relations. It appears utterly incredible that two organisms, if differing in a marked manner, should ever afterward converge so closely as to lead to a near approach to identity throughout their whole organization. In the case of the convergent pigs above referred to, evidence of their descent from two primitive stocks is

21. "Lectures on Man," Eng. translat. 1864, p. 468.
22. "Die Racen des Schweines," 1860, s. 46. "Vorstudien für Geschichte, etc., Schweineschädel," 1864, s. 104. With respect to cattle, see M. de Quatrefages, "Unité de l'Espèce Humaine," 1861, p. 119.

still plainly retained, according to Von Nathusius, in certain bones of their skulls. If the races of man were descended, as supposed by some naturalists, from two or more distinct species, which had differed as much, or nearly as much, from each other, as the orang differs from the gorilla, it can hardly be doubted that marked differences in the structure of certain bones would still have been discoverable in man as he now exists.

Although the existing races of man differ in many respects, as in color, hair, shape of skull, proportions of the body, etc., yet if their whole organization be taken into consideration they are found to resemble each other closely in a multitude of points. Many of these points are of so unimportant or of so singular a nature, that it is extremely improbable that they should have been independently acquired by aboriginally distinct species or races. The same remark holds good with equal or greater force with respect to the numerous points of mental similarity between the most distinct races of man. The American aborigines, Negroes, and Europeans, differ as much from each other in mind as any three races that can be named; yet I was incessantly struck, while living with the Fuegians on board the "Beagle," with the many little traits of character, showing how similar their minds were to ours; and so it was with a full-blooded negro with whom I happened once to be intimate.

He who will carefully read Mr. Tylor's and Sir J. Lubbock's interesting works[23] can hardly fail to be deeply impressed with the close similarity between the men of all races in tastes, dispositions, and habits. This is shown by the pleasure which they all take in dancing, rude music, acting, painting, tattooing, and otherwise decorating themselves—in their mutual comprehension of gesture-language—and, as I shall be able to show in a future essay, by the same expression in their features, and by the same inarticulate cries, when they are excited by various emotions. This similarity, or rather identity, is striking, when contrasted with the different expressions which may be observed in distinct species of monkeys. There is good evidence that the art of shooting with bows and arrows has not been handed down from any common progenitor of mankind, yet the stone arrow-heads, brought from the most distant parts of the world and manufactured at the most remote periods, are, as Nilsson has shown,[24] almost identical; and this fact can only be accounted for by the various races having similar inventive or mental powers. The same observation has

23. Tylor's "Early History of Mankind," 1865; for the evidence with respect to gesture-language, see p. 54. Lubbock's "Prehistoric Times," 2d edit. 1869.
24. "The Primitive Inhabitants of Scandinavia," Eng. translat. edited by Sir J. Lubbock, 1868, p. 104.

been made by archæologists[25] with respect to certain widely-prevalent ornaments, such as zigzags, etc.; and with respect to various simple beliefs and customs, such as the burying of the dead under megalithic structures. I remember observing in South America,[26] that there, as in so many other parts of the world, man has generally chosen the summits of lofty hills, on which to throw up piles of stones, either for the sake of recording some remarkable event, or for burying his dead.

Now, when naturalists observe a close agreement in numerous small details of habits, tastes, and dispositions, between two or more domestic races, or between nearly-allied natural forms, they use this fact as an argument that all are descended from a common progenitor who was thus endowed; and consequently that all should be classed under the same species. The same argument may be applied with much force to the races of man.

As it is improbable that the numerous and unimportant points of resemblance between the several races of man in bodily structure and mental faculties (I do not here refer to similar customs) should all have been independently acquired, they must have been inherited from progenitors who were thus characterized. We thus gain some insight into the early state of man, before he had spread step by step over the face of the earth. The spreading of man to regions widely-separated by the sea, no doubt, preceded any considerable amount of divergence of character in the several races; for otherwise we should sometimes meet with the same race in distinct continents; and this is never the case. Sir J. Lubbock, after comparing the arts now practised by savages in all parts of the world, specifies those which man could not have known, when he first wandered from his original birthplace; for if once learned they would never have been forgotten.[27] He thus shows that "the spear, which is but a development of the knife-point, and the club, which is but a long hammer, are the only things left." He admits, however, that the art of making fire probably had already been discovered, for it is common to all the races now existing, and was known to the ancient cave-inhabitants of Europe. Perhaps the art of making rude canoes or rafts was likewise known; but as man existed at a remote epoch, when the land in many places stood at a very different level, he would have been able, without the aid of canoes, to have spread widely. Sir J. Lubbock further remarks how improbable it is that our earliest ancestors could have "counted as high as ten, considering that so many races now in

25. Hodder M. Westropp, on Cromlechs, etc., "Journal of Ethnological Soc." as given in "Scientific Opinion," June 2, 1869, p. 3.
26. "Journal of Researches: Voyage of the 'Beagle,'" p. 46.
27. "Prehistoric Times," 1869, p. 574.

existence cannot get beyond four." Nevertheless, at this early period, the intellectual and social faculties of man could hardly have been inferior in any extreme degree to those now possessed by the lowest savages; otherwise primeval man could not have been so eminently successful in the struggle for life, as proved by his early and wide diffusion.

From the fundamental differences between certain languages, some philologists have inferred that when man first became widely diffused he was not a speaking animal; but it may be suspected that languages, far less perfect than any now spoken, aided by gestures, might have been used, and yet have left no traces on subsequent and more highly-developed tongues. Without the use of some language, however imperfect, it appears doubtful whether man's intellect could have risen to the standard implied by his dominant position at an early period.

Whether primeval man, when he possessed very few arts of the rudest kind, and when his power of language was extremely imperfect, would have deserved to be called man, must depend on the definition which we employ. In a series of forms graduating insensibly from some ape-like creature to man as he now exists, it would be impossible to fix on any definite point when the term "man" ought to be used. But this is a matter of very little importance. So again it is almost a matter of indifference whether the so-called races of man are thus designated, or are ranked as species or sub-species; but the latter term appears the most appropriate. Finally, we may conclude that when the principles of evolution are generally accepted, as they surely will be before long, the dispute between the monogenists and the polygenists will die a silent and unobserved death.

One other question ought not to be passed over without notice, namely, whether, as is sometimes assumed, each sub-species or race of man has sprung from a single pair of progenitors. With our domestic animals a new race can readily be formed from a single pair possessing some new character, or even from a single individual thus characterized, by carefully matching the varying offspring; but most of our races have been formed, not intentionally from a selected pair, but unconsciously by the preservation of many individuals which have varied, however slightly, in some useful or desired manner. If in one country stronger and heavier horses, and in another country lighter and fleeter horses, were habitually preferred, we may feel sure that two distinct sub-breeds would, in the course of time, be produced, without any particular pairs or individuals having been separated and bred from in either country. Many races have been thus formed, and their manner of formation is closely analogous with that of natural species. We know, also, that the horses which have been brought to the Falkland Islands have become, during successive generations, smaller and weaker, while those which have run wild on the Pampas have acquired larger and coarser heads; and such changes are manifestly due, not to any one pair, but to all the individuals having been subjected to the same conditions, aided, perhaps, by the principle of reversion. The new sub-breeds in none of these cases are descended from any single pair, but from many individuals which have varied in different degrees, but in the same general manner; and we may conclude that the races of man have been similarly produced, the modifications being either the direct result of exposure to different conditions, or the indirect result of some form of selection. But to this latter subject we shall presently return.

On the Extinction of the Races of Man.—The partial and complete extinction of many races and sub-races of man are historically known events. Humboldt saw in South America a parrot which was the sole living creature that could speak the language of a lost tribe. Ancient monuments and stone implements found in all parts of the world, of which no tradition is preserved by the present inhabitants, indicate much extinction. Some small and broken tribes, remnants of former races, still survive in isolated and generally mountainous districts. In Europe the ancient races were all, according to Schaaffhausen,[28] "lower in the scale than the rudest living savages;" they must therefore have differed, to a certain extent, from any existing race. The remains described by Prof. Broca[29] from Les Eyzies, though they unfortunately appear to have belonged to a single family, indicate a race with a most singular combination of low or simious and high characteristics, and is "entirely different from any other race, ancient or modern, that we have ever heard of." It differed, therefore, from the quaternary race of the caverns of Belgium.

Unfavorable physical conditions appear to have had but little effect in the extinction of races.[30] Man has long lived in the extreme regions of the North, with no wood wherewith to make his canoes or other implements, and with blubber alone for burning and giving him warmth, but more especially for melting the snow. In the Southern extremity of America the Fuegians survive without the protection of clothes, or of any building worthy to be called a hovel. In South Africa the aborigines wander over the most arid plains, where dangerous beasts abound. Man can withstand the deadly influence of the Terai at the foot of the Himalaya, and the pestilential shores of tropical Africa.

28. Translation in "Anthropological Review," Oct. 1868, p. 431.

29. "Transact. Internat. Congress of Prehistoric Arch." 1868, pp. 172–175. See also Broca (translation) in "Anthropological Review," Oct. 1868, p. 410.

30. Dr. Gerland, "Ueber das Aussterben der Naturvölker," 1868, s. 82.

Extinction follows chiefly from the competition of tribe with tribe, and race with race. Various checks are always in action, as specified in a former chapter, which serve to keep down the numbers of each savage tribe— such as periodical famines, the wandering of the parents and the consequent deaths of infants, prolonged suckling, the stealing of women, wars, accidents, sickness, licentiousness, especially infanticide, and, perhaps, lessened fertility from less nutritious food, and many hardships. If from any cause any one of these checks is lessened, even in a slight degree, the tribe thus favored will tend to increase; and when one of two adjoining tribes becomes more numerous and powerful than the other, the contest is soon settled by war, slaughter, cannibalism, slavery, and absorption. Even when a weaker tribe is not thus abruptly swept away, if it once begins to decrease, it generally goes on decreasing until it is extinct.[31]

When civilized nations come into contact with barbarians the struggle is short, except where a deadly climate gives its aid to the native race. Of the causes which lead to the victory of civilized nations, some are plain and some very obscure. We can see that the cultivation of the land will be fatal in many ways to savages, for they cannot, or will not, change their habits. New diseases and vices are highly destructive; and it appears that in every nation a new disease causes much death, until those who are most susceptible to its destructive influence are gradually weeded out;[32] and so it may be with the evil effects from spirituous liquors, as well as with the unconquerably strong taste for them shown by so many savages. It further appears, mysterious as is the fact, that the first meeting of distinct and separated people generates disease.[33] Mr. Sproat, who in Vancouver Island closely attended to the subject of extinction, believes that changed habits of life, which always follow from the advent of Europeans, induces much ill-health. He lays, also, great stress on so trifling a cause as that the natives becomes "bewildered and dull by the new life around them; they lose the motives for exertion, and get no new ones in their place."[34]

The grade of civilization seems a most important element in the success of nations which come in competition. A few centuries ago Europe feared the inroads of Eastern barbarians; now, any such fear would be ridiculous.

31. Gerland (ibid. s. 12) gives facts in support of this statement.

32. See remarks to this effect in Sir H. Holland's "Medical Notes and Reflections," 1839, p. 390.

33. I have collected ("Journal of Researches, Voyage of the 'Beagle,'" p. 435) a good many cases bearing on this subject: see also Gerland, ibid. s. 8. Poeppig speaks of the "breath of civilization as poisonous to savages."

34. Sproat, "Scenes and Studies of Savage Life," 1868, p. 284.

It is a more curious fact that savages did not formerly waste away, as Mr. Bagehot has remarked, before the classical nations, as they now do before modern civilized nations; had they done so, the old moralists would have mused over the event; but there is no lament in any writer of that period over the perishing barbarians.[35]

Although the gradual decrease and final extinction of the races of man is an obscure problem, we can see that it depends on many causes, differing in different places and at different times. It is the same difficult problem as that presented by the extinction of one of the higher animals— of the fossil horse, for instance, which disappeared from South America, soon afterward to be replaced, within the same districts, by countless troops of the Spanish horse. The New-Zealander seems conscious of this parallelism, for he compares his future fate with that of the native rat almost exterminated by the European rat. The difficulty, though great to our imagination, and really great if we wish to ascertain the precise causes, ought not to be so to our reason, as long as we keep steadily in mind that the increase of each species and each race is constantly hindered by various checks; so that if any new check, or cause of destruction, even a slight one, be super-added, the race will surely decrease in number; and as it has everywhere been observed that savages are much opposed to any change of habits, by which means injurious checks could be counterbalanced, decreasing numbers will sooner or later lead to extinction; the end, in most cases, being promptly determined by the inroads of increasing and conquering tribes.

On the Formation of the Races of Man.—It may be premised that when we find the same race, though broken up into distinct tribes, ranging over a great area, as over America, we may attribute their general resemblance to descent from a common stock. In some cases the crossing of races already distinct has led to the formation of new races. The singular fact that Europeans and Hindoos, who belong to the same Aryan stock and speak a language fundamentally the same, differ widely in appearance, while Europeans differ but little from Jews, who belong to the Semitic stock and speak quite another language, has been accounted for by Broca[36] through the Aryan branches having been largely crossed during their wide diffusion by various indigenous tribes. When two races in close contact cross, the first result is a heterogeneous mixture: thus Mr. Hunter, in describing the Santali or hill-tribes of India, says that hundreds of imper-

35. Bagehot, "Physics and Politics," "Fortnightly Review," April 1, 1868, p. 455.
36. "On Anthropology," translation, "Anthropolog. Review," Jan. 1868, p. 38.

ceptible gradations may be traced "from the black, squat tribes of the mountains to the tall olive-colored Bramin, with his intellectual brow, calm eyes, and high but narrow head"; so that it is necessary in courts of justice to ask the witnesses whether they are Santalis or Hindoos.[37] Whether a heterogeneous people, such as the inhabitants of some of the Polynesian islands, formed by the crossing of two distinct races, with few or no pure members left, would ever become homogeneous, is not known from direct evidence. But, as with our domesticated animals, a crossed breed can certainly, in the course of a few generations, be fixed and made uniform by careful selection,[38] we may infer that the free and prolonged intercrossing during many generations of a heterogeneous mixture would supply the place of selection, and overcome any tendency to reversion, so that a crossed race would ultimately become homogeneous, though it might not partake in an equal degree of the characters of the two parent-races.

Of all the differences between the races of man, the color of the skin is the most conspicuous and one of the best marked. Differences of this kind, it was formerly thought, could be accounted for by long exposure under different climates; but Pallas first showed that this view is not tenable, and he has been followed by almost all anthropologists.[39] The view has been rejected chiefly because the distribution of the variously-colored races, most of whom must have long inhabited their present homes, does not coincide with corresponding differences of climate. Weight must also be given to such cases as that of the Dutch families, who, as we hear on excellent authority,[40] have not undergone the least change of color, after residing for three centuries in South Africa. The uniform appearance in various parts of the world of gypsies and Jews, though the uniformity of the latter has been somewhat exaggerated,[41] is likewise an argument on the same side. A very damp or a very dry atmosphere has been supposed to be more influential in modifying the color of the skin than mere heat; but as D'Orbigny in South America, and Livingstone in Africa, arrived at diametrically opposite conclusions with respect to

37. "The Annals of Rural Bengal," 1868, p. 134.

38. "The Variation of Animals and Plants under Domestication," vol. ii. p. 95.

39. Pallas, "Act. Acad. St. Petersburg," 1780, part ii. p. 69. He was followed by Rudolphi, in his "Beyträge zur Anthropologie," 1812. An excellent summary of the evidence is given by Godron, "De l'Espèce," 1859, vol. ii. p. 246, etc.

40. Sir Andrew Smith, as quoted by Knox, "Races of Man," 1850, p. 473.

41. See De Quatrefages on this head, "Revue des Cours Scientifiques," Oct. 17, 1868, p. 731.

dampness and dryness, any conclusion on this head must be considered as very doubtful.[42]

Various facts, which I have elsewhere given, prove that the color of the skin and hair is sometimes correlated in a surprising manner with a complete immunity from the action of certain vegetable poisons and from the attacks of certain parasites. Hence it occurred to me, that negroes and other dark races might have acquired their dark tints by the darker individuals escaping during a long series of generations from the deadly influence of the miasmas of their native countries.

I afterward found that the same idea had long ago occurred to Dr. Wells.[43] That negroes, and even mulattoes, are almost completely exempt from the yellow fever, which is so destructive in tropical America, has long been known.[44] They likewise escape to a large extent the fatal intermittent fevers that prevail along, at least, 2,600 miles of the shores of Africa, and which annually cause one-fifth of the white settlers to die, and another fifth to return home invalided.[45] This immunity in the negro seems to be partly inherent, depending on some unknown peculiarity of constitution, and partly the result of acclimatization. Pouchet[46] states that the negro regiments, borrowed from the Viceroy of Egypt for the Mexican War, which had been recruited near the Soudan, escaped the yellow fever almost equally well with the negroes originally brought from various parts of Africa, and accustomed to the climate of the West Indies. That acclimatization plays a part is shown by the many cases in which negroes, after having resided for some time in a colder climate, have become to a certain extent liable to tropical fevers.[47] The nature of the climate under which the white races have long resided, likewise has some influence on them;

42. Livingstone's "Travels and Researches in S. Africa," 1857, p. 338, 329. D'Orbigny, as quoted by Godron, "De l'Espèce," vol. ii. p. 266.

43. See a paper read before the Royal Soc. in 1813, and published in his Essays in 1818. I have given an account of Dr. Wells's views in the Historical Sketch (p. xvi.) to my "Origin of Species." Various cases of color correlated with constitutional peculiarities are given in my "Variation of Animals under Domestication," vol. ii. pp. 227, 335.

44. See, for instance, Nott and Gliddon, "Types of Mankind," p. 68.

45. Major Tulloch, in a paper read before the Statistical Society, April 20, 1840, and given in the "Athenæum," 1840, p. 353.

46. "The Plurality of the Human Race" (translat.), 1864, p. 60.

47. Quatrefages, "Unité de l'Espèce Humaine," 1861, p. 205. Waitz, "Introduct. to Anthropology," translat. vol. i. 1863, p. 124. Livingstone gives analogous cases in his "Travels."

for, during the fearful epidemic of yellow fever in Demerara during 1837, Dr. Blair found that the death-rate of the immigrants was proportional to the latitude of the country whence they had come. With the negro the immunity, as far as it is the result of acclimatization, implies exposure during a prodigious length of time; for the aborigines of tropical America, who have resided there from time immemorial, are not exempt from yellow fever; and the Rev. B. Tristram states that there are districts in Northern Africa which the native inhabitants are compelled annually to leave, though the negroes can remain with safety.

That the immunity of the negro is in any degree correlated with the color of his skin is a mere conjecture: it may be correlated with some difference in his blood, nervous system, or other tissues. Nevertheless, from the facts above alluded to, and from some connection apparently existing between complexion and a tendency to consumption, the conjecture seemed to me not improbable. Consequently I endeavored, with but little success,[48] to ascertain how far it held good. The late Dr. Daniell, who had long lived on the West Coast of Africa, told me that he did not believe in any such relation. He was himself unusually fair, and had withstood the climate in a wonderful manner. When he first arrived as a boy on the coast,

---

48. In the spring of 1862 I obtained permission from the Director-General of the Medical Department of the Army, to transmit to the surgeons of the various regiments on foreign service a blank table, with the following appended remarks, but I have received no returns: "As several well-marked cases have been recorded with our domestic animals of a relation between the color of the dermal append-ages and the constitution; and it being notorious that there is some limited degree of relation between the color of the races of man and the climate inhabited by them, the following investigation seems worth consideration, namely, whether there is any relation in Europeans between the color of their hair and their liability to the diseases of the tropical countries. If the surgeons of the several regiments, when stationed in unhealthy tropical districts, would be so good as first to count, as a standard of comparison, how many men, in the force whence the sick are drawn, have dark and light colored hair, and hair of intermediate or doubtful tints; and if a similar account were kept by the same medical gentlemen of all the men who suffered from malarious and yellow fevers, or from dysentery, it would soon be apparent, after some thousand cases had been tabulated, whether there exists any relation between the color of the hair and constitutional liability to tropical diseases. Perhaps no such relation would be discovered, but the investigation is well worth making. In case any positive result were obtained, it might be of some practical use in selecting men for any particular service. Theoretically the result would be of high interest, as indicating one means by which a race of men inhabiting from a remote period an unhealthy tropical climate, might have become dark-colored by the better preservation of dark-haired or dark-complexioned indi-viduals during a long succession of generations."

an old and experienced negro chief predicted from his appearance that this would prove the case. Dr. Nicholson, of Antigua, after having attended to this subject, wrote to me that he did not think that dark-colored Europeans escaped the yellow fever better than those that were light-colored. Mr. J. M. Harris altogether denies[49] that Europeans with dark hair withstand a hot climate better than other men; on the contrary, experience has taught him, in making a selection of men for service on the coast of Africa, to choose those with red hair. As far, therefore, as these slight indications serve, there seems no foundation for the hypothesis, which has been accepted by several writers, that the color of the black races may have resulted from darker and darker individuals having survived in greater numbers, during their exposure to the fever-generating miasmas of their native countries.

Although with our present knowledge we cannot account for the strongly-marked differences in color between the races of man, either through correlation with constitutional peculiarities, or through the direct action of climate; yet we must not quite ignore the latter agency, for there is good reason to believe that some inherited effect is thus produced.[50]

We have seen in our third chapter that the conditions of life, such as abundant food and general comfort, affect in a direct manner the development of the bodily frame, the effects being transmitted. Through the combined influences of climate and changed habits of life, European settlers in the United States undergo, as is generally admitted, a slight but extraordinarily rapid change of appearance. There is, also, a considerable body of evidence showing that in the Southern States the house-slaves of the third generation present a markedly different appearance from the field-slaves.[51]

If, however, we look to the races of man, as distributed over the world, we must infer that their characteristic differences cannot be accounted for by the direct action of different conditions of life, even after exposure to them for an enormous period of time. The Esquimaux live exclusively on

49. "Anthropological Review," Jan. 1866, p. xxi.

50. See, for instance, Quatrefages ("Revue des Cours Scientifiques," Oct. 10, 1868, p. 724) on the effects of residence in Abyssinia and Arabia, and other analogous cases. Dr. Rolle (Der Mensch, seine Abstammung, etc., 1865, s. 99) states, on the authority of Khanikof, that the greater number of German families settled in Georgia have acquired in the course of two generations dark hair and eyes. Mr. D. Forbes informs me that the Quichuas in the Andes vary greatly in color, according to the position of the valleys inhabited by them.

51. Harlan, "Medical Researches," p. 532. Quatrefages ("Unité de l'Espèce Humaine," 1861, p. 128) has collected much evidence on this head.

animal food; they are clothed in thick fur, and are exposed to intense cold and to prolonged darkness; yet they do not differ in any extreme degree from the inhabitants of Southern China, who live entirely on vegetable food and are exposed almost naked to a hot, glaring climate. The unclothed Fuegians live on the marine productions of their inhospitable shores; the Botocudos of Brazil wander about the hot forests of the interior and live chiefly on vegetable productions; yet these tribes resemble each other so closely that the Fuegians on board the "Beagle" were mistaken by some Brazilians for Botocudos. The Botocudos, again, as well as the other inhabitants of tropical America, are wholly different from the Negroes who inhabit the opposite shores of the Atlantic, are exposed to a nearly similar climate, and follow nearly the same habits of life.

Nor can the differences between the races of man be accounted for, except to a quite insignificant degree, by the inherited effects of the increased or decreased use of parts. Men who habitually live in canoes may have their legs somewhat stunted; those who inhabit lofty regions have their chests enlarged; and those who constantly use certain sense-organs have the cavities in which they are lodged somewhat increased in size, and their features consequently a little modified. With civilized nations, the reduced size of the jaws from lessened use, the habitual play of different muscles serving to express different emotions, and the increased size of the brain from greater intellectual activity, have together produced a considerable effect on their general appearance, in comparison with savages.[52] It is also possible that increased bodily stature, with no corresponding increase in the size of the brain, may have given to some races (judging from the previously adduced cases of the rabbits) an elongated skull of the dolichocephalic type.

Lastly, the little-understood principle of correlation will almost certainly have come into action, as in the case of great muscular development and strongly-projecting supra-orbital ridges. It is not improbable that the texture of the hair, which differs much in the different races, may stand in some kind of correlation with the structure of the skin; for the color of the hair and skin are certainly correlated, as is its color and texture with the Mandans.[53] The color of the skin and the odor emitted by it are likewise in

52. See Prof. Schaaffhausen, translat. in "Anthropological Review," Oct. 1868, p. 429.

53. Mr. Catlin states ("North American Indians," 3d edit. 1842, vol. i. p. 49) that, in the whole tribe of the Mandans, about one in ten or twelve of the members of all ages and both sexes have bright silvery gray hair, which is hereditary. Now this hair is as coarse and harsh as that of a horse's mane, while the hair of other colors is fine and soft.

some manner connected. With the breeds of sheep the number of hairs within a given space and the number of the excretory pores stand in some relation to each other.[54] If we may judge from the analogy of our domesticated animals, many modifications of structure in man probably come under this principle of correlated growth.

We have now seen that the characteristic differences between the races of man cannot be accounted for in a satisfactory manner by the direct action of the conditions of life, nor by the effects of the continued use of parts, nor through the principle of correlation. We are therefore led to inquire whether slight individual differences, to which man is eminently liable, may not have been preserved and augmented during a long series of generations through natural selection. But here we are at once met by the objection that beneficial variations alone can be thus preserved; and as far as we are enabled to judge (although always liable to error on this head) not one of the external differences between the races of man are of any direct or special service to him. The intellectual and moral or social faculties must of course be excepted from this remark; but differences in these faculties can have had little or no influence on external characters. The variability of all the characteristic differences between the races, before referred to, likewise indicates that these differences cannot be of much importance; for, had they been important, they would long ago have been either fixed and preserved, or eliminated. In this respect man resembles those forms, called by naturalists protean or polymorphic, which have remained extremely variable, owing, as it seems, to their variations being of an indifferent nature, and consequently to their having escaped the action of natural selection.

We have thus far been baffled in all our attempts to account for the differences between the races of man; but there remains one important agency, namely, Sexual Selection, which appears to have acted as powerfully on man as on many other animals. I do not intend to assert that sexual selection will account for all the differences between the races. An unexplained residuum is left, about which we can in our ignorance only say that, as individuals are continually born with, for instance, heads a little rounder or narrower, and with noses a little longer or shorter, such slight differences might become fixed and uniform, if the unknown agencies which induced them were to act in a more constant manner, aided by long-continued intercrossing. Such modifications come under the provisional class, alluded to in our fourth chapter, which for the want of a better term

54. On the odor of the skin, Godron, "Sur l'Espèce," tom. ii. p. 217. On the pores in the skin, Dr. Wilckens, "Die Aufgaben der landwirth. Zootechnik," 1869, s. 7.

have been called spontaneous variations. Nor do I pretend that the effects of sexual selection can be indicated with scientific precision; but it can be shown that it would be an inexplicable fact if man had not been modified by this agency, which has acted so powerfully on innumerable animals, both high and low in the scale. It can further be shown that the differences between the races of man, as in color, hairiness, form of features, etc., are of the nature which it might have been expected would have been acted on by sexual selection. But in order to treat this subject in a fitting manner, I have found it necessary to pass the whole animal kingdom in review; I have therefore devoted to it the Second Part of this work. At the close I shall return to man, and, after attempting to show how far he has been modified through sexual selection, will give a brief summary of the chapters in this First Part.

9

Francis Galton, "Eugenics: Its Definition, Scope and Aims"

Francis Galton (1822–1911) introduced the term "eugenics" in 1883 in his Inquiries into Human Faculty and Its Development. *He had already expressed his views on race in 1869 in* Hereditary Genius *under the heading "The Comparative Worth of Different Races." The 1904 lecture that follows puts a relatively benign face on eugenics, although the idea of making eugenics a national issue combined with the idea of the "fittest races" was soon to have major consequences. In a move that was already an indication of what was to follow, eugenics was known in Germany as* Rassenhygiene, *or race hygiene.*

Eugenics is the science which deals with all influences that improve the inborn qualities of a race; also with those that develop them to the utmost advantage. The improvement of the inborn qualities, or stock, of some one human population, will alone be discussed here.

What is meant by improvement? What by the syllable *Eu* in Eugenics, whose English equivalent is *good?* There is considerable difference between goodness in the several qualities and in that of the character as a whole. The character depends largely on the *proportion* between qualities whose balance may be much influenced by education. We must therefore leave morals as far as possible out of the discussion, not entangling ourselves with the almost hopeless difficulties they raise as to whether a character as a whole is good or bad. Moreover, the goodness or badness of character is not absolute, but relative to the current form of civilisation. A fable will best explain what is meant. Let the scene be the Zoological Gardens in the quiet hours of the night, and suppose that, as in old fables, the animals are able to converse, and that some very wise creature who had easy access to all the cages, say a philosophic sparrow or rat, was engaged in collecting the opinions of all sorts of animals with a view of elaborating a system of absolute morality. It is needless to enlarge on the contrariety of ideals between the beasts that prey and those they prey upon, between

From *Essays in Eugenics*, 1909. Read before the Sociological Society at a Meeting in the School of Economics and Political Science (London University), on May 16th, 1904.

those of the animals that have to work hard for their food and the seden-
tary parasites that cling to their bodies and suck their blood, and so forth.
A large number of suffrages in favour of maternal affection would be
obtained, but most species of fish would repudiate it, while among the
voices of birds would be heard the musical protest of the cuckoo. Though
no agreement could be reached as to absolute morality, the essentials of
Eugenics may be easily defined. All creatures would agree that it was
better to be healthy than sick, vigorous than weak, well fitted than ill-fitted
for their part in life. In short that it was better to be good rather than bad
specimens of their kind, whatever that kind might be. So with men. There
are a vast number of conflicting ideals of alternative characters, of incompatible civilisations; but all are wanted to give fulness and interest to life.
Society would be very dull if every man resembled the highly estimable
Marcus Aurelius or Adam Bede. The aim of Eugenics is to represent each
class or sect by its best specimens; that done, to leave them to work out
their common civilisation in their own way.

A considerable list of qualities can be easily compiled that nearly every
one except "cranks" would take into account when picking out the best
specimens of his class. It would include health, energy, ability, manliness
and courteous disposition. Recollect that the natural differences between
dogs are highly marked in all these respects, and that men are quite as
variable by nature as other animals in their respective species. Special
aptitudes would be assessed highly by those who possessed them, as the
artistic faculties by artists, fearlessness of inquiry and veracity by scientists, religious absorption by mystics, and so on. There would be self-
sacrificers, self-tormentors and other exceptional idealists, but the representatives of these would be better members of a community than the
body of their electors. They would have more of those qualities that are
needed in a State, more vigour, more ability, and more consistency of
purpose. The community might be trusted to refuse representatives of
criminals, and of others whom it rates as undesirable.

Let us for a moment suppose that the practice of Eugenics should
hereafter raise the average quality of our nation to that of its better moiety
at the present day and consider the gain. The general tone of domestic,
social and political life would be higher. The race as a whole would be less
foolish, less frivolous, less excitable and politically more provident than
now. Its demagogues who "played to the gallery" would play to a more
sensible gallery than at present. We should be better fitted to fulfil our vast
imperial opportunities. Lastly, men of an order of ability which is now
very rare, would become more frequent, because the level out of which
they rose would itself have risen.

The aim of Eugenics is to bring as many influences as can be reasonably employed, to cause the useful classes in the community to contribute *more* than their proportion to the next generation.

The course of procedure that lies within the functions of a learned and active Society such as the Sociological may become, would be somewhat as follows:—

1. Dissemination of a knowledge of the laws of heredity so far as they are surely known, and promotion of their farther study. Few seem to be aware how greatly the knowledge of what may be termed the *actuarial* side of heredity has advanced in recent years. The *average* closeness of kinship in each degree now admits of exact definition and of being treated mathematically, like birth and death-rates, and the other topics with which actuaries are concerned.

2. Historical inquiry into the rates with which the various classes of society (classified according to civic usefulness) have contributed to the population at various times, in ancient and modern nations. There is strong reason for believing that national rise and decline is closely connected with this influence. It seems to be the tendency of high civilisation to check fertility in the upper classes, through numerous causes, some of which are well known, others are inferred, and others again are wholly obscure. The latter class are apparently analogous to those which bar the fertility of most species of wild animals in zoological gardens. Out of the hundreds and thousands of species that have been tamed, very few indeed are fertile when their liberty is restricted and their struggles for livelihood are abolished; those which are so and are otherwise useful to man becoming domesticated. There is perhaps some connection between this obscure action and the disappearance of most savage races when brought into contact with high civilization, though there are other and well-known concomitant causes. But while most barbarous races disappear, some, like the negro, do not. It may therefore be expected that types of our race will be found to exist which can be highly civilised without losing fertility; nay, they may become more fertile under artificial conditions, as is the case with many domestic animals.

3. Systematic collection of facts showing the circumstances under which large and thriving families have most frequently originated; in other words, the *conditions* of Eugenics. The names of the thriving families in England have yet to be learnt, and the conditions under which they have arisen. We cannot hope to make much advance in the science of Eugenics without a careful study of facts that are now accessible with difficulty, if at all. The definition of a thriving family, such as will pass muster for the moment at least is one in which the children have gained distinctly supe-

rior positions to those who were their class-mates in early life. Families may be considered "large" that contain not less than three adult male children. It would be no great burden to a Society including many members who had Eugenics at heart, to initiate and to preserve a large collection of such records for the use of statistical students. The committee charged with the task would have to consider very carefully the form of their circular and the persons entrusted to distribute it. The circular should be simple, and as brief as possible, consistent with asking all questions that are likely to be answered truly, and which would be important to the inquiry. They should ask, at least in the first instance, only for as much information as could be easily, and would be readily, supplied by any member of the family appealed to. The point to be ascertained is the *status* of the two parents at the time of their marriage, whence its more or less eugenic character might have been predicted, if the larger knowledge that we now hope to obtain had then existed. Some account would, of course, be wanted of their race, profession, and residence; also of their own respective parentages, and of their brothers and sisters. Finally, the reasons would be required why the children deserved to be entitled a "thriving" family, to distinguish worthy from unworthy success. This manuscript collection might hereafter develop into a "golden book" of thriving families. The Chinese, whose customs have often much sound sense, make their honours retrospective. We might learn from them to show that respect to the parents of noteworthy children, which the contributors of such valuable assets to the national wealth richly deserve. The act of systematically collecting records of thriving families would have the further advantage of familiarising the public with the fact that Eugenics had at length become a subject of serious scientific study by an energetic Society.

4. Influences affecting Marriage. The remarks of Lord Bacon in his essay on Death may appropriately be quoted here. He says with the view of minimising its terrors:

> "There is no passion in the mind of men so weak but it mates and masters the fear of death. Revenge triumphs over death; love slights it; honour aspireth to it; grief flyeth to it; fear pre-occupateth it."

Exactly the same kind of considerations apply to marriage. The passion of love seems so overpowering that it may be thought folly to try to direct its course. But plain facts do not confirm this view. Social influences of all kinds have immense power in the end, and they are very various. If unsuitable marriages from the Eugenic point of view were banned socially, or even regarded with the unreasonable disfavour which some attach to cousin-marriages, very few would be made. The multitude of marriage restrictions that have proved prohibitive among uncivilised people would require a volume to describe.

5. Persistence in setting forth the national importance of Eugenics. There are three stages to be passed through. *Firstly* it must be made familiar as an academic question, until its exact importance has been understood and accepted as a fact; *Secondly* it must be recognised as a subject whose practical development deserves serious consideration; and *Thirdly* it must be introduced into the national conscience, like a new religion. It has, indeed, strong claims to become an orthodox religious tenet of the future, for Eugenics co-operates with the workings of Nature by securing that humanity shall be represented by the fittest races. What Nature does blindly, slowly, and ruthlessly, man may do providently, quickly, and kindly. As it lies within his power, so it becomes his duty to work in that direction; just as it is his duty to succour neighbours who suffer misfortune. The improvement of our stock seems to me one of the highest objects that we can reasonably attempt. We are ignorant of the ultimate destinies of humanity, but feel perfectly sure that it is as noble a work to raise its level in the sense already explained, as it would be disgraceful to abase it. I see no impossibility in Eugenics becoming a religious dogma among mankind, but its details must first be worked out sedulously in the study. Over-zeal leading to hasty action would do harm, by holding out expectations of a near golden age, which will certainly be falsified and cause the science to be discredited. The first and main point is to secure the general intellectual acceptance of Eugenics as a hopeful and most important study. Then let its principles work into the heart of the nation, who will gradually give practical effect to them in ways that we may not wholly foresee.

10

Franz Boas,
"Instability of Human Types"

Franz Boas (1858–1942) is often referred to as the father of American an-
thropology. He is credited with liberating anthropology from the racial ide-
ology that had previously promoted the field. For Boas, the topic of
anthropology was not race but culture. Race was minimized. He did not
deny that race might be a factor, so that in certain respects questions of race
were sidestepped rather than addressed head-on. Nevertheless, this treatment
was not true of "Instability of Human Types," which Boas delivered at the
First Universal Races Congress held in London in July 1911. This was an
important congress attended by such scholars as W. E. B. Du Bois, Israel
Zangwill, Ferdinand Tönnies, and Harry H. Johnston. Boas was not the
first to challenge the permanence of racial characteristics, but he brought a
scientific sobriety to the issue.

When we try to judge the ability of races of man, we make the silent
assumption that ability is something permanent and stationary, that it
depends upon heredity, and that, as compared to it, environmental, modifying influences are, comparatively speaking, of slight importance. While
in a comparative study of the physical characteristics of races that are as
distinct as the white and the negro, or the negro and the Mongol, this
assumption might be accepted as a basis for further studies, its validity is
not so clear in a comparison of the mental characteristics of branches of
the same race. When, for instance, it is claimed that certain types of
Europe show better mental endowment than other types of Europe, the
assumption is made that these types are stable, and cannot undergo far-
reaching differences when placed in a new social or geographical
environment.

It would seem, therefore, that a study of the stability of race-types has
not only a fundamental biological importance, but that it will also determine our views of the relative mental endowment of different types of
man.

From G. Spiller, ed., *Papers on Inter-racial Problems, First Universal Races Con-*
gress, July 26–29, 1911.

A theoretical investigation of this problem will show that the assumption of an absolute stability of human types is not plausible. Observations on growth have shown that the amount of growth of the whole body depends upon more or less favourable conditions which prevail during the period of development. Unfavourable conditions retard growth; exceptionally favourable conditions accelerate it. A more detailed study of the phenomena of growth has shown that the development of different parts of the body does not proceed by any means at the same rate at a given period. Thus at the time of birth the bulk of the body and stature are very small, and increase with great rapidity until about the fourteenth year in girls, and the sixteenth year in boys. On the other hand, the size of the head increases rapidly only for one or two years; and from this time on the increment is, comparatively speaking, slight. Similar conditions prevail in regard to the growth of the face, which grows rapidly for a few years only, and later on increases, comparatively speaking, slowly. The amount of water contained in the brain also changes with a fair amount of rapidity during the early years of life, and remains about the same later on. It follows from this observation that if an individual is retarded by unfavourable conditions after a certain organ has obtained nearly its full development, while other organs are still in the process of rapid evolution, the former cannot be much influenced, while the latter may bear evidence of the unfavourable conditions which were controlling during a certain period of life. This must necessarily have the result that the proportions of the body of the adult will depend upon the general conditions of life prevailing during youth, and the effects of these conditions will be most noticeable in those organs which have the longest period of development.

It is a well-known fact that the central nervous system continues to develop in structure longer perhaps than any other part of the body, and it may therefore be inferred that it will be apt to show the most far-reaching influences of environment.

It follows from this consideration that social and geographical environment must have an influence upon the form of the body of the adult, and upon the development of his central nervous system.

This theoretical consideration is borne out by observation. The investigations of Bolk have shown clearly that an increase in stature has occurred in Europe during the last decades, due evidently to a change of environment; and the numerous investigations which have been made on the proportions of the body of the well-to-do and of the poor, of able students and poor students—all show characteristic differences, which may be explained in great part as effects of the retardation and acceleration to which we have referred.

It would seem, however, that besides the influences of more or less favourable environment which affect the form of the body during the period of growth, a number of other causes may modify the form of the body. Professor Ridgeway goes so far as to think that the stability of human types in definite areas and for long periods is an expression, not of the influence of heredity, but of the influence of environment; and that, on the other hand, the modifications of the human form which are found in the Mediterranean area, in Central Europe, and in North-western Europe, are due to the differences of climate, soil, and natural products. It does not seem to me that adequate proof can be given for modifications of the human form as far-reaching as those claimed by Professor Ridgeway, although we must grant the possibility of such influences. We have, however, good evidence which shows that the various European types undergo certain changes in a new environment. The observations on which this conclusion is based were made by me on emigrants from various European countries who live in the city of New York, and on their descendants.

The investigation of a large number of families has shown that every single measurement that has been studied has one value among individuals born in Europe, another one among individuals of the same families born in America. Thus, among the East European Jews the head of the European-born is shorter than the head of the American-born. It is wider among the European-born than it is among the American-born. At the same time the American-born is taller. As a result of the increase in the growth of head, and decrease of the width of head, the length-breadth index is considerably less than the corresponding index in the European-born. All these differences seem to increase with the time elapsed between the emigration of the parents and the birth of the child, and are much more marked in the second generation of American-born individuals.

Among the long-headed Sicilians similar observations have been made, but the changes are in a different direction. The stature does not change much; if anything, it is shorter among the American-born than among the European-born. The head is shorter among the American-born, and at the same time wider, than among the European-born. Thus a certain approach of the two distinct types may be observed.

It would of course be saying too much to claim that this approach expresses a tendency of diverse European types to assume the same form in America. Our studies prove only a modification of the type; but we are not able to determine what the ultimate amount of these modifications will be, and whether there is any real tendency of modifying diverse types in such a way that one particular American type should develop, rather than a limited modification of each particular European type.

The people of Bohemia and Hungary show also the effect of the changed environment. Among them both width of head and length of head decrease. The face becomes much narrower, the stature taller.

It is most remarkable that the change in head-form of American-born individuals occurs almost immediately after the arrival of their parents in America. A comparison of individuals born in Europe with those born in America shows that the change of head-form is almost abrupt at the time of immigration. The child born abroad, even if it is less than one year old at the time of arrival, has the head-form of the European-born. The child born in America, even if born only a few months after the arrival of the parents, has the head-form of the American-born. The failure of American environment to influence the foreign-born might be expected, because the total change of the head-index from early youth to adult life is very small. On the other hand, those measurements of the body which continue to change during the period of growth show a marked influence of American environment upon European-born individuals who arrive in America as young children. Thus the stature of European-born individuals increases the more the younger they were at the time of their arrival in America. The width of the faces decreases the more the younger the child that came to America.

These observations are of importance, because it might be claimed that the changes in head-form develop because the mechanical treatment of children in America differs from their treatment in Europe. The European child is swaddled, while the American child is allowed to lie free in the cradle. The change in the face diameters and in stature show, however, that such mechanical considerations alone cannot explain the changes that actually take place.

The results obtained by a rough comparison of European-born and American-born have been corroborated by a direct comparison of European-born parents and their own American-born children, and also by a comparison of the European immigrants who came to America in one particular year, and of their descendants born in America. In all these cases the same types of differences were found.

These observations seem to indicate a decided plasticity of human types; but I wish to repeat that the limits of this plasticity are not known to us. It follows, however, directly, that if the bodily form undergoes far-reaching changes under a new environment, concomitant changes of the mind may be expected. The same reasons which led us to the conclusion that more or less favourable conditions during the period of growth will have the greater influence the longer the period of development of a particular part of the body, make it plausible that a change of environment will influence those parts of the body most thoroughly which have the longest period of growth and development. I believe, therefore, that the American observations compel us to assume that the mental make-up of a certain type of man may be considerably influenced by his social and geographical environment. It is, of course, exceedingly difficult to give an actual proof of this conclusion by observation, because we know that the mental manifestations depend to a great extent upon the social group in which each individual grows up; but it is evident that the burden of proof is shifted upon those who claim absolute stability of mental characteristics of the same type under all possible conditions under which it may be found.

It may be pointed out here that the change of type which has been observed in America is in a way analogous to the difference of type that has been observed in Europe in a comparison between the urban population and the rural population. In all those cases in which thorough investigations have been made in regard to this problem, a difference in type has been found. The interpretation given in this phenomenon is, however, entirely different from the one attempted here. One group of observers, particularly Ridolfo Livi, believe that the type found in urban communities is largely due to the greater mixture of local types found in cities when compared to the open country. Others, notably Otto Ammon and Röse, believe that we have here evidence of natural selection, and that the better type survives. It seems to my mind that the latter theory cannot be substantiated, but that both mixture and change of type are sufficient to explain what is taking place in the transition from rural life to urban life.

It will naturally be asked, what produces changes in human types? Can these changes be so directed as to bring about an improvement of the race? I do not believe that these questions can be answered in the present state of our knowledge. The structural changes which must necessarily accompany the modifications of gross form are entirely unknown, and the physiological functions which are affected by the new environment cannot even be surmised. It seems, therefore, a vain endeavour to give a satisfactory explanation of the phenomenon at the present time. The investigation should be extended over numerous types, and carried on in different climates and different social environments, before we can hope to understand the correlation between bodily form and function and outward influences. The old idea of absolute stability of human types must, however, evidently be given up, and with it the belief of the hereditary superiority of certain types over others.

11

Alain Locke,
"The Concept of Race
as Applied to Social Culture"

Alain Locke (1885–1954) published "The Concept of Race as Applied to Social Culture" in 1924 while Chair of the Department of Philosophy at Howard University. The work arose out of a series of lectures first delivered in 1915 under the title Race Contacts and Interracial Relations. *Locke was an important figure in the Harlem Renaissance. Much of his work both at this time and later was focused specifically on African and African-American culture, but he coedited with Bernard Stern an anthology on race contacts and multiculturalism,* When Peoples Meet *(1942), that was far ahead of its time.*

In dealing with race and culture we undoubtedly confront two of the most inevitable but at the same time most unsatisfactory concepts involved in the broad-scale consideration of man and society. There is the general presumption and feeling that they have some quite vital and relevant connection, but as to the nature of this or even as to the scientific meaning of the individual concepts there is the greatest diversity of scientific opinion and theory. An analytic study of their highly variable meanings, confining this even to the more or less strictly scientific versions, would constitute two important and highly desirable treatises. But what we are here attempting is something quite more immediate and practical from the point of view of the use of these terms in the social sciences, and quite capable perhaps, if the analysis be successful, of settling some of these complexly controversial differences as to meaning by a process of elimination, namely an examination into their supposed relationship one to the other. For it seems that in the erroneous assumption of fixed relationships between the two, most of the serious difficulties and confusions lie. It will be our contention that far from being constants, these important aspects of human society are variables, and in the majority of instances not even paired variables, and that though they have at all times significant and definite relationships, they nevertheless are in no determinate way organically or causally connected. And if this should be so, whole masses of elaborately constructed social theory and cultural philosophizing fall

From *Howard Review*, 1, 1924.

with the destruction of a common basic assumption, that has been taken as a common foundation for otherwise highly divergent and even antagonistic theorizing. This position, differing from that of the school of interpretation which denies all significant connection between racial and cultural factors,[1] does not deny that race stands for significant social characters and culture-traits or represents in given historical contexts characteristic differentiations of culture-type. However, it does insist against the assumption of any such constancy, historical or intrinsic, as would make it possible to posit an organic connection between them and to argue on such grounds the determination of one by the other.

But the unwarranted assumption of race as a determinant of culture is still very current, and contemporary discussion, especially in ethnology, is still primarily concerned with the destructive criticism of this inveterate and chronic notion. We would by no means minimize the success and scientific service of such criticism as that of Boas in the field of anthropology and "race psychology," of Flinders-Petrie in archeology, of Finot, Babington, Hertz, and von Zollschan in social and political theory, and of Lowie and Wissler in ethnology,[2] in saying that as yet, however, we seem to be only at a transitional stage in the scientific consideration of the relationship of race to culture. In some revised and reconstructed form, we may anticipate the continued even if restricted use of these terms as more or less necessary and basic concepts that cannot be eliminated altogether, but that must nevertheless be so safe-guarded in this continued use as not to give further currency to the invalidated assumptions concerning them. It is too early to assume that there is no significant connection between race and culture because of the manifestly false and arbitrary linkage which has previously been asserted.

In the interval between these two stages of the discussion, as one might normally expect, there is considerable tendency to continue the corollaries of the older view even where the main position and hypothesis has been abandoned. Goldenweiser[3] is therefore quite justified in his insistence upon linking up these corollaries with the position of classical social evolutionism which gave them such vogue and standing, and disestablishing both by the same line of argument. For although this notion of race as a prime determining factor in culture was historically established by the

---

1. R. H. Lowie, *Culture and Ethnology*, Chap. II, 1923.

2. Franz Boas, *The Mind of Primitive Man*, (1911); W. M. Flinders-Petrie, *Race and Civilization* (Proc. Brit. Assoc., 1895); Jean Finot, *Race Prejudice* (Trans. 1907); W. D. Babington, *Fallacies of Race Theories;* Hertz, *Moderne Rassentheorien;* I. von Zollschan, *Das Rassenproblem* (Vienna, 1912).

3. A. Goldenweiser, *Early Civilization*, Chap. I, pp. 14–15.

theory and influence of de Gobineau,[4] its scientific justification has been associated with the doctrines of the strictly evolutionary interpretation of culture, especially with the influence of the social evolutionism of Spencer. The primary scientific use of this fixed linkage between race and culture was to justify the classical evolutionary scheme of a series of stepped stages in an historical progression of cultural development. In this connection it has been the analogue in the theory of society of the heredity factor in the biological field, and its stock notions of *race capacity* and *racial heredity* have had approximately the same phases of acceptance, repudiation, and revision. In their "classical" form they are now equally discredited by several lines of detailed evidence where the historical succession of stages does not coincide with those posited as the ground basis of the supposedly universal process of development,[5] and by the more intensive and objective study of primitive cultures which has shown how insidiously their consideration in the light of such evolutionary schemes has distorted their concrete facts and values. There is considerable warrant therefore for the position that wishes to exclude all further misinterpretation by a complete disassociation of the concept of race from the concept of culture.

This is the position of Lowie[6] who concludes after a brilliant and rigorous examination as to the inter-connection between culture and race that not only are cultural changes "manifestly independent of the racial factor," but that no race has permanent or even uniform alignment with reference to culture-type or cultural stages. His position, though one of the closest reasoned of any, is the most iconoclastic with respect to the assumption of any significant relation between race and culture, as may be estimated from the following passage:

> With great confidence we can say that since the same race at different times or in different subdivisions at the same time represents vastly different cultural stages, there is obviously no direct proportional between culture and race and if great changes of culture can occur without any change of race whatsoever, we are justified in considering it probable that a relatively minute change of hereditary ability might produce enormous differences.

But the extreme cultural relativism of Lowie leaves an open question as to the association of certain ethnic groups with definite culture-traits and culture types under circumstances where there is evidently a greater persistence of certain strains and characteristics in their culture than of other

---

4. de Gobineau, *Essai sur l'inegalite des races humains* (Paris, 1854).
5. Goldenweiser, *Early Civilization*, pp. 21–27. [Page 14 seems more appropriate.]
6. R. H. Lowie, *Culture and Ethnology*, p. 41.

factors. The stability of such factors and their resistance to direct historical modification marks out the province of that aspect of the problem of
race which is distinctly ethnological and which the revised notion of ethnic
race must cover. It seems quite clear that no adequate explanation can be
expected from the factors and principles of anthropological race distinctions. In the light of the most recent and accepted investigations any
attempt to explain one in terms of the other must be regarded as pseudoscientific. Nevertheless though there is lacking for the present any
demonstrable explanation, there are certain ethnic traits the peculiarly
stable and stock character of which must be interpreted as ethnically
characteristic. They are in no sense absolutely permanent, the best psychological evidence as yet gives us no reason for construing them as
inherent, yet they are factors not without an integral relationship one to
the other not satisfactorily explained as mere historical combinations.
Indeed it seems difficult and in some cases impossible to discover common
historical factors to account for their relative constancy. Few challenge the
specific factuality of these peculiarly resistant combinations of group
traits.

As Sapir[7] aptly says,

> Here, as so often, the precise knowledge of the scientist lags somewhat
> behind the more naive but more powerful insights of non-professional expe-
> rience and impression. To deny to the genius of a people an ultimate psycho-
> logical significance and to refer it to the specific historical development of
> that people is not, after all is said and done, to analyze it out of existence. It
> remains true that large groups of people everywhere tend to think and to act
> in accordance with established and all but instinctive forms, which are in a
> large measure peculiar to it.

The point that seems to be important to note and stress is that we do not
need to deny the existence of these characteristic racial molds in denying
that they are rooted in "inherent hereditary traits either of a biological or a
psychological nature."

If, instead of the anthropological, the ethnic characters had been more
in the focus of scientific attention, there probably would have resulted a
much more scientific and tenable doctrine of the relationship of race to
culture. Race would have been regarded as primarily a matter of social
heredity, and its distinctions due to the selective psychological "set" of
established cultural reactions. There is a social determination involved in
this which quite more rationally interprets and explains the relative sta-

---

7. E. Sapir, "Culture, Genuine and Spurious." *American Journal of Sociology* 29,
p. 406.

bility or so-called permanency that the old theorists were trying to account for on the basis of fixed anthropological characters and factors. To quote again from Sapir:[8]

The current assumption that the so-called "genius" of a people is ultimately reducible to certain inherent heredity traits of a biological and psychological nature does not, for the most part, bear very serious examination. Frequently enough, what is assumed to be an innate racial characteristic turns out on closer study to be the resultant of purely historical causes. A mode of thinking, a distinctive type of reaction, gets itself established in the course of a complex historical development as typical, as normal; it serves then as a model for the working over of new elements of civilization.

The best consensus of opinion then seems to be that race is a fact in the social or ethnic sense, that it has been very erroneously associated with race in the physical sense and is therefore not scientifically commensurate with factors or conditions which explain or have produced physical race characters and differentiation, that it has a vital and significant relation to social culture, and that it must be explained in terms of social and historical causes such as have caused similar differentiations of culture-type as pertain in lesser degree between nations, tribes, classes, and even family strains. Most authorities are now reconciled to two things,—first, the necessity of a thorough-going redefinition of the nature of race, and second, the independent definition of race in the ethnic or social sense together with the independent investigation of its differences and their causes apart from the investigation of the factors and differentiae of physical race. Of course eventually there may be some interesting correlation possible at the conclusion of these two lines of investigation, but up to the present they seem only to have needlessly handicapped and complicated one another and to have brought comparative ethnology and comparative anthropology both to a deadlock of confusion because of their incompatible points of view and incommensurable values. It is undoubtedly this necessity of a new start that Wissler[9] has in mind when he says, "So it is obvious that the relation between culture and race is a subject of more than passing interest, and though as yet not seriously investigated, the time is near at hand when its solution must be sought, if life is to be understood rationally and socially." Similarly we find Flinders-Petrie[10] in his address before the British Association saying "The definition of the nature of race is the most requisite element for any clear ideas about man," and then

8. *Ibid.*, pp. 405–406.
9. Wissler, C., *Man and Culture* (1923).
10. Flinders-Petrie, *Race and Civilization* (Proc. Brit. Assoc., 1895).

veering over to the strictly social definition of race by adding, "The only meaning a race can have is a group of persons whose type has become unified by their rate of assimilation and affection by their conditions exceeding the rate of change produced by foreign elements." Evidently the thought here is that blood intermixture is only one of the conducive conditions to cultural assimilation and absorption and that therefore *culture-type* or *social race* is the important fact and concept. Race in the vital and basic sense is simply and primarily the culture-heredity, and that in its blendings and differentiations is properly analyzed on the basis of conformity to or variance from culture-type.

Gault,[11] discussing Stevenson's study, *Socio-Anthropometry: An Interracial Critique,* and several studies of Indian cross-breeds, all of which draw conclusions that differences are due to blood-race factors, says:

> There is always the possibility that the Indian of mixed blood owes a degree of his superiority (we should say "difference") to the *social* stimuli of one or the other parent from earliest infancy: stimuli that from the beginning have induced a level of reactions that otherwise would have been lacking, and have built up personality complexes that are next to original nature as respects substantiality.

Thus even in instances where physical assimilation is the condition responsible for cultural assimilation, the latter takes place in terms of social factors. Divorced then by every line of objectively considered evidence from the anthropological notion and criteria of race with which its distinctions rarely if ever coincide, ethnic race or what Gault calls "sociologic type" becomes the most scientifically tenable and useful concept.

Instead therefore of regarding culture as expressive of race, race by this interpretation is regarded as itself a culture product. Goldenweiser[12] puts the matter this way; he says:

> Enough has been said to show that the view generally held of the relation between race and culture may well be reversed. According to the prevailing view, man is many and civilization one, meaning by this that the races differ significantly in potential ability and that only one, the white race, could have and has achieved civilization. The reverse view, forced upon the ethnologist and the historian by a more critical and open-minded survey of the facts, reads thus: *man is one, civilizations are many,* meaning by this that the races do not differ significantly in psychological endowment, that the variety of possible civilizations is great and of actual ones, considerable, and that many

11. Gault, R. H., *Social Psychology* (New York, 1923), p. 104.

12. Goldenweiser, *Early Civilization,* p. 14.

civilizations other than ours have achieved things of genuine and unique worth.

Perhaps the revolutionary significance of this can only be realized when we see it applied to specific descriptive analysis as in the case of Rivers'[13] use of the term race solely in a sense which means the people who had such and such culture-traits, whose customs dominated this or that period and set the pattern upon which a certain culture-type was developed.

Nothing seems more likely than that there will gradually develop out of this new and more objective analysis of culture a series of relatively divergent and basic culture-types, for each of which perhaps some more or less organic principle of development or evolution can be worked out, so that we may eventually get a standard of value for relative culture grading. Meanwhile we must grant the logic of the position of Lowie which is that the most objective study at present gives no warrant for the relative scientific grading of cultures. Meanwhile each culture must be treated as specific and as highly composite, and each ethnic group as the peculiar resultant of its own social history. This is what we mean then by this reversal of emphasis, that instead of the race explaining the cultural condition, the cultural conditions must explain the race traits, and that instead of artificially extracted units representing race types, the newer scientific approach demands that we deal with concrete culture-types which as often as not are composite racially speaking, and have only an artificial ethnic unity of historical derivation and manufacture.

Confident that this is the correct scientific conception of culture and its most warrantable scientific basis of approach and study, we return to the consideration of whether or not by such interpretation the concept of race is not entirely relegated from serious consideration in connection with it. So considerable is the shift of emphasis and meaning that at times it does seem that the best procedure would be to substitute for the term *race* the term *culture-group*. But what has become absolutely disqualified for the explanation of culture groups taken as totalities becomes in a much more scientific and verifiable way a main factor of explanation of its various cultural components. Race accounts for a great many of the specific elements of the cultural heredity, and the sense of race may itself be regarded as one of the operative factors in culture since it determines the stressed values which become the conscious symbols and tradition of the culture. Such stressed values are themselves factors in the process of culture making, and account primarily for the persistence and resistance of culture-traits. For these determine what is the dominant pattern in any

13. Compare Rivers, W. H., *Psychology and Ethnology* (London, 1926).

given culture, and it is toward these dominants as social norms that social conformation converges and according to which it eventually establishes the type. It is with respect to such principles of determination that the newer psychology of race must be worked out instead of with reference to assumed innate traits and capacities. The type itself may have been established by accident or fortuitous combinations of historical circumstances, but re-enforced by the sense of race as perhaps the most intense of the feelings of commonality, it becomes an accepted, preferred and highly resistant culture complex that seems to be and often is self-perpetuating.

Race operates as tradition, as preferred traits and values, and when these things change culturally speaking ethnic remoulding is taking place. Race then, so far as the ethnologist is concerned, seems to lie in that peculiar selective preference for certain culture-traits and resistance to certain others which is characteristic of all types and levels of social organization. And instead of decreasing as a result of contacts this sense and its accumulative results seems on the whole to increase, so that we get accumulative effect. It intensifies therefore with contacts and increases with the increasing complexity of the culture elements in any particular area. A diversity of cultural types temporarily at least accentuates the racial stresses involved, so that even when a fusion eventuates it takes place under the conditions determined by the resistance developed and the relative strength of the several cultural components.

Indeed, the evidence shows most cultures to be highly composite. Sometimes there seems to be a race relatively pure physically with a considerably mixed culture, sometimes, perhaps more frequently, a highly mixed race with a relatively fused culture. But in the large majority of cases the culture is only to be explained as the resultant of the meeting and reciprocal influence of several culture strains, several ethnic contributions. Such facts nullify two of the most prevalent popular and scientific fallacies, the ascription of a total culture to any one ethnic strain, and the interpretation of culture in terms of the intrinsic rather than the fusion values of its various constituent elements. Especially does this newer view insist upon the disassociation of the claims of political dominance and cultural productivity, and combat the traditional view that all or even the best elements of a culture are the contribution of the ethnic group which in a mixed culture has political dominance and is in dynastic control. Already a number of such politically proprietary claims have been disallowed and disestablished by the more intensive and objectively comparative study of culture-traits. Such procedure promises to redeem the fields of discussion which till recently have been so vitiated by racial and national bias that some ethnologists have been led to conclude the impossibility of the scientific evaluation of cultures. After all, the failure to maintain objective standards, relevant values, and parity of values ought not be taken as evidence that this is not possible. So great is the tendency to lapse back into the former positions of bias, that the rigid maintenance of objective description as the sole aim of the ethnologist may, however, be fully warranted for the time being.

But races may, and must eventually be compared with respect to their relative and characteristic abilities and tendencies with respect to cultural origins, cultural assimilation, cultural survival, and their concrete institutional contributions. But in every case absolute objective parity of condition and values must be maintained. An instance in point is Lowie's[14] own illustration in a discussion of the relative rating of cultures on the basis of cultural originality and assimilation. He says: "If the Japanese deserve no credit for having appropriated our culture, we must also carefully eliminate from that culture all elements not demonstrably due to the creative genius of our race before laying claim to the residue as our distinctive product." This seems simple enough to be axiomatic, yet as a principle of comparison one can find in treatise after treatise a score of breaches for every single observance of what ought to be a fundamental procedure. Irrelevant evaluation and invidious comparisons that do not even make the pretense of establishing either parity or equivalence of values abound, yet it is not to be corrected by excluding values, but rather through insistence upon the only properly scientific criteria—intrinsic values for the interpretation of any culture, and strictly commensurate or equivalent values as a basis of comparisons between them.

The chief source of error in the evaluation of cultures can be traced as the same source already described as responsible for the prevalent errors in the description of cultures. It is incumbent upon us to see clearly why the evolutionary formula has led in both these instances to such unsoundness of interpretation. It would seem that by putting all types and varieties into the same series, and this is the crux of the straight evolutionary point of view, the error of assuming basic common factors and commensurate values has almost irretrievably been made. Not that such factors may not exist, but that they are not to be discovered except from the point of view of a more objective and detailed comparison than has in most cases been attempted. Since the days of the Indo-Germanic myth, and its twin fancy the Aryan hypothesis, the desire and suppressed objective in many investigations has been to build a social pyramid of straight line progressive stages, and subtle variations of this point of view have been introducing error upon error into the interpretation of cultures, especially primitive and alien cultures which have naturally borne the brunt of the scheme

14. Lowie, *Culture and Ethnology*, pp. 32–33.

through having been distorted and pinched into alignment with the pre-conceived formula.[15] We have a clear and succinct statement of the re-sponsibility in this regard in the following passage:[16]

> The earlier anthropologists and sociologists, swayed by the biological theo-ries of evolution, posited parallel development in every people, following upon innate psychological tendencies. Complete systems, with stages of development culminating in our own particular type of civilization, were posited by such early writers as Morgan, Spencer, Tylor and others. How-ever, it has been found that the other cultural mechanism, that of diffusion, constituted a grave stumbling block to this a priori scheme of stage develop-ment, and it is now known that independent origins of inventions are infi-nitely more rare than was believed, and that they are conditioned not by innate psychological tendencies, but by the cultural milieu in which they occur.

Gradually it has become apparent that the procedure of using primitive cultures as the stock arguments and illustrations for societal evolution has disorganized the organic unity of these cultures, and merely used certain aspects of them as illustrating a comparative series which even if it were correct for the institution in question from which the accentuated culture-elements were taken, would not place correctly in scale as totalities the cultures respectively in question.

It follows then that the work of correction will have to begin at the very point where originally the errors and distortions have been introduced, namely, the more carefully objective study and organic interpretation of primitive cultures. This would be necessary from the purely corrective point of view, even if it were not also true as Wissler[17] says that "our clearest insight into the mechanisms of culture is attained when we exam-ine the more primitive marginal cultures of the world." After the applica-tion of the reconstructed notion of race as social in manifestation and derivation, this would seem to be the most important and promising revision of idea and method in the entire field of our discussion. As a straight methodological question then we get the following as the only correct and acceptable procedure in the study of any given culture—first, its analytic and complete description in terms of its own culture-elements, second, its organic interpretation in terms of its own intrinsic values as a vital mode of living, combined if possible with an historical account of its

15. Compare Goldenweiser, Chap. 1 and p. 125.

16. Herskovits and Willey, "The Cultural Approach to Sociology," *American Journal of Sociology* 29, p. 195.

17. Wissler, *Man and Culture*, p. 286.

development and derivation, and then finally and not till then its assign-ment to culture-type and interpretation as a stage of culture. Almost any culture so treated will be found to be radically different both in descrip-tion and evaluation from that account which would have been given it if immediately submitted on first analysis to the general scale and to univer-sal comparison. Let us call this the *principle of organic interpretation* and the other the *principle of cultural relativity*, and conclude that in combina-tion with the dynamic and social interpretation of race, the three are the methodological foundation and platform of the newer science of social culture. Especially in connection with the concept of race are all of the biased and partisan points of view and scales of evaluation obviated by such procedure so that it becomes possible to continue the term scien-tifically and usefully in the context of discussion to which it is most relevant, but into which until recently it has introduced primarily serious errors both of fact and of value.

12

Ashley Montagu,
"The Concept of Race in the Human
Species in the Light of Genetics"

Ashley Montagu (1905–1999) is considered one of the most influential public intellectuals of the twentieth century. He wrote or edited more than eighty books, many in multiple editions, as well as thousands of research articles, magazine pieces, book chapters, letters, commentaries, and lectures in a career that spanned three-fourths of the twentieth century. Among his best-known works on race are Man's Most Dangerous Myth, *published at the height of Nazism in 1942, and the seminal UNESCO* Statement on Race *(1952).*

It is said that when the theory of evolution was first announced it was received by the wife of the Canon of Worcester Cathedral with the remark, "Descended from the apes! My dear, we will hope it is not true. But if it is, let us pray that it may not become generally known."

I rather feel that the attempt to deprive the anthropologist of his belief in race is a piece of cruelty akin to that which sought to deprive the Canon's wife of her belief in special creation. Indeed, the anthropological conception of race and the belief in special creation have much in common. The prevailing attitude of mind is illustrated by the remark of a colleague who, when I gave him an account of this paper replied, somewhat like the Canon's wife, "My dear, I always thought that there was such a thing as race." I believe he had spoken more correctly had he said that he had always taken the idea for granted. Certainly, I had always taken the idea for granted, and I think all of us have done so. Indeed, the idea of race is one of the most fundamental if not *the* most fundamental of the concepts with which the anthropologist has habitually worked. To question the validity of this fundamental concept upon which we were intellectually brought up as if it were an axiom, was something which simply never occurred to one. One doesn't question the axioms upon which one's

Presented originally as a lecture, "The Meaninglessness of the Anthropological Conception of Race," before the American Association of Physical Anthropologists, Chicago, April, 1941, and originally published in *The Journal of Heredity*, Vol. 23, 1941, pp. 243–247. Copyright © 1963. Reprinted by permission of the author and Princeton University Press.

science, and one's activity in it, are based—at least, not usually. One simply takes them for granted.

But in science, as in life, it is a good practice, from time to time, to hang a question mark on the things one takes most for granted. In science such questioning is important because without it there is a very real danger that certain erroneous or arbitrary ideas which may originally have been used merely as a convenience, may become so fortified by technicality and so dignified by time that their original infirmities may be wholly concealed.

Blumenbach, in 1775 and in later years, foresaw this danger with respect to the usage of the term "race," and warned that it was merely to be used as a convenience helpful to the memory and no more. Herder, who was the first philosopher to make extensive use of Blumenbach's work wrote, in 1784 in his *Ideen zur Philosophie der Geschichte der Menschheit*, "I could wish the distinctions between the human species, that have been made from a laudable zeal for discriminating science, not carried beyond the due bounds. Some for instance have thought fit, to employ the term *races* for four or five divisions, originally made in consequence of country or complexion: but I see no reason for this appellation. Race refers to a difference of origin, which in this case does not exist, or in each of those countries, and under each of these complexions, comprises the most different races. . . . In short, there are neither four or five races, nor exclusive varieties, on this Earth. Complexions run into each other: forms follow the genetic character: and upon the whole, all are at last but shades of the same great picture, extending through all ages, and over all parts of the Earth. They belong not, therefore, so properly to systematic natural history, as to the physicogeographical history of man." When the last word has come to be said upon this subject it will, I am convinced, be very much in the words of Blumenbach and Herder. Meanwhile I propose to make a step in this direction here by showing that the concept of race is nothing but a whited sepulchre, a conception which in the light of modern experimental genetics is utterly erroneous and meaningless, and that it should therefore be dropped from the vocabulary of the anthropologist, for it has done an infinite amount of harm and no good at all.

The development of the idea of race may be clearly traced from the scholastic naturalization of Aristotle's doctrine of the Predicables of Genus, Species, Difference, Property and Accident. From thence it may be directly traced to the early days of the Age of Enlightenment when Linnaeus, in 1735, took over the concepts of Class, Species and Genus from the theologians to serve him as systematic tools. The term race was actually first introduced into the literature of Natural History by Buffon who, in the year 1749, used it to describe six groups of man.

The term merely represented an extension of the Aristotelian conception of Species, that is to say, it was a subdivision of a species. Buffon recognized that all human beings belonged to a single species, as did Linnaeus, and he considered it merely *convenient,* and I emphasize the word convenient, as did Blumenbach after him, to distinguish between certain geographic groups of man. Thus, at the very outset the term was understood to be purely arbitrary and a simple convenience.

The Aristotelian conception of Species, the theological doctrine of special creation and the Natural History of the Age of Enlightenment, as represented particularly by Cuvier's brilliant conception of Unity of Type, namely the idea that animals can be grouped and classified upon the basis of assemblages of structural characters which, more or less, they have in common, these three conceptions fitted together extremely well and together yielded the idea of the Fixity of Species. An idea which, in spite of every indication to the contrary in the years which followed, was gradually extended to the concept of race.

The Darwinian contribution was to show that species were not as fixed as was formerly believed, and that under the action of Natural Selection one species might give rise to another, that all animal forms might change in this way. It is, however, important to remember that Darwin conceived of evolution as a process involving continuous materials which, without the operation of Natural Selection, would remain unchanged. Hence under the Darwinian conception of species it was still possible to think of species as relatively fixed and immutable, with the modification that under the slow action of Natural Selection they were capable of change. For the nineteenth century anthropologist, therefore, it was possible to think of race, not as Buffon or Blumenbach did in the eighteenth century as an arbitrary convenience in classification, but as Cuvier at the beginning of the nineteenth century had done for all animals, as groups which could be classified upon the basis of the fact that they possessed an aggregate of common physical characters, and as Darwin later postulated, as groups which varied only under the conditions of Natural Selection, but which otherwise remained unchanged.

This is essentially a scholastic conception of species with the one additive fundamental difference that a species is considered to be no longer fixed and immutable. As far as the anthropological conception of race is concerned, the anthropologist who can afford to pass by the findings of experimental genetics, still thinks of race as the scholastics thought of species, as a knowable fixed whole the essence of which could be defined *per genus, species, propria et accidens.*

In fact, what the anthropologist has done has been to take a very crude eighteenth century notion which was originally offered as no more than an arbitrary convenience, and having erected a tremendous terminology and methodology about it, has deceived himself in the belief that he was dealing with an objective reality.

For nearly two centuries anthropologists have been directing their attention principally toward the task of establishing criteria by whose means races of mankind might be defined. All have taken completely for granted the one thing which required to be proven, namely, that the concept of race corresponded with a reality which could actually be measured and verified and descriptively set out so that it could be seen to be a fact. In short, that the anthropological conception of race is true which states that there exists in nature groups of human beings comprised of individuals each of whom possesses a certain aggregate of characters which individually and collectively serve to distinguish them from the individuals in all other groups.

Stated in plain English this is the conception of race which most anthropologists have held and which practically everyone else, except the geneticist, accepts. When, as in recent years, some anthropologists have admitted that the concept cannot be strictly applied in any systematic sense, they have thought to escape the consequences of that fact by calling the term a "general" one, and have proceeded to play the old game of blind man's buff with a sublimity which is almost enviable. For it is not vouchsafed to everyone to appreciate in its full grandeur the doctrine here implied. The feeling of dissatisfaction with which most anthropologists have viewed the many laborious attempts at classification of human races has not, on the whole, succeeded in engendering the disloyal suspicion that something was probably wrong somewhere. If there was a fault, it was generally supposed, it lay not with the anthropologist but with the material, with the human beings themselves who were the subject of classification and who always varied so much that it was difficult to put them into the group where they were conceived to belong, and this was definitely a nuisance, but happily one which could be overcome by the simple expedient of "averaging"—the principal task of the student of "race."

The process of averaging the characters of a given group, knocking the individuals together, giving them a good stirring, and then serving the resulting omelet as a "race" is essentially the anthropological process of race-making. It may be good cooking but it is not science, since it serves to confuse rather than to clarify. When an omelet is done it has a fairly uniform character, though the ingredients which have gone into its making may have been variable. This is what the anthropological conception of "race" is. It is an omelet which corresponds to nothing in nature. It is an indigestible dish conjured into being by an anthropological chef from a number of ingredients which are extremely variable in the characters which they present. The omelet called "race" has no existence outside the statistical frying-pan in which it has been reduced by the heat of the anthropological imagination.

It is this omelet conception of "race" which is so meaningless—meaningless because it is inapplicable to anything real. When anthropologists begin to realize that the proper description of a group does not consist in the process of making an omelet of it, but in the description of the character of the variability of the elements comprising it, its ingredients, they will discover that the fault lies not with the materials but with the conceptual tool with which they have approached its study.

That many differences exist between different groups of human beings is obvious, but the anthropological conception of these is erroneous, and the anthropological approach to the study of their relationships is unscientific and pre-Mendelian. Taxonomic exercises in the classification of assemblages of phenotypical characters will never succeed in elucidating the relationships of different groups of mankind to one another for the simple reason that it is not assemblages of characters which undergo change in the formation of the individual and of the group, but single units which influence the development of those characters. One of the great persisting errors involved in the anthropological conception of race has been due to the steady refusal to recognize this fact. The fact that it is not possible to classify the various groups of mankind by means of the characters which anthropologists customarily use, because these characters do not behave as pre-Mendelian, anthropologists think that they should behave, namely, as complexes of characters which are relatively fixed and are transmitted as complexes. Those characters instead behave in a totally different manner as the expressions of many independent units which have entered into their formation.

The materials of evolution are not represented by continuous aggregates which in turn determine particular aggregates of characters, but by discontinuous packages of chemicals, each of which is independent in its action and may be only partially responsible for the ultimate form of any character. These chemical packages are the genes, with which most anthropologists are still scarcely on terms of a bowing acquaintance. These genes retain both their independence and their individual character more or less indefinitely, although they are probably all inherently variable and, in time, capable of mutation. For these reasons any conception of race which operates as if inheritance were a matter of the transmission of gross aggregates of character is meaningless.

The principal agencies of evolutionary change in man are primarily gene variability and gene mutation, that is to say, through the rearrangement of gene combinations in consequence of the operation of many secondary factors, physical and social, and change in the character of genes themselves. In order to appreciate the meaning of the variety presented by mankind today it is indispensably necessary to understand the manner in which these agencies work. Thus, in man, it is practically certain that some forms of hair, and skin color, are due to mutation, while still other forms are due to various combinations of these mutant forms with one another as also with nonmutant forms. The rate of mutation for different genes in man is unknown, though it has been calculated that the gene for normal clotting mutates, for example, to the gene for hemophilia in one out of every 50,000 individuals per generation. It is highly probable, for example, that such a mutation occurred in the person of Queen Victoria's father, a fact which in the long run may perhaps prove her chief claim to fame. Mutation of the blood group genes is, however known to be very slow. Mutation of skin color genes is also very slow, while mutation of hair form genes is relatively frequent.

If we are ever to understand how the differing groups of mankind came to possess such characters as distinguish the more geographically isolated of them, and those of the less isolated more recently mixed, and therefore less distinguishable, groups, it should be obvious that we shall never succeed in doing so if we make omelets of the very ingredients, the genes, which it should be our purpose to isolate and map. We must study the frequencies with which such genes occur in different groups. If, roughly speaking, we assign one gene to every component of the human body it should be fairly clear that as regards the structure of man we are dealing with many thousands of genes. If we consider the newer genetic concepts which recognize that the adult individual represents the end-point in an interaction between all these genes, the complexities become even greater. The morphological characters which anthropologists have relied upon for their "racial" classifications have been very few indeed, involving a minute fraction of the great number of genes which it would actually be necessary to consider in attempting to make any real, that is to say, genetically analytic, classification of mankind.

To sum up, the indictment against the anthropological conception of race is (1) that it is artificial; (2) that it does not agree with the facts; (3) that it leads to confusion and the perpetuation of error, and finally, that for all these reasons it is meaningless, or rather more accurately such meaning as it possesses is false. Being so weighed down with false meaning it were better that the term were dropped altogether than that any attempt should be made to give it a new meaning.

If it be agreed that the human species is one and that it consists of a group of populations which, more or less, replace each other geographically or ecologically and of which the neighboring ones intergrade or hybridize wherever they are in contact, or are potentially capable of doing so, then it should be obvious that the task of the student interested in the character of these populations must lie in the study of the frequency distribution of the genes which characterize them—and not in the study of entities which have no meaning.

In conclusion, let me say that I realize how unsatisfactory this paper is, and that I cannot expect to have convinced you, in these few pages, of the meaninglessness of the anthropological concept of race. It may be that a notion so many times attacked during recent years is now passed beyond the reach both of scientific judgment and mortal malice, but in any event, may I be so bold as to hope that you will not feel as the Canon's wife felt about the threat to her belief in special creation?

This article was the subject of an unusual and gratifying procedure. The editor of the Journal of Heredity, *Dr. Robert C. Cook, considered it important enough to append to it the following editorial comments, which because of their interest are reprinted here.*

Dr. Ashley Montagu's interesting history of the term race, shows certain ways it has outgrown any usefulness, even becoming a menace. Some of his views may draw fire from geneticists, for humankind differs greatly in many characteristics variously distributed. If these differences are real enough to allow objective group-ings of people, such groups will differ just as much whether we call them "races" or invent a new term. If Dr. Montagu's idol smashing helps to clear the air it has served a very useful purpose.

The laboratory scientist shuns the market place and the politician's rostrum. Unfortunately folks accustomed to reach for a microphone refuse to stay out of the laboratory if they see a chance to gain even reluctant support for their pet nostrum. Because "race" is a word which inflames the emotions, much fanatical nonsense has been spoken and written about it. "Class" is another word called upon to carry an impossible genetic load, as the history of the eugenics movement testifies. Strange perversions, allegedly sanctioned by careful laboratory research, perplex and enslave millions of people.

Research workers in those sciences which may become social dynamite through perversion or prostitution of conclusions, may have to defend the integrity of their science whether they like it or not. This is emphasized in the depths of biological absurdity recently reached by champions of "racism" (a derivative word with very ugly connotations). Even the Norwegians have been read out of the Aryan fold by the dark-moustached "protector" of destiny-freighted blonds. The color of Nor-wegian hair and eyes has not changed. Rugged Norse individualism has made it impossible for the most "nordic" group in the world to accept the Procrustean savagery of the "new order."

With racism thus divorced by its leading proponent from shape of head and color of hair, eyes, and skin, it is essential that anthropologists and biologists clarify their own minds and inform lay people what actually are the differences between the human races. The study of human relationships through an analysis of gene distributions is as yet limited mainly to the blood groups and to P.T.C. taste reaction. The technique offers a hopeful approach which needs to be further explored.

As far as research and observation have been able to prove, the chromosome number of all the human races is the same, and all of the five, seven, or ten races (depending on who we follow) are inter-fertile. The blood of all races is built of the same pattern of agglutinins and antigens, and the appropriate blood type from one race can be transfused into any of the others without untoward effect. Thus in spite of the unquestionable physical differences (and less measurable mental and emotional differences) between groups of people, an imposing substrate of similarity underlies these differences. This must serve as a foundation for a world order willing to accept the differences as a challenge to developing useful specializations and not as a fatuous excuse for the enslavement or exploitation of one "race," class or nation by another.

13

W. E. B. Du Bois,
The Conservation of Races

William Edward Burghardt Du Bois (1868–1963) was born in Great Barrington, Massachusetts. He graduated with a degree in philosophy from Fisk, earned his Ph.D. in history from Harvard, and studied sociology in Berlin. His thesis, The Suppression of the African Slave Trade *(1896), inaugurated the Harvard Historical Series. His pioneering study of urban blacks,* The Philadelphia Negro *(1899), was the first such study to be conducted in America, and his much celebrated* The Souls of Black Folk *(1903) has become an American literary classic. Du Bois died in Ghana at the age of ninety-five as he was compiling material for his lifelong research project,* The Encyclopedia of the Negro.

The American Negro has always felt an intense personal interest in discussions as to the origins and destinies of races: primarily because back of most discussions of race with which he is familiar, have lurked certain assumptions as to his natural abilities, as to his political, intellectual and moral status, which he felt were wrong. He has, consequently, been led to deprecate and minimize race distinctions, to believe intensely that out of one blood God created all nations, and to speak of human brotherhood as though it were the possibility of an already dawning to-morrow.

Nevertheless, in our calmer moments we must acknowledge that human beings are divided into races; that in this country the two most extreme types of the world's races have met, and the resulting problem as to the future relations of these types is not only of intense and living interest to us, but forms an epoch in the history of mankind.

It is necessary, therefore, in planning our movements, in guiding our future development, that at times we rise above the pressing, but smaller questions of separate schools and cars, wage-discrimination and lynch law, to survey the whole question of race in human philosophy and to lay, on a basis of broad knowledge and careful insight, those large lines of policy and higher ideals which may form our guiding lines and boundaries in the practical difficulties of every day. For it is certain that all human striving

From the *American Negro Academy Occasional Papers*, 2, 1897.

must recognize the hard limits of natural law, and that any striving, no matter how intense and earnest, which is against the constitution of the world, is vain. The question, then, which we must seriously consider is this: What is the real meaning of Race; what has, in the past, been the law of race development, and what lessons has the past history of race development to teach the rising Negro people?

When we thus come to inquire into the essential difference of races we find it hard to come at once to any definite conclusion. Many criteria of race differences have in the past been proposed, as color, hair, cranial measurements and language. And manifestly, in each of these respects, human beings differ widely. They vary in color, for instance, from the marble-like pallor of the Scandinavian to the rich, dark brown of the Zulu, passing by the creamy Slav, the yellow Chinese, the light brown Sicilian and the brown Egyptian. Men vary, too, in the texture of hair from the obstinately straight hair of the Chinese to the obstinately tufted and frizzled hair of the Bushman. In measurement of heads, again, men vary; from the broad-headed Tartar to the medium-headed European and the narrow-headed Hottentot; or, again in language, from the highly-inflected Roman tongue to the monosyllabic Chinese. All these physical characteristics are patent enough, and if they agreed with each other it would be very easy to classify mankind. Unfortunately for scientists, however, these criteria of race are most exasperatingly intermingled. Color does not agree with texture of hair, for many of the dark races have straight hair; nor does color agree with the breadth of the head, for the yellow Tartar has a broader head than the German; nor, again, has the science of language as yet succeeded in clearing up the relative authority of these various and contradictory criteria. The final word of science, so far, is that we have at least two, perhaps three, great families of human beings—the whites and Negroes, possibly the yellow race. That other races have arisen from the intermingling of the blood of these two. This broad division of the world's races which men like Huxley and Raetzel have introduced as more nearly true than the old five-race scheme of Blumenbach, is nothing more than an acknowledgment that, so far as purely physical characteristics are concerned, the differences between men do not explain all the differences of their history. It declares, as Darwin himself said, that great as is the physical unlikeness of the various races of men their likenesses are greater, and upon this rests the whole scientific doctrine of Human Brotherhood.

Although the wonderful developments of human history teach that the grosser physical differences of color, hair and bone go but a short way toward explaining the different roles which groups of men have played in Human Progress, yet there are differences—subtle, delicate and elusive, though they may be—which have silently but definitely separated men into groups. While these subtle forces have generally followed the natural cleavage of common blood, descent and physical peculiarities, they have at other times swept across and ignored these. At all times, however, they have divided human beings into races, which, while they perhaps transcend scientific definition, nevertheless, are clearly defined to the eye of the Historian and Sociologist.

If this be true, then the history of the world is the history, not of individuals, but of groups, not of nations, but of races, and he who ignores or seeks to override the race idea in human history ignores and overrides the central thought of all history. What, then, is a race? It is a vast family of human beings, generally of common blood and language, always of common history, traditions and impulses, who are both voluntarily and involuntarily striving together for the accomplishment of certain more or less vividly conceived ideals of life.

Turning to real history, there can be no doubt, first, as to the widespread, nay, universal, prevalence of the race idea, the race spirit, the race ideal, and as to its efficiency as the vastest and most ingenious invention for human progress. We, who have been reared and trained under the individualistic philosophy of the Declaration of Independence and the laisser-faire philosophy of Adam Smith, are loath to see and loath to acknowledge this patent fact of human history. We see the Pharaohs, Caesars, Toussaints and Napoleons of history and forget the vast races of which they were but epitomized expressions. We are apt to think in our American impatience, that while it may have been true in the past that closed race groups made history, that here in conglomerate America *nous avons changer tout cela*—we have changed all that, and have no need of this ancient instrument of progress. This assumption of which the Negro people are especially fond, can not be established by a careful consideration of history.

We find upon the world's stage today eight distinctly differentiated races, in the sense in which History tells us the word must be used. They are, the Slavs of eastern Europe, the Teutons of middle Europe, the English of Great Britain and America, the Romance nations of Southern and Western Europe, the Negroes of Africa and America, the Semitic people of Western Asia and Northern Africa, the Hindoos of Central Asia and the Mongolians of Eastern Asia. There are, of course, other minor race groups, as the American Indians, the Esquimaux and the South Sea Islanders; these larger races, too, are far from homogeneous; the Slav includes the Czech, the Magyar, the Pole and the Russian; the Teuton includes the German, the Scandinavian and the Dutch; the English include the Scotch, the Irish and the conglomerate American. Under Romance nations the widely-differing Frenchman, Italian, Sicilian and

Spaniard are comprehended. The term Negro is, perhaps, the most indefinite of all, combining the Mulattoes and Zamboes of America and the Egyptians, Bantus and Bushmen of Africa. Among the Hindoos are traces of widely differing nations, while the great Chinese, Tartar, Corean and Japanese families fall under the one designation—Mongolian.

The question now is: What is the real distinction between these nations? Is it the physical differences of blood, color and cranial measurements? Certainly we must all acknowledge that physical differences play a great part, and that, with wide exceptions and qualifications, these eight great races of to-day follow the cleavage of physical race distinctions; the English and Teuton represent the white variety of mankind; the Mongolian, the yellow; the Negroes, the black. Between these are many crosses and mixtures, where Mongolian and Teuton have blended into the Slav, and other mixtures have produced the Romance nations and the Semites. But while race differences have followed mainly physical race lines, yet no mere physical distinctions would really define or explain the deeper differences—the cohesiveness and continuity of these groups. The deeper differences are spiritual, psychical, differences—undoubtedly based on the physical, but infinitely transcending them. The forces that bind together the Teuton nations are, then, first, their race identity and common blood; secondly, and more important, a common history, common laws and religion, similar habits of thought and a conscious striving together for certain ideals of life. The whole process which has brought about these race differentiations has been a growth, and the great characteristic of this growth has been the differentiation of spiritual and mental differences between great races of mankind and the integration of physical differences.

The age of nomadic tribes of closely related individuals represents the maximum of physical differences. They were practically vast families, and there were as many groups as families. As the families came together to form cities the physical differences lessened, purity of blood was replaced by the requirement of domicile, and all who lived within the city bounds became gradually to be regarded as members of the group; *i.e.*, there was a slight and slow breaking down of physical barriers. This, however, was accompanied by an increase of the spiritual and social differences between cities. This city became husbandmen, this, merchants, another warriors, and so on. The *ideals of life* for which the different cities struggled were different. When at last cities began to coalesce into nations there was another breaking down of barriers which separated groups of men. The larger and broader differences of color, hair and physical proportions were not by any means ignored, but myriads of minor differences disappeared, and the sociological and historical races of men began to approximate the present division of races as indicated by physical researches. At the same time the spiritual and physical differences of race groups which constituted the nations became deep and decisive. The English nation stood for constitutional liberty and commercial freedom; the German nation for science and philosophy; the Romance nations stood for literature and art, and the other race groups are striving, each in its own way, to develop for civilization its particular message, its particular ideal, which shall help to guide the world nearer and nearer that perfection of human life for which we all long, that

"one far off Divine event."

This has been the function of race differences up to the present time. What shall be its function in the future? Manifestly some of the great races of today—particularly the Negro race—have not as yet given to civilization the full spiritual message which they are capable of giving. I will not say that the Negro race has as yet given no message to the world, for it is still a mooted question among scientists as to just how far Egyptian civilization was Negro in its origin; if it was not wholly Negro, it was certainly very closely allied. Be that as it may, however, the fact still remains that the full, complete Negro message of the whole Negro race has not as yet been given to the world: that the messages and ideal of the yellow race have not been completed, and that the striving of the mighty Slavs has but begun. The question is, then: How shall this message be delivered; how shall these various ideals be realized? The answer is plain: By the development of these race groups, not as individuals, but as races. For the development of Japanese genius, Japanese literature and art, Japanese spirit, only Japanese, bound and welded together, Japanese inspired by one vast ideal, can work out in its fullness the wonderful message which Japan has for the nations of the earth. For the development of Negro genius, of Negro literature and art, of Negro spirit, only Negroes bound and welded together, Negroes inspired by one vast ideal, can work out in its fullness the great message we have for humanity. We cannot reverse history; we are subject to the same natural laws as other races, and if the Negro is ever to be a factor in the world's history—if among the gaily-colored banners that deck the broad ramparts of civilization is to hang one uncompromising black, then it must be placed there by black hands, fashioned by black heads and hallowed by the travail of 200,000,000 black hearts beating in one glad song of jubilee.

For this reason, the advance guard of the Negro people—the 8,000,000 people of Negro blood in the United States of America—must soon come to realize that if they are to take their just place in the van of Pan-Negroism, then their destiny is *not* absorption by the white Americans. That if in America it is to be proven for the first time in the modern world that not only Negroes are capable of evolving individual men like Toussaint, the Saviour, but are a nation stored with wonderful possibilities of culture, then their destiny is not a servile imitation of Anglo-Saxon culture, but a stalwart originality which shall unswervingly follow Negro ideals.

It may, however, be objected here that the situation of our race in America renders this attitude impossible; that our sole hope of salvation lies in our being able to lose our race identity in the commingled blood of the nation; and that any other course would merely increase the friction of races which we call race prejudice, and against which we have so long and so earnestly fought.

Here, then, is the dilemma, and it is a puzzling one, I admit. No Negro who has given earnest thought to the situation of his people in America has failed, at some time in life, to find himself at these cross-roads; has failed to ask himself at some time: What, after all, am I? Am I an American or am I a Negro? Can I be both? Or is it my duty to cease to be a Negro as soon as possible and be an American? If I strive as a Negro, am I not perpetuating the very cleft that threatens and separates Black and White America? Is not my only possible practical aim the subduction of all that is Negro in me to the American? Does my black blood place upon me any more obligation to assert my nationality than German, or Irish or Italian blood would?

It is such incessant self-questioning and the hesitation that arises from it, that is making the present period a time of vacillation and contradiction for the American Negro; combined race action is stifled, race responsibility is shirked, race enterprises languish, and the best blood, the best talent, the best energy of the Negro people cannot be marshalled to do the bidding of the race. They stand back to make room for every rascal and demagogue who chooses to cloak his selfish deviltry under the veil of race pride.

Is this right? Is it rational? Is it good policy? Have we in America a distinct mission as a race—a distinct sphere of action and an opportunity for race development, or is self-obliteration the highest end to which Negro blood dare aspire?

If we carefully consider what race prejudice really is, we find it, historically, to be nothing but the friction between different groups of people; it is the difference in aim, in feeling, in ideals of two different races; if, now, this difference exists touching territory, laws, language, or even religion, it is manifest that these people cannot live in the same territory without fatal collision; but if, on the other hand, there is substantial agreement in laws, language and religion; if there is a satisfactory adjustment of economic life, then there is no reason why, in the same country and on the same street, two or three great national ideals might not thrive and develop, that men of different races might not strive together for their race ideals as well, perhaps even better, than in isolation. Here, it seems to me, is the reading of the riddle that puzzles so many of us. We are Americans, not only by birth and by citizenship, but by our political ideals, our language, our religion. Farther than that, our Americanism does not go. At that point, we are Negroes, members of a vast historic race that from the very dawn of creation has slept, but half awakening in the dark forests of its African fatherland. We are the first fruits of this new nation, the harbinger of that black to-morrow which is yet destined to soften the whiteness of the Teutonic to-day. We are that people whose subtle sense of song has given America its only American music, its only American fairy tales, its only touch of pathos and humor amid its mad money-getting plutocracy. As such, it is our duty to conserve our physical powers, our intellectual endowments, our spiritual ideals; as a race we must strive by race organization, by race solidarity, by race unity to the realization of that broader humanity which freely recognizes differences in men, but sternly deprecates inequality in their opportunities of development.

For the accomplishment of these ends we need race organizations: Negro colleges, Negro newspapers, Negro business organizations, a Negro school of literature and art, and an intellectual clearing house, for all these products of the Negro mind, which we may call a Negro Academy. Not only is all this necessary for positive advance, it is absolutely imperative for negative defense. Let us not deceive ourselves at our situation in this country. Weighted with a heritage of moral iniquity from our past history, hard pressed in the economic world by foreign immigrants and native prejudice, hated here, despised there and pitied everywhere; our one haven of refuge is ourselves, and but one means of advance, our own belief in our great destiny, our own implicit trust in our ability and worth. There is no power under God's high heaven that can stop the advance of eight thousand thousand honest, earnest, inspired and united people. But—and here is the rub—they *must* be honest, fearlessly criticising their own faults, zealously correcting them; they must be *earnest*. No people that laughs at itself, and ridicules itself, and wishes to God it was anything but itself ever wrote its name in history; it *must* be inspired with the Divine faith of our black mothers, that out of the blood and dust of battle will march a victorious host, a mighty nation, a peculiar people, to speak to the nations of earth a Divine truth that shall make them free. And such a people must be united; not merely united for the organized theft of political spoils, not united to disgrace religion with whoremongers and ward-heelers; not united merely to protest and pass resolutions, but united to stop the ravages of consumption among the Negro people, united to keep black boys from loafing, gambling and crime; united to guard the purity of black women and to reduce that vast army of black prostitutes that is today marching to hell; and united in serious organizations, to determine by careful conference and thoughtful interchange of opinion the broad lines of policy and action for the American Negro.

This, is the reason for being which the American Negro Academy has. It aims at once to be the epitome and expression of the intellect of the black-blooded people of America, the exponent of the race ideals of one of the world's great races. As such, the Academy must, if successful, be

(*a*). Representative in character.
(*b*). Impartial in conduct.
(*c*). Firm in leadership.

It must be representative in character; not in that it represents all interests or all factions, but in that it seeks to comprise something of the *best* thought, the most unselfish striving and the highest ideals. There are scattered in forgotten nooks and corners throughout the land, Negroes of some considerable training, of high minds, and high motives, who are unknown to their fellows, who exert far too little influence. These the Negro Academy should strive to bring into touch with each other and to give them a common mouthpiece.

The Academy should be impartial in conduct; while it aims to exalt the people it should aim to do so by truth—not by lies, by honesty—not by flattery. It should continually impress the fact upon the Negro people that they must not expect to have things done for them—they MUST DO FOR THEMSELVES; that they have on their hands a vast work of self-reformation to do, and that a little less complaint and whining, and a little more dogged work and manly striving would do us more credit and benefit than a thousand Force or Civil Rights bills.

Finally, the American Negro Academy must point out a practical path of advance to the Negro people; there lie before every Negro today hundreds of questions of policy and right which must be settled and which each one settles now, not in accordance with any rule, but by impulse or individual preference; for instance: What should be the attitude of Negroes toward the educational qualification for voters? What should be our attitude toward separate schools? How should we meet discriminations on railways and in hotels? Such questions need not so much specific answers for each part as a general expression of policy, and nobody should be better fitted to announce such a policy than a representative honest Negro Academy.

All this, however, must come in time after careful organization and long conference. The immediate work before us should be practical and have direct bearing upon the situation of the Negro. The historical work of collecting the laws of the United States and of the various States of the Union with regard to the Negro is a work of such magnitude and importance that no body but one like this could think of undertaking it. If we could accomplish that one task we would justify our existence.

In the field of Sociology an appalling work lies before us. First, we must unflinchingly and bravely face the truth, not with apologies, but with solemn earnestness. The Negro Academy ought to sound a note of warning that would echo in every black cabin in the land: *Unless we conquer our present vices they will conquer us;* we are diseased, we are developing criminal tendencies, and an alarmingly large percentage of our men and women are sexually impure. The Negro Academy should stand and proclaim this over the housetops, crying with Garrison: *I will not equivocate, I will not retreat a single inch, and I will be heard.* The Academy should seek to gather about it the talented, unselfish men, the pure and noble-minded women, to fight an army of devils that disgraces our manhood and our womanhood. There does not stand today upon God's earth a race more capable in muscle, in intellect, in morals, than the American Negro, if he will bend his energies in the right direction; if he will

> Burst his birth's invidious bar
> And grasp the skirts of happy chance,
> And breast the blows of circumstance,
> And grapple with his evil star.

In science and morals, I have indicated two fields of work for the Academy. Finally, in practical policy, I wish to suggest the following *Academy Creed:*

1. We believe that the Negro people, as a race, have a contribution to make to civilization and humanity, which no other race can make.

2. We believe it the duty of the Americans of Negro descent, as a body, to maintain their race identity until this mission of the Negro people is accomplished, and the ideal of human brotherhood has become a practical possibility.

3. We believe that, unless modern civilization is a failure, it is entirely feasible and practicable for two races in such essential political, economic and religious harmony as the white and colored people of America, to develop side by side in peace and mutual happiness, the peculiar contribution which each has to make to the culture of their common country.

4. As a means to this end we advocate, not such social equality between these races as would disregard human likes and dislikes, but such a social equilibrium as would, throughout all the complicated relations of life, give due and just consideration to culture, ability, and moral worth, whether they be found under white or black skins.

5. We believe that the first and greatest step toward the settlement of the present friction between the races—commonly called the Negro Problem—lies in the correction of the immorality, crime and laziness among the Negroes themselves, which still remains as a heritage from slavery. We believe that only earnest and long continued efforts on our own part can cure these social ills.

6. We believe that the second great step toward a better adjustment of the relations between the races, should be a more impartial selection of ability in the economic and intellectual world, and a greater respect for personal liberty and worth, regardless of race. We believe that only earnest efforts on the part of the white people of this country will bring much needed reform in these matters.

7. On the basis of the foregoing declaration, and firmly believing in our high destiny, we, as American Negroes, are resolved to strive in every honorable way for the realization of the best and highest aims, for the development of strong manhood and pure womanhood, and for the rearing of a race ideal in America and Africa, to the glory of God and the uplifting of the Negro people.

14

Anthony Appiah,
"The Uncompleted Argument:
Du Bois and the Illusion of Race"

Kwame Anthony Appiah is Professor of African-American Studies at Harvard University. The books that he has published include Assertions and Conditionals *(1985),* For Truth in Semantics *(1986),* Necessary Questions *(1989), and* In My Father's House *(1992). His essay on Du Bois has been the source of much debate. He takes up the question of racial identity and social policy in* Color Consciousness *(1998), coedited with Amy Gutman.*

Introduction

Contemporary biologists are not agreed on the question of whether there are any human races, despite the widespread scientific consensus on the underlying genetics. For most purposes, however, we can reasonably treat this issue as terminological. What most people in most cultures ordinarily believe about the significance of "racial" difference is quite remote, I think, from what the biologists *are* agreed on. Every reputable biologist will agree that human genetic variability between the populations of Africa or Europe or Asia is not much greater than that within those populations; though *how much* greater depends, in part, on the measure of genetic variability the biologist chooses. If biologists want to make interracial difference seem relatively large, they can say that "the proportion of genic variation attributable to racial differences is . . . 9–11%."[1] If they want to make it seem small, they can say that, for two people who are both Caucasoid, the chances of difference in genetic constitution at one site on a given chromosome are currently estimated at about 14.3 percent, while for any two people taken at random from the human population, they are

From Henry Louis Gates, Jr., ed., *Race, Writing and Difference* (Chicago: University of Chicago Press, 1986). Reprinted with permission.

1. Masatoshi Nei and Arun K. Roychoudhury, "Genetic Relationship and Evolution of Human Races," *Evolutionary Biology* 14 (1983): 11; all further references to this work, abbreviated "GR," will be included in the text.

estimated at about 14.8 percent. (I will discuss why this is considered a measure of genetic difference in section 2.) The statistical facts about the distribution of variant characteristics in human populations and sub-populations are the same, whichever way the matter is expressed. Apart from the visible morphological characteristics of skin, hair, and bone, by which we are inclined to assign people to the broadest racial categories—black, white, yellow—there are few genetic characteristics to be found in the population of England that are not found in similar proportions in Zaire or China; and few too (though more) which are found in Zaire but not in similar proportions in China or in England. All this, I repeat, is part of the consensus (see "GR," pp. 1–59). A more familiar part of the consensus is that the differences between peoples in language, moral affections, aesthetic attitudes, or political ideology—those differences which most deeply affect us in our dealings with each other—are not biologically determined to any significant degree.

These claims will, no doubt, seem outrageous to those who confuse the question of whether biological difference accounts for our differences with the question of whether biological similarity accounts for our similarities. Some of our similarities as human beings in these broadly cultural respects—the capacity to acquire human languages, for example, or, more specifically, the ability to smile—*are* to a significant degree biologically determined. We can study the biological basis of these cultural capacities and give biological explanations of our exercise of them. But if biological difference between human beings is unimportant in these explanations—and it is—then racial difference, as a species of biological difference, will not matter either.

In this essay, I want to discuss the way in which W. E. B. Du Bois—who called his life story the "autobiography of a race concept"—came gradually, though never completely, to assimilate the unbiological nature of races. I have made these few prefatory remarks partly because it is my experience that the biological evidence about race is not sufficiently known and appreciated but also because they are important in discussing Du Bois. Throughout his life, Du Bois was concerned not just with the meaning of race but with the truth about it. We are more inclined at present, however, not to express our understanding of the intellectual development of people and cultures as a movement toward the truth; I shall sketch some of the reasons for this at the end of the essay. I will begin, therefore, by saying what I think the rough truth is about race, because, against the stream, I am disposed to argue that this struggle toward the truth is exactly what we find in the life of Du Bois, who can claim, in my view, to have thought longer, more engagedly, and more publicly about race than any other social theorist of our century.

"The Conservation of Races"

Du Bois' first extended discussion of the concept of race is in "The Conservation of Races" (1897), a paper he delivered to the American Negro Academy in the year it was founded. The "American Negro," he declares, has "been led to . . . minimize race distinctions" because "back of most of the discussions of race with which he is familiar, have lurked certain assumptions as to his natural abilities, as to his political, intellectual and moral status, which he felt were wrong." Du Bois continues: "Nevertheless, in our calmer moments we must acknowledge that human beings are divided into races," even if when we "come to inquire into the essential difference of races we find it hard to come at once to any definite conclusion." For what it is worth, however, the "final word of science, so far, is that we have at least two, perhaps three, great families of human beings—the whites and Negroes, possibly the yellow race."[2]

Du Bois is not, however, satisfied with the final word of nineteenth-century science. For, as he thinks, what matter are not the "grosser physical differences of color, hair and bone" but the "differences—subtle, delicate and elusive, though they may be—which have silently but definitely separated men into groups" ("CR," p. 75).

> While these subtle forces have generally followed the natural cleavage of common blood, descent and physical peculiarities, they have at other times swept across and ignored these. At all times, however, they have divided human beings into races, which, while they perhaps transcend scientific definition, nevertheless, are clearly defined to the eye of the historian and sociologist.
>
> If this be true, then the history of the world is the history, not of individuals, but of groups, not of nations, but of races. . . . What, then, is a race? It is a vast family of human beings, generally of common blood and language, always of common history, traditions and impulses, who are both voluntarily and involuntarily striving together for the accomplishment of certain more or less vividly conceived ideals of life. ["CR," pp. 75–76]

We have moved, then, away from the "scientific"—that is, biological and anthropological—conception of race to a sociohistorical notion. Using this sociohistorical criterion—the sweep of which certainly encourages the thought that no biological or anthropological definition is possible—Du Bois considers that there are not three but eight "distinctly

2. W. E. B. Du Bois, "The Conservation of Races," *W. E. B. Du Bois Speaks: Speeches and Addresses, 1890–1919*, ed. Philip S. Foner (1897; New York, 1970), pp. 73, 74, 75; all further references to this work, abbreviated "CR," will be included in the text.

differentiated races, in the sense in which history tells us the word must be used" ("CR," p. 76). The list is an odd one: Slavs, Teutons, English (both in Great Britain and America), Negroes (of Africa and, likewise, America), the Romance race, Semites, Hindus and Mongolians.

> The question now is: What is the real distinction between these nations? Is it the physical differences of blood, color and cranial measurements? Certainly we must all acknowledge that physical differences play a great part. . . . But while race differences have followed mainly physical race lines, yet no mere physical distinctions would really define or explain the deeper differences— the cohesiveness and continuity of these groups. The deeper differences are spiritual, psychical, differences—undoubtedly based on the physical, but infinitely transcending them. ["CR," p. 77]

Each of the various races is

> striving, . . . in its own way, to develop for civilization its particular message, its particular ideal, which shall help to guide the world nearer and nearer that perfection of human life for which we all long, that "one far off Divine event." ["CR," p. 78]

For Du Bois, then, the problem for the Negro is the discovery and expression of the message of his or her race.

> The full, complete Negro message of the whole Negro race has not as yet been given to the world.
> The question is, then: how shall this message be delivered; how shall these various ideals be realized? The answer is plain: by the development of these race groups, not as individuals, but as races. . . . For the development of Negro genius, of Negro literature and art, of Negro spirit, only Negroes bound and welded together, Negroes inspired by one vast ideal, can work out in its fullness the great message we have for humanity.
> For this reason, the advance guard of the Negro people—the eight million people of Negro blood in the United States of America—must soon come to realize that if they are to take their just place in the van of Pan-Negroism, then their destiny is *not* absorption by the white Americans. ["CR," pp. 78, 79][3]

3. This talk of racial absorption (and similar talk of racial extinction) reflects the idea that Afro-Americans might disappear because their genetic heritage would be diluted by the white one. This idea might be considered absurd in any view propounding the notion of a racial essence: either a person has it or they don't. But this way of thinking conceives of racial essences as being like genes, though Mendelian genetics was not yet "rediscovered" when Du Bois wrote this piece.

Du Bois ends by proposing his Academy Creed, which begins with words that echo down almost a century of American race relations:

1. We believe that the Negro people, as a race, have a contribution to make to civilization and humanity, which no other race can make.
2. We believe it the duty of the Americans of Negro descent, as a body, to maintain their race identity until this mission of the Negro people is accomplished, and the ideal of human brotherhood has become a practical possibility. ["CR," p. 84]

What can we make of this analysis and prescription?

On the face of it, Du Bois' argument in "The Conservation of Races" is that "race" is not a scientific—that is, biological—concept. It is a sociohistorical concept. Sociohistorical races each have a "message" for humanity—a message which derives, in some way, from God's purpose in creating races. The Negro race has still to deliver its full message, and so it is the duty of Negroes to work together—through race organizations—so that this message can be delivered.

We do not need the theological underpinnings of this argument. What is essential is the thought that through common action Negroes can achieve, by virtue of their sociohistorical community, worthwhile ends which will not otherwise be achieved. On the face of it, then, Du Bois' strategy here is the antithesis in the classic dialectic of reaction to prejudice.

The thesis in this dialectic—which Du Bois reports as the American Negro's attempt to "minimize race distinctions"—is the denial of difference. Du Bois' antithesis is the acceptance of difference, along with a claim that each group has its part to play; that the white race and its racial Other are related not as superior to inferior but as complementaries; that the Negro message is, with the white one, part of the message of humankind.

I call this pattern the classic dialectic for a simple reason: we find it in feminism also—on the one hand, a simple claim to equality, a denial of substantial difference; on the other, a claim to a special message, revaluing the feminine Other not as the helpmeet of sexism, but as the New Woman.

Du Bois is probably thinking of "passing for white"; in views of inheritance as the blending of parental "blood," the more that black "blood" is diluted, the more it is likely that *every* person of African descent in America *could* pass for white. That, of course, would be a kind of extinction of the Negro. It is interesting that those who discussed this issue assumed that it would not cause the extinction of the white race also and the creation of a "hybridized" human race. But, as I say, such speculation is ruled out by the rise of Mendelian genetics.

Because this *is* a classic dialectic, my reading of Du Bois' argument is a natural one. I believe that it is substantially correct. But to see that it is correct, we need to make clear that what Du Bois attempts, despite his own claims to the contrary, is not the transcendence of the nineteenth-century scientific conception of race—as we shall see, he relies on it—but rather, as the dialectic requires, a revaluation of the Negro race in the face of the sciences of racial inferiority. We can begin by analyzing the sources of tension in Du Bois' allegedly sociohistorical conception of race, which he explicitly sets over against the scientific conception. The tension is plain enough in his references to "common blood"; for this, dressed up with fancy craniometry, a dose of melanin, and some measure for hair-curl, is what the scientific notion amounts to. If he has fully transcended the scientific notion, what is the role of this talk about "blood"?

We may leave aside for the moment the common "impulses" and the voluntary and involuntary "strivings." These must be due either to a shared biological inheritance, "based on the physical, but infinitely transcending" it; to a shared history; or, of course, to some combination of these. If Du Bois' notion is purely sociohistorical, then the issue is common history and traditions; otherwise, the issue is, at least in part, a common biology. We shall know which only when we understand the core of Du Bois' conception of race.

The claim that a race generally shares a common language is also plainly inessential: the "Romance" race is not of common language nor, more obviously, is the Negro. And "common blood" can mean little more than "of shared ancestry," which is already implied by talk of a "vast family." At the center of Du Bois' conception, then, is the claim that a race is "a vast family of human beings, . . . always of common history [and] traditions." So, if we want to understand Du Bois, our question must be: What is a family of common history?

We already see that the scientific notion, which presupposes common features in virtue of a common biology derived from a common descent, is not fully transcended. A family can, it is true, have adopted children, kin by social rather than biological law. By analogy, therefore, a vast human family might contain people joined not by biology but by an act of choice. But it is plain that Du Bois cannot have been contemplating this possibility: like all of his contemporaries, he would have taken for granted that race is a matter of birth. Indeed, to understand the talk of "family," we must distance ourselves from its sociological meaning. A family is almost always culturally defined only through either patrilineal or matrilineal descent. But if an individual drew a "conceptual" family tree back over five hundred years and assumed that he or she was descended from each ancestor in only one way, it would have more than a million branches at the top. Although, in such a case, many individuals would be represented by more than one branch—that far back we are all going to be descended from many people by more than one route—it is plain that either a matrilineal or patrilineal conception of our family histories drastically underrepresents the biological range of our ancestry. Biology and social convention go startlingly different ways. Let's pretend, secure in our republicanism, that the claim of the queen of England to the throne depends partly on a single line from one of her ancestors nine hundred years ago. If there were no overlaps in her family tree, there would be more than fifty thousand billion such lines, though there have never been that many people on the earth; even with reasonable assumptions about over-laps, there are millions of such lines. We chose one line, even though most of the population of England is probably descended from William the Conqueror by *some* uncharted route. Biology is democratic: all parents are equal. Thus, to speak of two people as being of common ancestry requires that, before some historical point in the past, a large proportion of the branches in their respective family trees coincided.[4]

Already, then, Du Bois requires, as the scientific conception does, a common ancestry (in the sense just defined) with whatever—if anything—that ancestry biologically entails. But apparently this does not commit him to the scientific conception, for there are many groups of common ancestry—ranging from humanity in general to narrower groups such as the Slavs, Teutons, and Romance people taken together—which do not, for Du Bois, constitute races. Thus, Du Bois' "common history," which must be what is supposed to distinguish Slav from Teuton, is an essential part of his conception. The problem is whether a common his-tory can be a criterion which distinguishes one group of human beings—extended in time—from another. Does adding a notion of common his-tory allow us to make the distinctions between Slav and Teuton or between English and Negro? The answer is no.

Consider, for example, Du Bois himself. As the descendant of Dutch ancestors, why doesn't his relation to the history of Holland in the four-teenth century (which he shares with all people of Dutch descent) make him a member of the Teutonic race? The answer is straightforward: the Dutch were not Negroes; Du Bois is. But it follows from this that the history of Africa is part of the common history of Afro-Americans not simply because Afro-Americans descended from various peoples who

4. I owe this way of thinking about the distance between social and biological ancestry to chapter 6 of R. B. Le Page and A. Tabouret-Keller's forthcoming book, *Acts of Identity*. I am very grateful to Professor Le Page for allowing me to see a typescript.

played a part in African history but rather because African history is the history of people of the same race.

My general point is this: in order to recognize two events at different times as part of the history of a single individual, we have to have a criterion for identity of the individual at each of those times, independent of his or her participation in the two events. In the same way, when we recognize two events as belonging to the history of one race, we have to have a criterion for membership in the race at those two times, independent of the participation of the members in the two events. To put it more simply: sharing a common group history cannot be a criterion for being members of the same group, for we would have to be able to identify the group in order to identify *its* history. Someone in the fourteenth century could share a common history with me through our membership in a historically extended race only if something accounts both for his or her membership in the race in the fourteenth century and for mine in the twentieth. That something cannot, on pain of circularity, be the history of the race. Whatever holds Du Bois' races together conceptually cannot be a common history; it is only because they are bound together that members of a race at different times can share a history at all. If this is true, Du Bois' reference to a common history cannot be doing any work in his individuation of races. And once we have stripped away the sociohistorical elements from Du Bois' definition of race, we are left with the true criterion.

Consequently, not only the talk of language, which Du Bois admits is neither necessary (the Romance race speaks many languages) nor sufficient (Afro-Americans and Americans generally speak the same language) for racial identity, must be expunged from the definition; now we have seen that talk of common history and traditions must go too. We are left with common descent and the common impulses and strivings that I put aside earlier. Since common descent and the characteristics which flow from it are part of the scientific conception of race, these impulses are all that remain to do the job that Du Bois had claimed for a sociohistorical conception: namely, to distinguish his conception from the biological one. Du Bois claims that the existence of races is "clearly defined to the eye of the historian and sociologist" ("CR," p. 75). Since biology acknowledges common ancestry as a criterion, whatever extra insight is provided by sociohistorical understanding can be gained only by observing the common impulses and strivings. Reflection suggests, however, that this cannot be true. For what common impulses—whether voluntary or involuntary—do the Romance people share that the Teutons and the English do not?

Du Bois had read the historiography of the Anglo-Saxon school, which accounted for the democratic impulse in America by the racial tradition of the Anglo-Saxon moot. He had read American and British historians in earnest discussion of the "Latin" spirit of Romance peoples; and perhaps he had believed some of it. Here perhaps may be the source of the notion that history and sociology can observe the differing impulses of races.

In all these writings, however, such impulses are allegedly discovered to be the a posteriori properties of racial and national groups, not criteria of membership in them. It is, indeed, because the claim is a posteriori that historical evidence is relevant to it. And if we ask what common impulses history has detected which allow us to recognize the Negro, we shall see that Du Bois' claim to have found a criterion of identity in these impulses is mere bravado. If, without evidence about his or her impulses, we can say who is a Negro, then it cannot be part of what it is to be a Negro that he or she has them; rather, it must be an a posteriori claim that people of a common race, defined by descent and biology, have impulses, for whatever reason, in common. Of course, the common impulses of a biologically defined group may be historically caused by common experiences, common history. But Du Bois' claim can only be that biologically defined races happen to share, for whatever reason, common impulses. The common impulses cannot be a criterion of group membership. And if that is so, we are left with the scientific conception.

How, then, is it possible for Du Bois' criteria to issue in eight groups, while the scientific conception issues in three? The reason is clear from the list. Slavs, Teutons, English, Hindus, and Romance peoples each live in a characteristic geographical region. (American English—and, for that matter, American Teutons, American Slavs, and American Romance people—share recent ancestry with their European "cousins" and thus share a relation to a place and certain languages and traditions.) Semites and Mongolians each inhabit a rather larger geographical region also. Du Bois' talk of common history conceals his superaddition of a geographical criterion: group history is, in part, the history of people who have lived in the same place.[5]

The criterion Du Bois actually uses amounts to this: people are members of the same race if they share features in virtue of being descended largely from people of the same region. Those features may be physical— hence Afro-Americans are Negroes—or cultural—hence Anglo-

5. This seems to me the very notion that the biologists have ended up with: a population is a group of people (or, more generally, organisms) occupying a common region (or, more generally, an environmental niche), along with people largely descended from that original group who now live in other regions. See Nei and Roychoudhury, "Gene Differences between Caucasian, Negro, and Japanese Populations," *Science* 177 (Aug. 1972): 434–35, and "Genetic Relationship," p. 4.

Americans are English. Focusing on one sort of feature—"grosser . . . differences of color, hair and bone"—defines "whites and Negroes, possibly the yellow race" as the "final word of science, so far." Focusing on a different feature—language or shared customs—defines instead Teutons, Slavs, and Romance peoples. The tension in Du Bois' definition of race reflects the fact that, for the purposes of European historiography (of which his Harvard and University of Berlin training had made him aware), it was the latter that mattered; but for the purposes of American social and political life, it was the former.

The real difference in Du Bois' conception, therefore, is not that his definition of race is at odds with the scientific one. It is, rather, as the classic dialectic requires, that he assigns to race a moral and metaphysical significance different from that of his contemporaries. The distinctive claim is that the Negro race has a positive message, a message not only of difference but of value. And that, it seems to me, is the significance of the sociohistorical dimension: the strivings of a race are, as Du Bois viewed the matter, the stuff of history.

> The history of the world is the history, not of individuals, but of groups, not of nations, but of races, and he who ignores or seeks to override the race idea in human history ignores and overrides the central thought of all history. ["CR," p. 75]

By studying history, we can discern the outlines of the message of each race.

"Crisis": August 1911

We have seen that, for the purpose that concerned him most—understanding the status of the Negro—Du Bois was thrown back on the scientific definition of race, which he officially rejected. But the scientific definition (Du Bois' uneasiness with which is reflected in his remark that races "perhaps transcend scientific definition") was itself threatened as he spoke at the first meeting of the Negro Academy. In the later nineteenth century most thinking people (like too many even today) believed that what Du Bois called the "grosser differences" were a sign of an inherited racial essence which accounted for the intellectual and moral deficiency of the "lower" races. In "The Conservation of Races" Du Bois elected, in effect, to admit that color was a sign of a racial essence but to deny that the cultural capacities of the black-skinned, curly-haired members of humankind were inferior to those of the white-skinned, straighter-haired ones. But the collapse of the sciences of racial inferiority led Du Bois to deny the

connection between cultural capacity and gross morphology—the familiar impulses and strivings of his earlier definition.

We can find evidence of his change of mind in an article in the August
1911 issue of the *Crisis*.

> The leading scientists of the world have come forward[6] . . . and laid down in
> categorical terms a series of propositions which may be summarized as
> follows:
>
>   1. (a) It is not legitimate to argue from differences in physical charac-
> teristics to differences in mental characteristics. . . .
>
>   2. The civilization of a . . . race at any particular moment of time offers
> no index to its innate or inherited capacities.[7]

These results have been amply confirmed since then. And we do well, I
think, to remind ourselves of the current picture.

Human characteristics are genetically determined, to the extent that
they are determined, by sequences of DNA in the chromosome—in other
words, by genes.[8] The region of a chromosome occupied by a gene is
called a locus. Some loci are occupied in different members of a population by different genes, each of which is called an allele; and a locus is said
to be polymorphic in a population if there is at least one pair of alleles for
it. Perhaps as many as half the loci in the human population are polymorphic; the rest, naturally enough, are monomorphic.

Many loci have not just two alleles but several, and each has a frequency
in the population. Suppose a particular locus has n alleles, which we can
call 1, 2, and so on up to n; then we can call their frequencies $x_1, x_2, \ldots,$
to x_n. If we consider two randomly chosen members of a population and
look at the same locus on one chromosome of each of them, the probability
that they'll have the same allele at that locus is just the probability that
they'll both have the first allele $(x_1{}^2)$, plus the probability that they'll both
have the second $(x_2{}^2)$, plus the probability that they'll both have the nth

6. This claim was prompted by G. Spiller; see *Papers in Inter-Racial Problems
Communicated to the First Universal Races Congress Held at the University of London, July 26–29, 1911,* ed. Spiller (1911; Secaucus, N.J., 1970).

7. Du Bois, "Races," *Crisis,* August 1911, pp. 157–58.

8. Strictly we should say that the character of an organism is fixed by genes, along
with sequences of nucleic acid in the cytoplasm and some other features of the
cytoplasm of the ovum. But these latter sources of human characteristics are
largely swamped by the nucleic DNA and are, in any case, substantially similar in
almost all people. It is the latter fact that accounts, I think, for their not being
generally mentioned.

$(x_n{}^2)$. We can call this number the expected homozygosity at that locus: for it is just the proportion of people in the population who would be homozygous at that locus—having identical alleles at that locus on each of the relevant chromosomes—provided the population is mating at random.[9]

Now if we take the average value of the expected homozygosity for all loci, polymorphic and monomorphic (which, for some reason, tends to get labeled *J*), we have a measure of the chance that two people, taken at random from the population, will share the same allele at a locus on a chromosome taken at random. This is a good measure of how similar a randomly chosen pair of individuals should be expected to be in their biology *and* a good (though rough) guide to how closely the populations are genetically related.

I can now express simply one measure of the extent to which members of these human populations we call races differ more from each other than they do from members of the same race. For example, the value of *J* for Caucasoids—based largely on samples from the English population—is estimated to be about 0.857, while that for the whole human population is estimated at 0.852.[10] The chances, in other words, that two people taken at random from the human population will have the same characteristic at a locus, are about 85.2 percent, while the changes for two (white) people taken from the population of England are about 85.7 percent. And since 85.2 is 100 minus 14.8 and 85.7 is 100 minus 14.3, this is equivalent to what I said in the introduction: the chances of two people who are both Caucasoid differing in genetic constitution at one site on a given chromosome are about 14.3 percent, while, for any two people taken at random from the human population, they are about 14.8 percent. The conclusion is obvious: given only a person's race, it is hard to say what his or her

9. It follows from these definitions that where a locus is monomorphic, the expected homozygosity is going to be one.

10. These figures come from Nei and Roychoudhury, "Genetic Relationship," and I have used the figures derived from looking at proteins, not blood-groups, since they claim these are likely to be more reliable. I have chosen a measure of "racial" biological difference that makes it look spectacularly small, but I would not wish to imply that it is not the case, as these authors say, that "genetic differentiation is real and generally statistically highly significant" (pp. 8, 11, 41). I would dispute their claim that their work shows the existence of a biological basis for the classification of human races; what it shows is that human populations differ in their distributions of genes. That *is* a biological fact. The objection to using this fact as a basis of a system of classification is that far too many people don't fit into just one category that can be so defined.

biological characteristics will be, except in respect of the "grosser" features of color, hair, and bone (the genetics of which are, in any case, rather poorly understood)—features of "morphological differentiation," as the evolutionary biologist would say. As Nei and Roychoudhury express themselves, somewhat coyly, "The extent of genic differentiation between human races is not always correlated with the degree of morphological differentiation" ("GR," p. 44).

To establish that race is relatively unimportant in explaining biological differences between people, where biological difference is measured in the proportion of differences in loci on the chromosome, is not yet to show that race is unimportant in explaining cultural difference. It could be that large differences in intellectual or moral capacity are caused by differences at very few loci and that, at these loci, all (or most) black-skinned people differ from all (or most) white-skinned or yellow-skinned ones. As it happens, there is little evidence for any such proposition and much against it. But suppose we had reason to believe it. In the biological conception of the human organism, in which characteristics are determined by the pattern of genes in interaction with environments, it is the presence of the alleles (which give rise to these moral and intellectual capacities) that accounts for the observed differences in those capacities in people in similar environments. So the characteristic racial morphology—skin and hair and bone—could only be a sign of those differences if it were (highly) correlated with those alleles. Furthermore, even if it were so correlated, the causal explanation of the differences would be that they differed in those alleles, not that they differed in race. Since there are no such strong correlations, even those who think that intellectual and moral character are strongly genetically determined must accept that *race* is at best a poor indicator of capacity.

But it was earlier evidence, pointing similarly to the conclusion that "the genic variation within and between the three major races of man . . . is small compared with the intraracial variation" ("GR," p. 40) and that differences in morphology were not correlated strongly with intellectual and moral capacity, which led Du Bois in the *Crisis* to an explicit rejection of the claim that biological race mattered for understanding the status of the Negro:

> So far at least as intellectual and moral aptitudes are concerned, we ought to speak of civilizations where we now speak of races. . . . Indeed, even the physical characteristics, excluding the skin color of a people, are to no small extent the direct result of the physical and social environment under which it is living. . . . These physical characteristics are furthermore too indefinite

and elusive to serve as a basis for any rigid classification or division of human groups.[11]

This is straightforward enough. Yet it would be too swift a conclusion to suppose that Du Bois here expresses his deepest convictions. After 1911, he went on to advocate Pan-Africanism, as he had advocated Pan-Negroism in 1897, and whatever Afro-Americans and Africans, from Ashanti to Zulu, share, it is not a single civilization.

Du Bois managed to maintain Pan-Africanism while officially rejecting talk of race as anything other than a synonym for color. We can see how he did this by turning to his second autobiography, *Dusk of Dawn*, published in 1940.

"Dusk of Dawn"

In *Dusk of Dawn*—the "essay toward an autobiography of a race concept"—Du Bois explicitly allies himself with the claim that race is not a scientific concept.

It is easy to see that scientific definition of race is impossible; it is easy to prove that physical characteristics are not so inherited as to make it possible to divide the world into races; that ability is the monopoly of no known aristocracy; that the possibilities of human development cannot be circumscribed by color, nationality, or any conceivable definition of race.[12]

But we need no scientific definition, for

all this has nothing to do with the plain fact that throughout the world today organized groups of men by monopoly of economic and physical power, legal enactment and intellectual training are limiting with determination and unflagging zeal the development of other groups; and that the concentration particularly of economic power today puts the majority of mankind into a slavery to the rest. [*D*, pp. 137–38]

Or, as he puts it pithily a little later,

the black man is a person who must ride "Jim Crow" in Georgia. [*D*, p. 153]

11. Du Bois, "Races," p. 158.
12. Du Bois, *Dusk of Dawn: An Essay toward an Autobiography of a Race Concept* (1940; New York, 1975), p. 137. All further references to this work, abbreviated *D*, will be included in the text.

Yet, just a few pages earlier, he has explained why he remains a Pan-Africanist, committed to a political program which binds all this indefinable black race together. The passage is worth citing extensively.

Du Bois begins with Countée Cullen's question, "What is Africa to me?" and answers,

> Once I should have answered the question simply: I should have said "fatherland" or perhaps better "motherland" because I was born in the century when the walls of race were clear and straight; when the world consisted of mut[u]ally exclusive races; and even though the edges might be blurred, there was no question of exact definition and understanding of the meaning of the word. . . .
>
> Since then [the writing of "The Conservation of Races"] the concept of race has so changed and presented so much of contradiction that as I face Africa I ask myself: what is it between us that constitutes a tie which I can feel better than I can explain? Africa is, of course, my fatherland. Yet neither my father nor my father's father ever saw Africa or knew its meaning or cared overmuch for it. My mother's folk were closer and yet their direct connection, in culture and race, became tenuous; still, my tie to Africa is strong. On this vast continent were born and lived a large portion of my direct ancestors going back a thousand years or more. The mark of their heritage is upon me in color and hair. These are obvious things, but of little meaning in themselves; only important as they stand for real and more subtle differences from other men. Whether they do or not, I do not know nor does science know today.
>
> But one thing is sure and that is the fact that since the fifteenth century these ancestors of mine and their other descendants have had a common history; have suffered a common disaster and have one long memory. The actual ties of heritage between the individuals of this group, vary with the ancestors that they have in common [with] many others: Europeans and Semites, perhaps Mongolians, certainly American Indians. But the physical bond is least and the badge of color relatively unimportant save as a badge; the real essence of this kinship is its social heritage of slavery; the discrimination and insult; and this heritage binds together not simply the children of Africa, but extends through yellow Asia and into the South Seas. It is this unity that draws me to Africa. [*D,* pp. 116–17]

This passage is affecting, powerfully expressed. We might like to be able to follow it in its conclusions. But we should not; since the passage seduces us into error, we should begin distancing ourselves from the appeal of its argument by noticing how it echoes an earlier text. Color and hair are unimportant save "as they stand for real and more subtle differences," Du Bois says here, and we recall the "subtle forces" that "generally followed the natural cleavage of common blood, descent and physical peculiarities" of "The Conservation of Races." There it was an essential part of the argument that these subtle forces—"impulses" and "strivings"— were the common property of those who shared a "common blood"; here, Du Bois does "not know nor does science" whether this is so. But if it is not so, then, on Du Bois' own admission, these "obvious things" are "of little meaning." If they are of little meaning, then his mention of them marks, on the surface of his argument, the extent to which he cannot quite escape the appeal of the earlier conception of race.

Du Bois' yearning for the earlier conception which he prohibited himself from using accounts for the pathos of the gap between the unconfident certainty that Africa is "of course" his fatherland and the concession that it is not the land of his father or his father's father. What use is such a fatherland? What use is a motherland with which your own mother's connection is "tenuous"? What does it matter that a large portion of his ancestors have lived on that vast continent, if there is no subtler bond with them than brute—that is, culturally unmediated—biological descent and its entailed "badge" of hair and color?

Even in the passage that follows Du Bois' explicit disavowal of the scientific conception of race, the references to "common history"—the "one long memory," the "social heritage of slavery"—only lead us back into the now familiar move of substituting a sociohistorical conception of race for the biological one; but that is simply to bury the biological conception below the surface, not to transcend it. Because he never truly "speaks of civilization," Du Bois cannot ask if there is not in American culture—which undoubtedly *is* his—an African residue to take hold of and rejoice in, a subtle connection mediated not by genetics but by intentions, by meaning. Du Bois has no more conceptual resources here for explicating the unity of the Negro race—the Pan-African identity—than he had in "The Conservation of Races" half a century earlier. A glorious non sequitur must be submerged in the depths of the argument. It is easily brought to the surface.

If what Du Bois has in common with Africa is a history of "discrimination and insult," then this binds him, by his own account, to "yellow Asia and . . . the South Seas" also. How can something he shares with the whole nonwhite world bind him to only a part of it? Once we interrogate the argument here, a further suspicion arises that the claim to this bond may be based on a hyperbolic reading of the facts. Du Bois' experience of "discrimination and insult" in his American childhood and as an adult citizen of the industrialized world was different in character from that experienced by, say, Kwame Nkrumah in colonized West Africa; it is absent altogether in large parts of "yellow Asia." What Du Bois shares with the nonwhite world is not insult but the *badge* of insult; and the badge, without the insult, is the very skin and hair and bone which it is impossible to connect with a scientific definition of race.

Concluding Unscientific Postscript

Du Bois died in Nkrumah's Ghana, led there by the dream of Pan-Africanism and the reality of American racism. If he escaped that racism, he never completed the escape from race. The logic of his argument leads naturally to the final repudiation of race as a term of difference and to speaking instead "of civilizations where we now speak of races." The logic is the same logic that has brought us to speak of genders where we spoke of sexes, and a rational assessment of the evidence requires that we should endorse not only the logic but the premises of each argument. I have only sketched the evidence for these premises in the case of race, but it is all there in the scientific journals. Discussing Du Bois has been largely a pretext for adumbrating the argument he never quite managed to complete.

I think the argument worth making because I believe that we—scholars in the academy—have not done enough to share it with our fellow citizens. One barrier facing those of us in the humanities has been methodological. Under Saussurian hegemony, we have too easily become accustomed to thinking of meaning as constituted by systems of differences purely internal to our endlessly structured *langues*.[13] Race, we all assume, is, like all other concepts, constructed by metaphor and metonymy; it stands in, metonymically, for the Other; it bears the weight, metaphorically, of other kinds of difference.

Yet, in our social lives away from the text-world of the academy, we take reference for granted too easily. Even if the concept of race *is* a structure of oppositions—white opposed to black (but also to yellow), Jew opposed to Gentile (but also to Arab)—it is a structure whose realization is, at best, problematic and, at worst, impossible. If we can now hope to understand the concept embodied in this system of oppositions, we are nowhere near finding referents for it. The truth is that there are no races: there is nothing in the world that can do all we ask "race" to do for us. The evil that is done is done by the concept and by easy—yet impossible— assumptions as to its application. What we miss through our obsession with the structure of relations of concepts is, simply, reality.

---

13. Post-structuralism is not a step forward here, as Terry Eagleton has observed (see *Literary Theory: An Introduction* [Oxford, 1983], pp. 143–44).

Talk of "race" is particularly distressing for those of us who take culture seriously. For, where race works—in places where "gross differences" of morphology are correlated with "subtle differences" of temperament, belief, and intention—it works as an attempt at a metonym for culture; and it does so only at the price of biologizing what *is* culture, or ideology. To call it "biologizing" is not to consign our concept of race to biology. What is present there is not our concept but our word only. Even the biologists who believe in human races use the term "race," as they say, "without any social implication" ("GR," p. 4). What exists "out there" in the world—communities of meaning, shading variously into each other in the rich structure of the social world—is the province not of biology but of hermeneutic understanding.

I have examined these issues through the writings of Du Bois, with the burden of his scholarly inheritance, and have tried to transcend the system of oppositions which, had Du Bois accepted it, would have left him opposed to the (white) norm of form and value. In his early work, Du Bois took race for granted and sought to revalue one pole of the opposition of white to black. The received concept is a hierarchy, a vertical structure, and Du Bois wished to rotate the axis, to give race a "horizontal" reading. Challenge the assumption that there can be an axis, however oriented in the space of values, and the project fails for loss of presuppositions. In his later work, Du Bois—whose life's work was, in a sense, an attempt at just this impossible project—was unable to escape the notion of race he had explicitly rejected. We may borrow his own metaphor: though he saw the dawn coming, he never faced the sun. And we must surely admit that he is followed in this by many in our culture today; we too live in the dusk of that dawn.

15

Leopold Senghor,
"What Is 'Negritude'?"

*Leopold Senghor, the Senegalese poet, philosopher, and politician, was born
in 1906. He moved to France in 1928 and began teaching in 1936, a career
he pursued until 1945. He returned to Senegal in 1945, becoming its first
president from 1961 to 1980. Aimé Cesaire, under the inspiration of the
Harlem Renaissance, had conceived the negritude movement primarily as
political, but for Senghor it was more literary. The text printed here was
extracted from a lecture that Senghor delivered at Oxford University in
1961. In addition to summarizing the basic idea of negritude, Senghor attempted in this lecture to answer some of the criticisms directed against the
movement.*

Paradoxically, it was the French who first forced us to seek its essence, and
who then showed us where it lay . . . when they enforced their policy of
assimilation and thus deepened our despair. . . . Early on, we had become
aware within ourselves that assimilation was a failure; we could assimilate
mathematics or the French language, but we could never strip off our
black skins nor root out our black souls. And so we set out on a fervent
quest for the Holy Grail: our *Collective Soul.* And we came upon it.

It was not revealed to us by the "official France" of the politicians who,
out of self interest and political conviction defended the policy of assimilation. Its whereabouts was pointed out to us by that handful of freelance
thinkers—writers, artists, ethnologists, and prehistorians—who bring
about cultural revolutions in France. It was, to be quite precise, our
teachers of Ethnology who introduced us to the considerable body of work
already achieved in the understanding of Africa, by the University of
Oxford.

What did we learn from all those writers, artists and teachers? That the
early years of colonisation and especially, even before colonisation, the
slave trade had ravaged black Africa like a bush fire, wiping out images and
values in one vast carnage. That negroid civilisation had flourished in the
Upper Paleolithic Age, and that the Neolithic Revolution could not be
explained without them. That their roots retained their vigour, and would
one day produce new grass and green branches. . . .

From *West Africa*, November 4, 1961. Reprinted with permission.

Negritude is *the whole complex of civilised values—cultural, economic, social and political—which characterise the black peoples,* or, more precisely, the Negro-African world. All these values are essentially informed by intuitive reason, because this sentient reason, the reason which comes to grips, expresses itself emotionally, through that self-surrender, that coalescence of subject and object; through myths, by which I mean the archetypal images of the collective Soul; above all through primordial rhythms, synchronised with those of the Cosmos. In other words, the sense of communion, the gift of myth-making, the gift of rhythm, such are the essential elements of Negritude, which you will find indelibly stamped on all the works and activities of the black man. . . .

In opposition to European racialism, of which the Nazis were the symbol, we set up an "anti-racial racialism." The very excesses of Naziism, and the catastrophes it engendered, were soon to bring us to our senses. Such hatred, such violence, above all, such weeping and such shedding of blood produced a feeling of revulsion—it was so foreign to our continent's genius: our *need to love.* And then the anthropologists taught us that there is no such thing as a pure race: scientifically speaking, races do not exist. They went one better and forecast that, with a mere two hundred million people, we would in the end disappear as a "black race," through miscegenation. At the same time they did offer us some consolation. "The focal points of human development," wrote Teilhard de Chardin, in 1939, "always seem to coincide with the points of contact and anastomosis of several nerve paths," that is, in the ordinary man's language, of several races. If then we were justified in fostering the values of Negritude, and arousing the energy slumbering within us, it must be in order to pour them into the mainstream of cultural miscegenation (the biological process taking place spontaneously). They must flow towards the meeting point of all Humanity; they must be our contribution to the Civilisation of the Universal.

Biological miscegenation, then, takes place spontaneously, provoked by the very laws which govern Life, and in the face of all policies of Apartheid. It is a different matter in the realm of culture. Here, we remain wholly free to cooperate or not, to provoke or prevent the synthesis of cultures. This is an important point. For, as certain biologists point out, the psychological mutations brought about by education are incorporated in our genes, and are then transmitted by heredity. Hence the major role played by *"Culture."*

Seen within this prospect of the Civilisation of the Universal, the colonial policies of Great Britain and France have proved successful complements to each other, and black Africa has benefited. The policies of the former tended to reinforce the traditional native civilisation. As for

France's policy, although we have often reviled it in the past, it too ended with a credit balance, through forcing us actively to assimilate European civilisation. This fertilised our sense of Negritude. Today, our Negritude no longer expresses itself as opposition to European values, but as a *complement* to them. Henceforth, its militants will be concerned, as I have often said, *not to be assimilated, but to assimilate.* They will use European values to arouse the slumbering values of Negritude, which they will bring as their contribution to the Civilisation of the Universal.

Nevertheless, we still disagree with Europe: not with its values any longer (with the exception of Capitalism) but with its theory of the Civilisation of the Universal. . . . In the eyes of the Europeans, the "exotic civilisations" are static in character, being content to live by means of archetypal images, which they repeat indefinitely. The most serious criticism is that they have no idea of the *pre-eminent dignity of the human person.* My reply is this. Just as much as black Africa, taking this as an example, Europe and its North American offspring live by means of archetypal images. For what are Free Enterprise, Democracy, Communism, but *myths,* around which hundreds of millions of men and women organise their lives? Negritude itself is a myth (I am not using the word in any pejorative sense), but a living, dynamic one, which evolves with its circumstances into a form of humanism. Actually, our criticism of the [European] thesis is that it is monstrously anti-humanist. For if European civilisation were to be imposed, unmodified, on all Peoples and Continents, it could only be by force. That is its first disadvantage. A more serious one is that it would not be *humanistic,* for it would cut itself off from the complementary values of the greater part of humanity. As I have said elsewhere, it would be a universal civilisation; it would not be the Civilisation of the Universal.

Whereas our revised Negritude is humanistic, I repeat, it welcomes the complementary values of Europe and the white man, and indeed, of all other races and continents. But it welcomes them in order to fertilise and re-invigorate its own values, which it then offers for the construction of a civilisation which shall embrace all Mankind. The *Neo-Humanism* of the twentieth century stands at the point where the paths of all Nations, Races and Continents cross, "where the Four Winds of the Spirit blow."

16

Linda Alcoff,
"Mestizo Identity"

Linda Martin Alcoff is Professor of Philosophy and Women's Studies at Syracuse University. Alcoff is coeditor, with Elizabeth Potter, of Feminist Epistemologies *(1993). Also, she is the author of numerous articles that have been published in journals. In this essay, Alcoff presents an account of mixed-race identity that draws upon the philosophic literature of Latin America. She defends the idea of mestizo identity as an alternative to the standard view of the self presupposed in current policy debates.*

We Latin Americans have never been able to take our racial or cultural identity for granted:

> Who are we? asks the Liberator [Venezuelan] Simon Bolivar: ". . . we are not Europeans, we are not Indians, but a species in between. . . . we find ourselves in the difficult position of challenging the natives for title of possession, and of upholding the country that saw us born against the opposition of the invaders. . . . It is impossible to identify correctly to what human family we belong."[1]

Part European, part indigenous, half colonialist aggressor, half colonized oppressed, we have never had an unproblematic relationship to the questions of culture, identity, race, ethnicity, or even liberation. Still, Latin American thought has been structured to a great extent by European ideas about race and culture—ideas which value racial purity and cultural authenticity—and the contradiction between those ideas and Latin American reality has produced a rich tradition of philosophical work on the concept of cultural identity and its relation to the self. In a situation where there is no hope of attaining purity, a different set of practices and concepts around identity has emerged, one not without its own racisms, but

From Naomi Zack, ed., *American Mixed Race,* Rowman and Littlefield, 1995. Reprinted with permission.

1. Leopoldo Zea, "Identity: A Latin American Philosophical Problem," *The Philosophical Forum* 20 (Fall–Winter 1988–89): 37.

one that might evoke the beginnings of an alternative vision for mestizo peoples throughout the world.

This chapter is situated within Anglo-American discourses about identity and subjectivity. My aim is to contribute to new thinking about racial identity without purity for mixed-race peoples in the United States. It may be thought that there already exists in the North American context an available alternative to racial purity, that is, assimilationism and the imagery of the melting pot. I discuss this in the second section and show why I believe it to be inadequate. I then draw from the work of Latin Americans and Latino philosophers and theorists to find transformative notions of identity, authenticity, and multiculturalism that can usefully inform debates here.

Raced Purely or Purely Erased

Sometimes I feel like a socio-genetic experiment
A petri-dish community's token of infection.
                              —Disposable Heroes of Hiphoprisy[2]

For a variety of reasons that I explore in the next section, Spanish colonizers generally did not operate through practices of genocide, but quickly began intermarrying with indigenous people. The result is that, although there are pockets in some countries where the people are almost wholly indigenous, nearly all the Hispanics of the region share indigenous or African heritage as well. Neocolonial relations between the United States and Latin America have created the conditions to continue this practice of intermarrying (the joke in Panama today is that the most lasting effect of the U.S. invasion is to be found neither in politics nor in the drug trade but in the several hundred marriages that resulted). My own family is a typical case. Neocolonial relations between Panama and the United States created the conditions in which my cholito (mixed Spanish, Indian, and African) Panamanian father married a white Anglo-Irish woman from the United States to produce my sister and me. And through his subsequent liaisons, I have a range of siblings from black to brown to tan to freckled, spanning five countries and three continents, at last count (Panama, Costa Rica, Spain, Venezuela, and the United States). Ours is truly the postcolonial, postmodernist family, an open-ended set of indeterminate national, cultural, racial, and even linguistic allegiances.

2. Epigraph to part 1: "Sociogenic Experiments," by Disposable Heroes of Hiphoprisy.

However, despite the normality of mestizo identity in Latin America, my own experience of my identity has been painful and at times confusing. In Panama, my sister and I were prized for our light skin. Because I was exceptionally light with auburn hair, my father named me "Linda," meaning pretty. There, the mix itself did not pose any difficulties; the issue of concern was the *nature* of the mix—lighter or darker—and we were of the appropriately valued lighter type. When my parents divorced, my sister and I moved with our mother to her parents' home in central Florida, and here the social meanings of our racial identity were wholly transformed. We were referred to as her "Latin daughters," and the fact that we were mixed made us objects of peculiarity. In the central Florida of the 1950s, a biracial system and the one-drop rule still reigned, and our mixed-race status meant that we could occupy white identity only precariously.[3] As much as was possible, we began to pass as simply white, which I was able to do more easily than my sister (she was older, darker, and spoke only Spanish at first). But for both of us, this coerced incorporation into the white Anglo community induced feelings of self-alienation, inferiority, and a strong desire to gain recognition and acceptance within the white community. It also, however, helped us to see through the Jim Crow system, for, through the experience of having racist whites unknowingly accept us, we could see all too clearly the speciousness of the biracial illusion as well as the hurtfulness and irrationality of racial hierarchies and systems of exclusion. I remember standing in the lunch line one day at school while a friend made racist remarks, feeling revolted by her attitude, and also thinking "you could be talking about me."

In cultures defined by racialized identities and divided by racial hierarchies, mixed white–nonwhite persons face an unresolvable status ambiguity. They are rejected by the dominant race as impure and therefore inferior, but also disliked by the oppressed race for their privileges of

3. Latinos in the Florida of the 1950s were generally classified as "almost white" or as "black" depending on their color. But most lived in Miami and Tampa, which were even then cosmopolitan cities very different from the "deep south" cities in north Florida and other southern states. The biggest source of ostracism for Latinos then, as now, was language. Today, the many dark-skinned Latinos who have moved to south Florida are ostracized not only by white Anglos but by African Americans as well for their use of Spanish. Anglos of all colors ridicule the sound of the language, share jokes about uncomprehending sales clerks, and commiserate across their own racial and ethnic differences about the "difficulties" of living in a bilingual city. The experience of Latinos in the United States makes it very clear that so-called racial features never operate alone to determine identity but are always mediated by language, culture, nationality, and sometimes religion.

closer association with domination. Surprisingly consistent repudiations of mixing are found across differences of social status: oppressed and dominant communities disapprove of open mixing, both fail to acknowledge and accept mixed offspring, and both value a purity for racial identity. Thus, the mixed-race person has been denied that social recognition of self that Hegel understood as necessarily constitutive of self-consciousness and full self-development.[4] For those of us who could pass, our community acceptance was always at the price of misrecognition and the troubling knowledge that our social self was grounded on a lie.[5]

Interestingly, this problem has not been restricted to a single political ideology: left and right political discourses have placed a premium on racial purity. For the right, race mixing is a form of "pollution" that requires intermittent processes of ethnic cleansing, which can take the form of genocide, segregation, or simply rural terrorism (the kind practiced by the Ku Klux Klan, the Confederate Knights of America, and the White Aryan Resistance). The very concept of "rape as genocide"—the belief that a massive transcommunity orchestrated series of rapes will result in the genocide of a culture—assumes purity as a necessary and prized cultural identity attribute. Right-wing nationalist movements have also been grounded, in some cases, on the claimed need for a separate political formation that is coextensive with a racial or ethnic identity; here the state becomes the representative of a race or ethnic group and the arbiter over questions of group inclusion.[6] The state must then make it its business to oversee the reproduction of this group, thus to engage in what Michel Foucault called bio-power, to ensure a continuation of its constituency.[7]

For the left, cultural autonomy and community integrity are held up as having an intrinsic value, resulting in mixed-race persons treated as sym-

4. "Self-consciousness exists in itself and for itself, in that, and by the fact that it exists for another self-consciousness; that is to say, it *is* only by being acknowledged or 'recognized'." G. W. F. Hegel, *The Phenomenology of Mind*, trs. J. B. Baillie (New York: Harper, 1967), p. 229.

5. For a moving and insightful literary description of this situation, see Nella Larsen's brilliant novel, *Quicksand* (New Brunswick, N.J.: Rutgers University Press, 1993).

6. For example, it seems likely that the problem Israeli feminists are having in gaining acceptance for a reproductive rights agenda has to do not only with the close association between the Israeli state and Judaism, but also because the state's self-understood legitimation requires the literal reproduction of Jewish identity.

7. Michael Foucault, *The History of Sexuality, 1*, trs. Robert Hurley (New York: Random House, 1980).

bols of colonial aggression or cultural dilution. The very demand for self-determination too often presupposes an authentic self, with clear, unambiguous commitments and allegiances. Thus, as Richard Rodriguez suggests sarcastically, the "Indian [has] become the mascot of an international ecology movement," but not just any Indian. "The industrial countries of the world romanticize the Indian who no longer exists [i.e., the authentic, culturally autonomous Indian without any connection to capitalist economic formations], ignoring the Indian who does—the Indian who is poised to chop down his rain forest, for example. Or the Indian who reads the *New York Times.*"[8] The mythic authentic voice of the oppressed, valorized by the left, is culturally *un*changed, racially *un*mixed, and, as a matter of fact, extinct. The veneration of authenticity leads the left to disregard (when they do not scorn) the survivors of colonialism.

Thus, in many cultures today, mixed-race people are treated as the corporeal instantiation of a lack—the lack of an identity that can provide a public status. They (we) are turned away from as if from an unpleasant sight, the sight and mark of an unclean copulation, the product of a taboo, the sign of racial impurity, cultural dilution, colonial aggression, or even emasculation. Which particular attribution is chosen will reflect the particular community's cultural self-understanding and its position as dominant or subordinate. But the result is usually the same: Children with impure racial identities are treated as an unwanted reminder of something shameful or painful and are alienated (to a greater or lesser extent) from every community to which they have some claim of attachment.

Some theorists have suggested that when such a rigidity around racial identity manifests itself among oppressed people, it is the result of their internalization of oppression and acceptance of racist, self-denigrating cultural values.[9] But I am not sure that this is the cause in every case, or the whole story—the problem may be deeper, in that foundational concepts of self and identity are founded on purity, wholeness, and coherence. A self that is internally heterogeneous beyond repair or resolution becomes a candidate for pathology in a society where the integration of self is taken to be necessary for mental health. We need to reflect upon this premium put on internal coherence and racial purity and how this is manifested in Western concepts and practices of identity as a public persona as well as subjectivity as a foundational understanding of the self. We need to consider what role this preference for purity and racial sepa-

8. Richard Rodriguez, *Days of Obligation* (New York: Penguin, 1992), p. 6.
9. See, e.g., Maria P. P. Root, "Within, Between, and Beyond Race," in *Racially Mixed People in America,* ed. Maria P. P. Root (Newbury Park, Calif.: Sage, 1992), pp. 3–11.

rateness has had on dominant formulations of identity and subjectivity, and what the effects might be if this preference was no longer operative.

Behind my claim that an important relationship exists between purity and racial identity is of course the presupposition that an important relationship exists between race and identity, a relationship that may not always exist but one that appears quite resistant to imminent change. Today, it is easily apparent that acceptance and status within a community are tied to one's racial identification and *identifiability*. In the United States, census forms, as well as application forms of many types, confer various sorts of benefits or resources according to racial identity, thus affecting one's social status. Less formally, one's ability to be accepted in various kinds of social circles, religious groups, and neighborhoods is tied to one's (apparent) race. And I would also argue that not only social status is affected here, but one's lived interiority as well. Such things as government benefits and employment opportunities have an effect on one's subjectivity, one's sense of oneself as a unique, individuated person and as competent, acceptable, or inferior. Dominant discourses, whether they are publically regulated and institutionalized or more amorphous and decentralized, can affect the lived experience of subjectivity. Discourses and institutions implicitly invoke selves that have specific racial identities, which are correlated to those selves' specific legal status, discursive authority, epistemic credibility, and social standing.

During the building of the Panama Canal, workers were divided and identified by the United States owned and run Panama Canal Commission as "gold" (whites) and "silver" (West Indian blacks), denoting the form of currency in which they were paid. Gold and silver workers were given separate and differently constructed living quarters, different currency for wages, and different commissaries; they were assigned different tasks and also attributed different characteristics. In Canal Commission documents, gold workers were described as loyal, earnest, responsible, self-sacrificing, and enthusiastic. Silver workers were described as shiftless, inconstant, exasperating, irresponsible, carefree, "yet as reliable a workman as our own American cottonfield hand."[10] Here race explicitly determined economic and social status, but it also was understood by the dominant white authorities to be the determinate constitutive factor of subjectivity— involving personal character traits and internal constitution (blacks were thought to be more resistant to yellow fever).[11] Such publically instituted

10. Frederic J. Haskin, *The Panama Canal* (Garden City, New York: Doubleday, 1913), p. 162.

11. See Stephen Frenkel's Ph.D. dissertation on the construction of the "other" in the building of the Panama Canal, Syracuse University, 1992.

and circulated associations between race and subjectivity will always have an effect on the self-perceptions of those persons so described. The convincing portrait that has been drawn of subjectivity as constitutively relational by such theorists as Hegel, Fanon, and Irigaray, must persuade us that no self can withstand completely the substantive recognitions from external sources. Thus, racialized identities affect not only one's public status but one's experienced selfhood as well.

To the extent that this public and private self involves a racial construction, this self, outside of Latin America, has been constructed with a premium on purity and separation. The valorization of cultural integrity and autonomy found in diverse political orientations, from left to right, brings along with it the valorization of purity over dilution, of the authentic voice over the voice of collusion, and of autonomy over what might be called "bio-political intercourse."

Erasures of Race

What, then, is the American, this new man? . . . He is an American, who, leaving behind him all his ancient prejudices and manners, receives new ones from the new mode of the life he has embraced, the new government he obeys, and the new rank he holds.
—Hector St. Jean de Crèvecoeur, 1782[12]

If it is generally true that selves are constituted in relationship to communities that have been racially constructed, what happens when there are multiple, conflicting communities through which a self is constituted? What would a concept of the self look like that did not valorize purity and coherence? If we reject the belief that retaining group integrity is an intrinsic good, how will this affect our political goals of resisting the oppression of racialized groups?

Within the United States, assimilationism has been the primary alternative to a racial purity and separateness, but it has notoriously been restricted to European ethnicities, and it has worked to assimilate them all to a Northern European WASP norm—thus Jewish and Roman Catholic Southern Europeans were more difficult to assimilate to this norm and never quite made it into the melting pot. And of course, the melting pot failed to diminish racial hierarchies because it was never really intended to include different races; no proponent of the melting pot ideology ever promoted miscegenation.[13]

12. Quoted in John Hope Franklin, *Race and History* (Baton Rouge: Louisiana State University Press, 1989), pp. 321–2.
13. See Franklin, *Race and History.*

Moreover, as Homi Bhabha remarks, "Fixity, as the sign of cultural/historical/racial difference in the discourse of colonialism, is a paradoxical mode of representation: it connotes rigidity and a unchanging order as well as disorder, degeneracy and daemonic repetition."[14] The fluidity of cultural identity promoted by the assimilationist discourse actually was used to bolster Northern European–Americans' claims to cultural superiority: Their (supposed) "fluidity" was contrasted with and presented as a higher cultural achievement than the (supposed) fixity and rigidity of colonized cultures. Here, fixity symbolized inferiority and flexibility symbolized superiority (although of course, in reality, the designation of "fixity" meant simply the inability or unwillingness to conform to the Northern European norm). This paradox of the meaning of fixity explains how it was possible that, simultaneous to the Panama Canal Commission's construction of rigid racial groups working on the Canal, the ideology at home (i.e., the United States) was dominated by the melting pot imagery. The WASPS could be fluid, tolerant, and evolving, but the natives could not. The very fluidity of identity that one might think would break down hierarchies was used to justify them. Given this, a prima facie danger exists in drawing on assimilationist rhetoric, as it was espoused in the United States, to reconfigure relations of domination.

Ironically, the fact of the matter is that throughout Latin America and the Caribbean, a true melting pot of peoples, cultures, and races was created unlike anything north of the border. The liberal, modernist-based vision of assimilation succeeded best in the premodernist, Roman Catholic, Iberian-influenced countries, while the proponents of secularism and modernism to the north were too busy to notice. Rodriguez points out that, still today,

> Mexico City is modern in ways that "multiracial," ethnically "diverse" New York is not yet. Mexico City is centuries more modern than racially "pure," provincial Tokyo. . . . Mexico is the capital of modernity, for in the sixteenth century, . . . Mexico initiated the task of the twenty-first century—the renewal of the old, the known world, through miscegenation. Mexico carries the idea of a round world to its biological conclusion.[15]

Today, the liberalism that spawned assimilationism has metamorphosed into an ethic of appreciation for the diversity of cultures. In the name of preserving cultural diversity, and in the secret hope of appropriating native wisdom and the stimulation that only exotica can provide a consumption-weary middle class, indigenous cultures and peoples are

14. Homi Bhabha, *The Location of Culture* (New York: Routledge, 1994), p. 66.
15. Rodriguez, pp. 24–25.

commodified, fetishized and fossilized as standing outside of history and social evolution (if they are not totally different than "us," then they will not be exotic enough to have commodity value). Thus, an image of the American Indian straddling a snowmobile (as appeared in the *Times*) evokes affected protestations from educated Anglos about the tragic demise of a cultural identity, as if American Indian identity can only exist where it is pure, unsullied, fixed in time and place.[16] The project of "protecting" the cultural "integrity" of indigenous peoples in the guise of cultural appreciation secures a sense of superiority for those who see their own cultures as dynamic and evolving. Anglo culture can grow and improve through what it learns from "native" cultures, and thus the natives are prized for an exchange value that is dependent on their stagnation.

In North America, then, assimilationism and its heir apparent, cultural appreciation, have not led to a true mixing of races or cultures, or to an end to the relations of domination between cultures. However, interestingly, the concept and the practice of assimilation resonates very differently in South and Central America. As I discuss in the third section of this chapter, for Mexican philosophers such as Samuel Ramos and Leopoldo Zea, assimilation did not require conformity to a dominant norm; instead, assimilation was associated with an antixenophobic cosmopolitanism that sought to integrate diverse elements into a new formation.

What can account for the different practices and theories of assimilation in North and South cultures? And what were the elements involved in U.S. assimilationism that allowed it to coexist with racism rather than come into conflict with it? Finding the answer to such questions can be instructive for the project of developing a better alternative to identify constructions than those based on racial purity. Toward this, I have already suggested that assimilationism in the North was organized around an implicit normative identity (WASP) to which others were expected to conform; hence its exclusive application to Northern Europeans. And I have also suggested that the flexibility of identity claimed by assimilationists was used to bolster WASP claims to cultural superiority over the supposedly rigid peoples and cultures that could not be made to conform. I offer two further elements toward such an answer, one taken from cultural history and the other involving the Enlightenment concept of secular reason.

Latin American and North American countries have different cultural genealogies based on the different origins of their immigrants: respectively, Roman Catholic Iberia and Germano-Protestant England. In North

16. Rodriguez, p. 6.

America, race mixing generally was perceived with abhorrence. In the countries colonized by Spain, by contrast, "elaborate racial taxonomies gained official recognition from the outset . . . and these casta designations became distinct identities unto themselves, with legal rights as well as disabilities attaching to each."[17] After independence, the casta system was eliminated from official discourses, and racial discrimination was made illegal, because such practices of discrimination obviously could not work in countries where as few as 5 percent of the population were *not* mestizo of some varied racial combination.

According to Carlos Fernández and the historian A. Castro, this contrast in the practices around racial difference can be accounted for in the historical differences between "Nordic" and "Latin" cultures.

> Due primarily to its imperial character, the Roman world of which Spain (Hispania) was an integral part developed over time a multiethnically tolerant culture, a culture virtually devoid of xenophobia. The Romans typically absorbed the cultures as well as the territories of the peoples they conquered. Outstanding among their cultural acquisitions were the Greek tradition and, later, the Judaic tradition. It was the Roman co-optation of Judaic Christianity that the Spanish inherited as Catholicism.[18]

Thus, in the missionary zeal of the Spanish Christians can be found the spirit of Roman imperialism, as well as its cosmopolitanism.

By contrast, the Germanic peoples of Northern Europe "emerged into history at the margins of the Roman empire, constantly at war with the legions, not fully conquered or assimilated into Roman life." Fernández hypothesizes that this "condition of perpetual resistance against an alien power and culture" produced the generally negative attitude of the Germans toward foreigners, especially because the Roman legions with which they fought included numerous ethnic groups. This attitude had profound historical results: "The persistence of the German peoples, born of their struggles against the Romans, can also be seen later in history as an important element in the Protestant schism with Rome accomplished by the German Martin Luther. It is no coincidence that Protestantism is primarily a phenomenon of Northwestern Europe while Catholicism is mainly associated with Southern Europe."[19]

Now this of course is not the whole story as to why genocide was so widespread in North America and not in the South: "The difference in

17. Carlos A. Fernández, "La Raza and the Melting Pot: A Comparative Look at Multiethnicity," in Root, p. 135.

18. Fernández, p. 135.

19. Fernández, p. 136.

the size and nature of the Native American populations in Anglo and Latin America also helps account for the emergence of different attitudes about race."[20] In the North, the indigenous peoples were generally nomadic and seminomadic, not very numerous, and there was a great technological distance between them and the European settlers; in the South, the indigenous peoples were numerous and "lived a settled, advanced (even by European standards) agricultural life with large cities and developed class systems."[21] So the resultant integrations between race and cultural formations that developed differently in the North and the South were the product not just of different European traditions but also their interaction with the different cultures in the New World.

And certainly Roman imperialism was not less oppressive than Germanic forms of domination; both perpetrated a strategy of domination. But it is instructive to note the different forms domination can take, and the different legacies each form has yielded in the present. In the North, the melting pot stopped at the border of German-Anglo ethnicities. To venture beyond that border endangered their incorporation into a Roman superpower, ethnically and racially diverse but centered always in Rome. Thus, for Nordic peoples, assimilation and cultural integrity were posed in conflict, and to maintain the distinctness of their borders, they were willing to commit sweeping annihilations. For Rome and Hispania, however, assimilation meant expansion, development, growth. Cultural supremacy did not require isolationism or separation but precisely the constant absorption and blending of difference into an ever larger, more complex, heterogeneous whole. Border control was thus not the highest priority or even considered an intrinsic good. This is why the concept of assimilationism has never had the same meaning in the South as it has in the North, either conceptually or in practice.

The second part of the story involves the Enlightenment concept of secular reason. The northern variant of assimilationism was strongly tied to the development of a Liberal antifeudal ideology that espoused humanism against the aristocracy and secularism against the fusion of church and civil society. The Enlightenment in Northern Europe put forward a vision of universal humanism with equality and civil freedoms for all citizens of a secular state. Diverse ethnicities and religious allegiances could coexist and unite under the auspices of a larger community founded on natural law, and that natural law could be discerned through the use of secular reason, which was conceived as the common denominator across cultural differences. Thus, reason became the means through which the Nordic

20. Fernández, p. 136.
21. Fernández, p. 137.

immigrants to America could relax their borders enough to create a new ethnically mixed society.

But why was the banner of reason incapable of expanding beyond WASP communities? To understand this it helps to recall that the European Enlightenment was flourishing at exactly the same time that European countries were most successfully colonizing the globe—exploiting, enslaving, and in some cases eliminating indigenous populations.[22] But what can account for this juxtaposition between the invocations of liberty for all and the callous disregard of the liberty as well as well-being of non-Europeans? To answer this we need to look more critically at what grounded the claims to liberty.

Universalist humanism was based on a supposedly innate but unevenly developed capacity to reason, a reason conceptualized as entirely mental and thus capable of transcending the particularities of material contexts and specific individuals. Leopoldo Zea has written about the political uses that colonialism has made of the Western notion of reason.[23] Where the Frankfurt School analyzed the connection between Enlightenment reason and social domination, Zea provides a piece of the analysis noticeably missing from their account: the connection between reason and colonialism. "The marginalization of non-European peoples with respect to Europeans," Zea argues, "is related to a Eurocentric view of reason, which leads to the perception that non-Western people are inferior to Europeans in their capacity to reason, hence, in their status of human beings. Political questions of autonomy and the right of self-governance hang in the balance."[24] Universal standards and articulations of rationality are implicated in socially organized practices and institutions that implement colonial and neocolonial policies. When the paradigm of reason, construed as culturally neutral, is defined as the scientific practices of European-based countries, the result is a flattering contrast between Europe and its colonies. Reason is counterposed to ignorance, philosophies of mind to folk psychologies, religion to superstition, and history to myth, producing a cultural hierarchy that vindicates colonialist arrogance. And because this hierarchy is justified through a concept that is presented as culturally neutral, it cannot be assailed by political arguments nor can it be identified

---

22. Just as feminist historians have countered the usual assessment of the Renaissance, arguing that in this period women's situation actually worsened and so there was no renaissance for women, so it has been argued that the Enlightenment offered nothing for those peoples of the world newly colonized. These epoch-dividing categories reflected the perspectives of the dominant.

23. Quoted in Ofelia Schutte, *Cultural Identity and Social Liberation in Latin American Thought* (Albany: State University Press of New York, 1993), p. 86.

24. Ibid.

as an intellectual product of a particular culture. Thus its political effects become unassailable. Following this, Zea points out that the issue of identity must not be mistakenly thought to have relevance only within a conceptual or cultural realm. "It is a problem located in the public sector—in the public conception of reason and in the use of power."[25]

The capacity for reasoning and science on the Western model requires an ability to detach oneself, to be objective, to subdue one's own passionate attachments and emotions. Such a personality type was associated with Northern Europeans and contrasted with the passionate natures of Latin temperaments and the inferior intellects of darker peoples. Thus a humanism based on secular reason, far from conflicting with racism and cultural chauvinism, supported their continuation. In its most benign form, reason could only support Europe's role as beneficent teacher for the backward Other, but could never sustain a relationship of equality. It is for this reason that Zea concludes,

> The racial mestizahe that did not bother the Iberian conquerors and colonizers was to disturb greatly the creators of the new empires of America, Asia, and Africa. Christianity blessed the unity of men and cultures regardless of race, more a function of their ability to be Christian. But modern civilization stressed racial purity, the having or lacking of particular habits and customs proper to a specific type of racial and cultural humanity.[26]

Thus, secularization actually promoted racial purity by replacing Christian values with culturally specific habits and customs. In challenging what is still a powerful orthodoxy—the claim that secularization has only progressive effects—Zea's critique of modernism strikes more deeply than even much of postmodernism. To pretend that these existing concepts—of reason, of philosophy, and of religion—can be extracted from their cultural history and purged of their racial associations and racial content is a delusion. Reason, it turns out, is white, at least in its specific articulations in Western canonical discourses. Therefore, an account of the core of human nature that is based on a reasoning capacity is a racialized concept of the self *passing* for a universal one.

Given this history, then, it is no longer a surprise that the concept and practice of assimilationism that developed in this Northern European context sought to maintain its borders against the devouring capacities and polluting effects of other cultures, and to unite its diverse ethnic groups on the basis of a criterion that simultaneously excluded others (i.e., the capacity for reason and science in the mode of Northern Europe). Whether the concept of reason can be reconstructed is not my project

25. Ibid.
26. Zea, "Identity: A Latin American Philosophical Problem," p. 37.

here, though I certainly support such a project. Rather my question here is, can the concept of assimilation be transformed and salvaged? This discussion will begin in the final section of this chapter.

But first, I want to look briefly at one other, more current, alternative to conceptions of identity based on purity—the very recently developed notion of nomad subjectivity in the work of Gilles Deleuze and Felix Guattari.[27] This concept is not analogous to assimilationism in being widely disseminated within dominant cultural discourses, but it is influential in many academic, theoretical circles and it gains support from some formulations of the new global world over. Nomad subjectivity announces that fluidity and indeterminateness will break up racial and cultural hierarchies that inflict oppression and subordination. Freed from state-imposed structures of identity by the indeterminate flows of capital, nomad subjectivity deterritorializes toward becoming like "a nomad, an immigrant, and a gypsy."[28] Within language, as within subjectivity,

> There is no longer any proper sense or figurative sense, but only a distribution of states that is part of the range of the word. The thing and other things are no longer anything but intensities overrun by deterritorialized sound or words that are following their lines of escape. . . . Instead, it is now a question of a becoming that includes the maximum of difference as a difference of intensity, the crossing of a barrier. . . . [29]

The flow of deterritorialization does not move between points but "has abandoned points, coordinates, and measure, like a drunken boat. . . ."[30] Deterritorializations thus have the effect of deconstructing racial and morphological identity categories along with national, cultural, and ethnic ones, and so the result is not a multiply situated subject but a nomadic subject without the concreteness implied by situation.

This sort of view obviously connects more generally to a postmodernist notion of the indeterminate self, a self defined only by its negation of or

---

27. See Gilles Deleuze and Felix Guattari, *Kafka: Toward a Minor Literature,* trs. Dana Polan (Minneapolis: University of Minnesota Press, 1986); *Anti Oedipus,* trs. Robert Hurley et al. (Minneapolis: University of Minnesota Press, 1983); and *A Thousand Plateaus,* trs. Brian Massumi (Minneapolis: University of Minnesota Press, 1987). For a critique, see Caren Kaplan, "Deterritorializations: The Rewriting of Home and Exile in Western Feminist Discourse," *Cultural Critique* (Spring 1987):187–98.

28. *Kafka: Toward a Minor Literature,* p. 19.

29. Ibid., p. 22.

30. *A Thousand Plateaus,* p. 296.

resistance to categories of identity.[31] And there is a strand of this in academic feminism among theorists who repudiate identity-based politics in the name of antiessentialism. Liberation is associated with the refusal to be characterized, described, or classified, and the only true strategy of resistance can be one of negation, a kind of permanent revolution on the metaphysical front. Unfortunately, nomadic subjectivity works no better than assimilationist doctrine to interpellate mixed identity: the nomad self is bounded to no community and represents an absence of identity rather than a multiply entangled and engaged identity. This is not the situation of mixed-race peoples who have deep (even if problematic) ties to specific communities; to be a free-floating unbound variable is not the same as being multiply categorized and ostracized by specific racial communities. It strikes me that the postmodern nomadic vision fits far better the multinational CEO with fax machine and cellular phone in hand who is bound to, or by, no national agenda, tax structure, cultural boundary, or geographical border. And what this suggests is that a simplistic promotion of fluidity will not suffice.

I am concerned with the way in which a refusal of identity might be useful for the purposes of the current global market. The project of global capitalism is to transform the whole world into postcolonial consumers and producers of goods in an acultural world commodity market, the Benetton-like vision where the only visible differences are those that can be commodified and sold. Somewhere between that vision and the vision of a purist identity construction that requires intermittent ethnic cleansing we must develop a different alternative, an alternative which can offer a normative reconstruction of raced-identity applicable to mixed-race peoples.

Mestiza Race

> Jose Vasconcelos, Mexican philosopher, envisaged una raza mestiza, una mezcla de razas afines, una raza de color—la primera raza sintesis del globo. He called it a cosmic race, la raza cosmica, a fifth race embracing the four major races of the world. Opposite to the theory of the pure Aryan. . . . his theory is one of inclusivity.
>
> —Gloria Anzaldúa[32]

31. See, e.g., Paul Smith, *Discerning the Subject* (Minneapolis: University of Minnesota Press, 1988). See also my review of this book in *American Literary History* (Summer 1993): 335–46.

32. Gloria Anzaldúa, *Borderlands/La Frontera* (San Francisco: Spinsters/Aunt Lute, 1987), p. 77.

We must begin to look South, where there already exists a long tradition of philosophical work on the intersections of identity, multiplicity, and politics. The specifically philosophical treatment of identity will certainly seem odd to Anglo philosophers, who on the whole leave such cultural specificities to sociologists or anthropologists, and instead prefer to concentrate on problems considered to have universal relevance and applicability. I am reminded here of a story that Michael Kimmel told recently at a talk he gave. As a graduate student in the History of Consciousness program at the University of California–Santa Cruz, he was taking a seminar in feminist theory when a debate occurred about the importance of race versus gender. In the midst of the discussion, bell hooks asked Bettina Aptheker what she saw when she looked in the mirror. Aptheker replied, "I see a woman." hooks responded that when she looked in the mirror, she saw a black woman. Kimmel reported feeling very uncomfortable at that moment, because he realized that when he looked in the mirror, what he saw was a human being. When your own particular and specific attributes are dominant *and* valorized, they can be taken for granted and ignored.

Because of their interest in contributing to the thinking about identity issues, many Latin American philosophers have developed a different understanding of the nature of philosophy itself. If philosophy is defined as raising only universal, general, and abstract problems, beyond the issues facing concrete individuals in the everyday world, there is no space within philosophy for discussions about cultural identity, and so such issues are left to the social sciences. Zea argues that such a view exemplifies the desire to be godlike on the part of philosophers, to transcend the "concrete capacity of vision of the one who asks."[33] Drawing on the views of Hans-Georg Gadamer and Karl-Otto Apel, Zea suggests that we need not abandon theoretical discourse to reject this delimitation of philosophical problems to abstract and universal issues:

> At stake here is not a choice [e.g., between theory and practice] but a reconstruction of problems that are inescapably linked among themselves because they have an origin in man. The philosopher does not have to give up being a philosopher to face the many problems of a reality different from theory. Without ceasing to be a philosopher he can philosophically, rationally, confront man's daily problems and seek possible solutions.[34]

So, without ceasing to be a philosopher, let me return to the problem of racial identity.

33. Zea, "Identity: A Latin American Philosophical Problem," pp. 33–34.
34. Ibid., p. 34.

First, it seems clear that, within the context of racially based and organized systems of oppression, racial identity will continue to be a salient internal and external component of identity. Systems of oppression, segregated communities, and practices of discrimination create a collective experience and a shared history for a racialized grouping. It is that shared experience and history, more than any physiological or morphological features, that cements the community and creates connections with others along racial lines. And that history cannot be deconstructed by new scientific accounts that dispute the characterization of race as a natural kind.[35] Accounts of race as a social and historical identity, though this brings in elements that are temporally contingent and mutable, will probably prove to have more persistence than accounts of race that tie it to biology. Ironically, history will probably have more permanence than biology.

Moreover, I would argue that, given current social conditions, any materialist account of the self must take into account the element of race. This is not to deny that generic and universalist concepts of human being are both possible and necessary. Despite my concern expressed in the last section against formulating a universal humanism based on reason, connections do exist between persons that endure across differences of sexuality, race, culture, even class. My view is not that such connections do not exist, or that they are trivial, or that in all cases a universalist humanism is politically pernicious. However, if we restrict a philosophical analysis of identity and subjectivity to only those elements that can be universally applied, our resulting account will be too thin to do much philosophical work. In the concrete everydayness of "actually existing" human life, the variabilities of racial designation mediate experience in ways we are just beginning to recognize.

Another reason to maintain the racial dimension of formulations of identity is that universalist pretensions often produce alienation in those whose identities are not dominant. When such false universalisms become influential in oppressed communities, the result is that, for example, non-white peoples internalize the perspective of white identity. In *The Bluest Eye*, Toni Morrison dramatically captures this phenomenon for the young black child who wants blond hair and blue eyes. Simone de Beauvoir and Sandra Bartky have written about a form of female alienation in which women see themselves and their bodies through a generalized male gaze that rates and ranks attributes, and disciplines behavior to a degree worthy

35. See Naomi Zack, "Race and Philosophic Meaning," in *American Philosophical Association Newsletter on Philosophy and the Black Experience* 94, no. 1 (Fall 1994), pp. 14–20.

of Foucault's description of the Benthamite panopticon. And Samuel Ramos has argued that the veneration of Europe has led Mexicans to live "with a view of the world alien to their own cultural reality," in effect, "to live outside their 'being.'"[36]

Such patterns of alienation have profound effects on the capacity for self-knowledge, a capacity that philosophers as diverse as Plato and Hegel have seen as critical for the possibility of any knowledge whatsoever. If knowledge represents a concrete vision correlated to a particular social location, then the alienation one suffers from one's own perspectival vision will have ramifications throughout one's life. And for mixed-race persons, this problem can be particularly difficult to overcome. For them (us), it is not a question of reorienting perspective from the alien to the familiar, because no ready-made, available perspective captures their contradictory experience. Without a social recognition of mixed identity, the mixed-race person is told to choose one or another perspective. This creates not only alienation, but the sensation of having a mode of being that is an incessant, unrecoverable lack and an unsurpassable inferiority. This blocks the possibility of self-knowledge. The epistemic authority and credibility that accrue to nearly everyone, at least with respect to their "ownmost" perspective, is denied to the mixed-race person. Vis-à-vis each community or social location to which she or he might claim a connection, she or he can never claim authority to speak unproblematically for or from that position. Ramos warns that, without a connection to an ongoing history and community, "one lives only for the day . . . without regard to past or future."[37] Only communities have continuity beyond individual life; cast off from all communities, the individual has no historical identity, and thus is unlikely to value the community's future.

Identity is not, of course, monopolized by race, nor does race operate on identity as an autonomous determinant. Mixed-race persons probably notice more than others the extent to which "race" is a social construction, ontologically dependent on a host of contextual factors. The meanings of both race and such things as skin color are mediated by language, religion, nationality, and culture, to produce a racialized identity. As a result, a single individual's racial identity can change across communities, and a family's race can change across history. In the Dominican Republic, "black" is defined as Haitian, and dark-skinned Dominicans do not self-identify as black but as dark Indians or mestizos. Coming to the United States, Dominicans "become" black by the dominant standards. In the United States, I generally pass as a white angla; as soon as I land in

36. Schutte, *Cultural Identity*, p. 75.
37. Ibid., p. 77.

Panama, I am recognized as Panamanian. In England, South Asians are identified as blacks. Every year in South Africa, numbers of people petition the government to change their official racial classification, resulting in odd official announcements from the Home Affairs Minister that, for example, "nine whites became coloured, 506 coloureds became white, two whites became Malay . . . 40 colored became black, 666 blacks became coloured, 87 colored became Indian. . . ."[38] The point here is not that racial identities are often misidentified, but that race does not stand alone; race identity is mediated by other factors, political as well as sociological ones. And appearance is also socially mediated; the dominant perspective in the United States on a person's racial identity or whether they "look" Latino or black is not natural. Appearances "appear" differently across cultural contexts.

Because nationality, culture, and language are so critical to identity, some propose that, for example, nationality should be taken as a more important distinguishing characteristic than race. Nationality could provide a strong connection across racialized communities, increasing their unity and sympathetic relationships. This phenomenon is emerging in the United States today as minority communities become antiimmigrant, even when the immigrants are of the same racial features or share a cultural background. Thus African-American school kids fight with West Indians in Brooklyn, and Cubans disdain the Central Americans flooding into Miami. Such conflict is sometimes based on class, but it is also based on a claim to the so-called "American" identity. In this way, U.S. minorities can ally with the (still) powerful white majority against new immigrants, and perhaps share in the feeling if not the reality of dominance. An identification that places nationality over race thus ensures, at least for the present, an increase in antiimmigrant violence.

The point of the preceding discussion is to suggest that race cannot and should not be eliminated as a salient identity in the near future. In my view, it should not be replaced by nationality, and its erasure only conceals the ongoing dominance of white Northern European values and perspectives. Some have argued that, given the socially constructed character of race, and the largely detrimental effects that racial classifications have had on all nonwhite peoples and mixed-race persons in particular, all forms of racial identity should be rejected. I would argue rather for developing a positive reconstruction of mixed-race identity. I will end by suggesting some ways this might be developed.

---

38. Quoted in Trinh T. Minh-Ha, *When the Moon Waxes Red* (New York: Routledge, 1991), p. 73. Notice that, as she points out, no whites applied to become black.

In her book *Borderlands/La Frontera*, Gloria Anzaldúa has offered a powerful and lyrical vision of the difficulties mixed-race persons endure. She writes:

> The ambivalence from the clash of voices results in mental and emotional states of perplexity. Internal strife results in insecurity and indecisiveness. The mestiza's dual or multiple personality is plagued by psychic restlessness.[39]

Contrast that description with Deleuze and Guattari's romantic portrait of the nomad and the schizophrenic, as a paradigm of liberation.

Anzaldúa worries that the shame and rootlessness of the mestizo can lead to excessive compensation, especially in the form of machismo. She writes:

> In the Gringo world, the Chicano suffers from excessive humility and self-effacement, shame of self and self-deprecation. Around Latinos he suffers from a sense of language inadequacy and its accompanying discomfort; with Native Americans he suffers from a racial amnesia which ignores our common blood, and from guilt because the Spanish part of him took their land and oppressed them. He has an excessive compensatory hubris when around Mexicans from the other side. It overlays a deep sense of racial shame . . . which leads him to put down women and even to brutalize them.[40]

For Anzaldúa, an alternative positive articulation of mestiza consciousness and identity must be developed to provide some degree of coherence and to avoid the incessant cultural collisions or violent compensations that result from the shame and frustration of self-negation.

Toward this, Anzaldúa sees the mixed-race person as engaged in the valuable though often exhausting role of border crosser, negotiator, and mediator between races, and sometimes also between cultures, nations, and linguistic communities. The mixed person is a traveler often within her own home or neighborhood, translating and negotiating the diversity of meanings, practices, and forms of life. This vision provides a positive alternative to the mixed-race person's usual representation as lack or as the tragically alienated figure.

Such figures who can negotiate between cultures have of course been notoriously useful for the dominant, who can use them to better understand and thus control their colonized subjects. Thus, such figures as Malinche and Pocahontas are often reviled for their cooperation with

39. Anzaldúa, *Borderlands/La Frontera*, p. 78.
40. Ibid., p. 83.

dominant communities and their love for specific individuals from those communities. There is no question that such border negotiation can exacerbate oppression. Today large numbers of bilingual and biracial individuals are recruited by the U.S. military and the F.B.I. to infiltrate suspected gangs or communities and countries designated as U.S. enemies. To my dismay, many Latinos in the U.S. military were deployed in the invasion of Panama. Here again, an allegiance based on nationality is used to circumvent what might be a stronger racial or cultural tie.

I suspect that for mixed-raced persons, especially those who have suffered some degree of rejection from the communities to which they have some attachment, such jobs hold a seductive attraction as a way to overcome feelings of inferiority and to find advantage for the first time in the situation of being mixed. Where I agree with Anzaldúa is the positive spin she puts on the mixed-race identity. (And I must say to Anglos who may have read her book, don't underestimate the radical nature of what she has done: her use of a mix of languages, including English, Spanish, Tex-Mex, and indigenous languages, is a practice that is reviled by most Spanish speaking people in the United States and Latin America, even including most Mexican Americans. Her insistence on linguistic mixes is very liberating.) But where I would place a note of caution concerns the uses to which such border crossings can be put: they are not all to the good.

Another element worth exploring is Samuel Ramos's concept of an assimilation that does not demand conformity to the dominant or consist in a kind of imitation. Rather, assimilation in Ramos's sense is an incorporation or absorption of different elements. This is similar to the Hegelian concept of sublation in the sense of a synthesis that does not simply unite differences but develops them into a higher and better formulation. In the context of Latin America, Ramos called for a new self-integration that would appropriate its European and Indian elements. "The practice of imitating European culture must be replaced by the assimilation of such a culture. 'Between the process of imitation and that of assimilation there lies the same difference,' he notes, 'as there is between what is mechanical and what is organic.'"[41] Ramos believes that this process of active assimilation cannot occur without reflective self-knowledge. An imitative stance toward the other, and a conformity to dominant norms, will occur unless the empty self-image of the Mexican is replaced by a more substantive perspective indexed to one's own cultural, political, and racial location.

I believe that the concept of mestizo consciousness and identity can contribute toward the development of such a perspective, by creating a

41. Schutte, *Cultural Identity*, p. 80.

linguistic, public, socially affirmed identity for mixed-race persons. Mestizo consciousness is a double vision, a conscious articulation of mixed identity, allegiances, and traditions. As I quote Anzaldúa above, Jose Vasconcelos called this new identity the cosmic race, la raza cosmica, based on a rich inclusivity and mutability rather than purity. All forms of racial mixes could be included in this identity, thus avoiding the elaborate divisions that a proliferation of specific mixed identities could produce. Such a vision is not captured by the "United Colors of Benetton," but by the organic integration of a new human blend such as the world has never seen.

Only recently have I finally come to some acceptance of my ambiguous identity. I am not simply white nor simply Latina, and the gap that exists between my two identities—indeed, my two families—a gap that is cultural, racial, linguistic, and national, feels too wide and deep for me to span. I cannot bridge the gap, so I negotiate it, standing at one point here, and then there, moving between locations as events or other people's responses propel me. I never reach shore: I never wholly occupy either the Angla or the Latina identity. Paradoxically, in white society I feel my Latinness, in Latin society I feel my whiteness, as that which is left out, an invisible present, sometimes as intrusive as an elephant in the room and sometimes more as a pulled thread that alters the design of my fabricated self. Peace has come for me by living that gap, and no longer seeking some permanent home onshore. What I seek now is no longer a home, but perhaps a lighthouse, that might illuminate this place in which I live, for myself as much as for others.

17

Michael Hanchard, "Black Cinderella? Race and the Public Sphere in Brazil"

Michael Hanchard teaches political science in the department of political science at Northwestern University. He is author of Orpheus and Power: Afro-Brazilian Social Movements in Rio de Janeiro and São Paulo, Brazil, 1945–1988 *(1994). Hanchard employs Jürgen Habermas's notion of the public sphere to understand the racial policy toward black people in Brazil—a policy that has been historically a matter of cultural, as well as legal, practice.*

On June 26, 1993 an incident in Vitória, capital city of Espírito Santo, Brazil, drove another nail into the coffin of the ideology of Brazilian racial democracy. Ana Flávia Peçanha de Azeredo, a nineteen-year-old college student, was accosted and punched in the face by a forty-year-old woman and her eighteen-year-old son in the service elevator of an apartment building where Ms. Peçanha was visiting a friend. The physical assault was the result of an argument between the three over Ana Flávia's use of the elevator. The mother and son did not like the fact that this young black woman not only had entered their building and held up the social elevator to talk to a friend, forcing them to use the service elevator, but also that she had dared to tell them to respect her after they informed her that "black and poor don't have a place here" in the building where they lived.[1]

This incident, like so many other acts of racist violence in Brazil, would have gone unnoticed if Ana Flávia's father, Albuino Azeredo, was not the governor of the state of Espírito Santo. With the resources available to him, Governor Azeredo employed lawyers and physicians to examine his daughter's situation, and filed suit against Teresina and Rodrigo Stange, the alleged assailants. If convicted of racial discrimination under Article Five of the federal Constitution, both mother and son could be sent to

Michael Hanchard, "Black Cinderella? Race and the Public Sphere in Brazil," *Public Culture* 7:1 (Fall 1994), pp. 165–85. Copyright 1994. All rights reserved. Reprinted by permission of Duke University Press.

I would like to thank Kit Belgum, Claudia Briones, Richard Graham and Hendrick Kraay for their helpful comments on an earlier version of this paper.

1. See "A Cinderela Negra" in *Veja*, 7 de Julho, 1993, p. 66–71.

prison for one to five years. Ironically, the Brazilian press referred to Ana Flávia as the black Cinderella, with her father the Governor playing the role of prince. One may wonder, however, which Cinderella were they referring to? The one who is fitted with the errant glass slipper and who lives with the prince happily ever after, or the one who wears worn-out clothing and spends her days performing domestic labor? In fact, as a woman of African descent, Ana Flávia is neither. She is closer to a composite of status-filled and status-less roles in Brazilian society; considered a member of Brazil's elite when identified by birth, treated as a lowly, powerless member of society when identified by race.

The tale of black Cinderella is resonant with many of the constitutional, legal, cultural and societal issues of Afro-Brazilians within the Brazilian public sphere. It encapsulates the intersection of race, citizenship and modernity in a society that in theory is committed to liberal-democratic principles, but in practice still struggles with the legacies of patron-clientelism, racial slavery and oppression. The above incident might seem commonsensical enough from a comparative perspective, but within the context of Brazilian racial politics it further confirms the denial of full citizenship to people of African descent in Brazil during this most recent period of democratization. Comparatively, it also attests to the pervasiveness of black subjectivity in societies under the template of modernity, both inside and outside the West. The public sphere, far from being simply the location of bourgeois culture's prized subject—the individual—has also been the place where the West's others have been displaced and marginalized, inside and outside its borders. Indeed, as I will argue in this explication and critique of notions of the public sphere put forth by several social and political theorists, it has been upheld as the benchmark of modernity, the principal indicator of political and socio-economic development.

People of African descent, however, have been granted contingent and partial citizenship within these spheres, and only as a consequence of their own political struggles that have gone beyond the boundaries of liberal discourse. What I would like to demonstrate in this essay is the symbolic functions of Afro-Brazilians within Brazilian society as bearers of non-citizenship, in accordance with racist ideologies and practices by the Brazilian state and in civil society during the nineteenth and twentieth centuries. In short Afro-Brazilians—like many other Afro-diasporic populations—have been depicted as embodying the antithesis of modernity.

This depiction, however, has two specific implications for scholarly intervention. First, it highlights modernity's limitations in terms of racial politics, and the manner in which its ideals have been intrinsically racialized. Second, it highlights the abstractness of theorizing on citizenship and the public sphere by theorists like Charles Taylor and Jürgen Habermas, as well as the radical disjuncture between ideals of the public sphere and their historical embodiments.

While many theorists have considered racism within the public sphere as a mere aberration along the road to modernity, I suggest that the distinctly oppressive conditions under which people of African descent have lived partially constitute modernity and the public sphere. Racial differences is but one of modernity's internal contradictions and disjunctures; it has been a criteria of both citizenship and noncitizenship.

Through a brief analysis of the Afro-Brazilian public sphere I examine how the dialectics of race and modernity are embodied in Brazilian racial politics. This in turn suggests first that Afro-Brazilians have been accorded partial and contingent access to the public sphere, a domain which has been defined explicitly and implicitly as white. While this in itself is no innovative conclusion, it can be utilized to interrogate the notion of the bourgeois public sphere as the sole arena or possibility for cultural articulation. This then leads to my second point: through segregation and other forms of racial alienation, alternative public spheres operate within a broadly defined public sphere. Marginalized groups create territorial and epistemological communities for themselves as a consequence of their subordinate location within the bourgeois public sphere. Along these lines, Afro-Brazilians have constructed public spheres of their own which critique Brazil's societal and political norms.

Race and the Public Sphere

In his pathbreaking work, *The Structural Transformation of the Public Sphere,* Jürgen Habermas defines the bourgeois public sphere as "the sphere of private people come together as a public; they soon claimed the public sphere regulated from above against the public authorities themselves, to engage them in a debate over the general rules governing relations in the basically privatized but publicly relevant sphere of commodity exchange and social labor."[2] The important historical precedent, within Habermas's interpretation, lies in the confrontation between "public authority," namely, depersonalized state power, and individual propertied subjects over the "private sphere of society that has become publicly

2. Jürgen Habermas, *The Structural Transformation of the Public Sphere* (Cambridge, MA: MIT Press, 1991), 27.

relevant."[3] With the advent of capitalism, commerce and the related growth of mass news and information, propertied subjects came to use reason in ways formerly reserved for private concerns such as the domestic economy and household management and private business interests. This interface would radically shift the locus of power from feudal landlords to state institutions and socially engaged, private citizens who had become public.

Rather than engage in an extended discussion of Habermas's explication of the public sphere, for which there is already an extensive literature,[4] I shall point out several contradictions that emerged from this historical precedent and have been commented upon by public sphere specialists and social theorists more generally. While the creation of this new public sphere did supplant the old, becoming the dominant, most logical social forum and institution in countries like France, Germany,[5] Britain and Denmark, it did not automatically sever the formerly dominant modes of economic and political relations.[6] Unpropertied social groups, who were never *private* citizens under the previous socioeconomic order, still remained outside the category of citizen within the new public sphere. The mark of difference—education, religious affiliations, dress, habits, speech, language, an entire way of life—haunted these unpropertied social groups as they were reinscribed into newly subordinate social relationships.

Thus the bourgeois public sphere was simultaneously expansive and exclusive. It burgeoned with new forms of social inequality to parallel new forms of public authority and financial organization. Yet the working classes were neither entirely nor permanently outside the new social order, since universal suffrage, freedom of assembly and association, provided certain sectors of working-class groups the opportunity to contest the

---

3. Habermas, *Structural Transformation*, 19.

4. For critiques of the exclusionary character of Habermas's public sphere, or rather, considerations of the evolution of micro-public spheres for groups and subjects excluded from participatory roles within the bourgeois version see Nancy Fraser, "Rethinking the Public Sphere: A Contribution to the Critique of Actually Existing Democracy," in Craig Calhoun, ed. *Jürgen Habermas and the Public Sphere* (Cambridge, MA: MIT Press, 1991), 109–142 and in the same volume Mary Ryan, "Gender and Public Access: Women and Politics in 19th Century America," 259–288.

5. Rogers Brubaker, *Citizenship and Nationhood in France and Germany* (Cambridge, MA: Harvard University Press, 1992).

6. Cedric Robinson, *Black Marxism* (London: Zed, 1983).

inequalities of the new order, and in the process, construct what I shall call micro-public spheres, that is spheres of public articulation that were not limited to, but dominated by the idioms, norms and desires of working-class women and men.[7]

The bourgeois public sphere's ability to be perceived not as one space among several, but as the only forum for all social groups to engage in normative debate—either amongst themselves or between two or more groups—was the crowning ideological achievement of bourgeois culture. Another way to view this (mis)perception relates to the evolving presumption that the bourgeois public sphere superseded private/public relations of the feudal order and, all previously subordinate subjects and groups henceforth operated as social and political equals. The reality, however, was that "the oligarchy of capital was replacing the oligarchy of birth."[8] Habermas clearly recognized this contradiction within the remaking of civil society. Yet other social theorists, particularly liberal ones and architects of modernity in the New World did not, and in some cases ignored it completely. This misconception has led *the* public sphere to become reified by most analysts of it and of its virtues and problems. The most serious consequence of this reification is the equation of an ideal type public sphere with Western polities, thus ignoring the internal contradictions within Western polities themselves concerning the realities of racial and ethnic difference.

Race, Modernity and the Public Sphere in the New World

Habermas has suggested that the philosophical discourses of modernity are distinguished by their orientation towards the future, their need to negate previous conceptions of time and history. In *The Philosophical Discourses of Modernity*, Habermas applies Hegel's understanding of modernity: "Modernity can and will no longer borrow the criteria by which it takes its orientation from the models supplied by another epoch; *it has to*

7. The work of E. P. Thompson, *The Making of the English Working Class* (New York: Vintage Books, 1966), Paul Willis, *Learning to Labor* (New York: Columbia University Press, 1981), Raymond Williams, *The Country and the City* (New York: Oxford University Press, 1975), and George Orwell, *The Road to Wigan Pier* (San Diego: Harcourt Brace Jovanovich, 1958) provides evidence of a public sphere of working classes that is quite distinct from more affluent counterparts.

8. Emilia Viotti da Costa, *The Brazilian Empire: Myths and Histories* (Chicago: University of Chicago Press, 1985), 55.

create its normativity out of itself. Modernity sees itself cast back upon itself without any possibility of escape."[9]

Yet modernity cannot efface history entirely. It needs history for points of reference from which to distinguish itself. A much greater impediment to complete historical denial was the discovery of the New World and the slave trade. This discovery led to the presence of New World and African people and/or their artifacts and other forms of production in the West, as well as in emergent New World nations. By the end of the nineteenth century, elites in most American nations decided to appropriate French or U.S. models of republicanism and liberal democracy in the transition from colony to free nation-state.[10] The fundamental contradiction in cultural terms that emerged from this was the presence of non-Western peoples amidst projects of modernity and the public sphere in the New World. Latin American elites and intellectuals had less difficulty reconciling European modernity's break with the past in nation-states with no previous *national*-state history (Cuba, Brazil, Colombia and Argentina, for example), than in accounting for the presence of sizable populations of "premodern people." Such populations were regarded as being without reason and rationality; they were treated as the ant colonies of Latin American modernity—excavating mines, constructing cities, harvesting crops, tending to children. They enabled those very same elites to become modern like their Western models.

In Brazil and many other Latin American countries, the shift from slave to wage labor was not as momentous an event as the shift from feudalism to capitalism in Europe. However the repercussions of this shift profoundly affected the dynamics of social interaction between landed and landless groups, as well as among white, indigenous and African-derived populations. This shift signalled the inauguration of *the modern moment* in Latin America, in which various nations in this region of the world attempted to pattern themselves after the nation-states and civilizations of Western Europe. Yet the modern moment in Latin America differed from its Western European model due to the relatively late growth of industry, mass communications networks and centralized state power. Furthermore, the landowning classes were not rendered obsolete but rather transformed their mode of social dominance. These historical differences complicated the evolution of an ideal type public sphere, for the slaveowners and landowners occupied the sociological location of the bourgeoisie with-

9. Jürgen Habermas, *The Philosophical Discourses of Modernity* (Cambridge, MA: MIT Press, 1987), 7.

10. Harold Davis, *Latin American Social Thought* (Washington, DC: The University Press of Washington, D.C., 1961).

out actually constituting a bourgeoisie themselves. Thus, the collision between feudal and slave labor on the one hand, and capitalist wage labor on the other, was not as radical as it may have appeared. The dominant ideological amalgam in Brazil came to be known as conservative liberalism. Viotti characterizes conservative liberalism as a contradiction between liberal discourse and liberal practice, the expressed interest in the bourgeoisie's economic project without its attendant political and "valuative" responsibilities, like respect for the rights of individuals.[11] Thus slavery and patron-clientelism fused with liberal rhetoric to create a much more ambiguous setting for civil society than in European nation-states.

The specific consequences for the various African slave populations in Brazil was first, that they were the last slave population in the New World to be granted emancipation.[12] Elites justified the long delay in unchaining the enslaved on the grounds that Brazilian slavery was actually less harsh than the working conditions of peasants and wage laborers in Southern Europe, and that slaves were actually spared the horrors of savage Africa by being transported to the more civilized and enlightened Brazil. This justification, buttressed by purported cultural differences between Portuguese and other European civilizations underpinned the now well known myth of racial democracy.[13] The realities of Afro-Brazilian life by 1888, when slavery was abolished, were quite different. In 1871 slavery was clearly on the wane, and planters in the province of São Paulo decided to subsidize Southern European immigration to Brazil in order to develop a European proletariat, even though there were more free Afro-Brazilians than slaves in the province of São Paulo.[14] It was a simultaneous expression of racial and economic interests through state implementation of racially and economically specific policies.

These policies basically disqualified freedpersons from objective market competition in the emergent capitalist marketplace, thus limiting their prospects regardless of occupational differentiation within Afro-Brazilian communities. Large landowners in most cases refused to hire former slaves, in part on the grounds that they were recalcitrant and demanded specific conditions under which they would labor, but largely due to their desire to engage in economic relationships with those whom they most

11. Viotti, *The Brazilian Empire,* 55.

12. Robert Conrad, *Children of God's Fire* (Princeton: Princeton University Press, 1983).

13. Gilbert Freyre, *The Masters and the Slaves* (New York: Alfred A. Knopf, 1946).

14. George Reid Andrews, *Blacks and Whites in São Paulo, Brazil. 1888–1988* (Madison: University of Wisconsin, 1988).

resembled, even in subordinate roles. European immigrant labor was preferred despite the fact that many Afro-Brazilians were skilled laborers at
the time of abolition, and already had the skills which Italian and other
immigrants were just developing.[15] Previously freed Afro-Brazilians did
not fare much better even though by 1872, seventy-four percent of all
Afro-Brazilians were free (as compared to six percent in the South of the
United States on the eve of emancipation).[16]

The employment practices were consistent with the marginalization of
enslaved and free blacks during the period of national formation that
culminated in Brazil's independence from Portugal. The first national
elections of 1821 for a centralized government—one year before
independence—created the electoral conditions for the Brazilian elite to
participate in public debate about Brazil's transformation into an independent monarchy, but excluded those who remained enslaved until 1888.[17]
Bastos suggests that the 1821 election was a defining moment in Brazilian
political culture, for the new constitutional order helped integrate previously marginalized groups such as small merchants, artisans, salespeople
and others by elevating them to the status of citizens. These groups were
similar to those who constituted the petit bourgeoisie in revolutionary
France by the late-eighteenth century. The Constitution of 1824 defined
Brazil as a constitutional monarchy; it gave black freedmen the right to
vote, but they could not be chosen as electors.[18]

The slave population was well aware of the struggles between monar-
chial nationalists and loyalists to the Portuguese Crown. In fact, slaves and
mulattos were key participants on both sides. Moreover, Africans in Bahia,
like their counterparts in other slave societies in the New World, used
moments of elite crisis in Brazil to their own advantage, fomenting revolts
and rebellions at critical moments of disunity among these elites who were
largely rural landholders that had maintained their power after indepen-

15. Warren Dean, *Rio Claro: A Brazilian Plantation System, 1820–1920* (Palo
Alto: Stanford University Press, 1976).

16. See Herbert S. Klein, "Nineteenth Century Brazil," in David Cohen and Jack
P. Greene, eds. *Neither Slave nor Free: The Freedman of African Descent in the Slave
Societies of the New World* (Baltimore: Johns Hopkins University Press, 1972);
309–334, 319.

17. Lùcia Maria Bastos P. Neves, "As eleiçoes na construção do emperior
Brasileiro: Os limites de uma nova practica da cultura politica Luso-Brasileira
(1820–1823)." Paper presented at the workshop on Political Representation and
Nation Building in Nineteenth-Century Latin America, University of Texas, Austin, March 7–9, 1994.

18. Brazil, *Constituição politica do Imperio do Brasil*, Art. 94 in combination with
Articles 6 and 91, quoted in Graham.

dence in 1822.[19] Revolts in 1835 and 1837 in Bahia led to waves of repression not only against blacks, but also against the poor and other urban elements who remained politically excluded after independence. In Salvador, Bahia, local officials responded to the 1835 revolt by African-Brazilians by imposing stringent laws that monitored the movement of freed and enslaved blacks. Porters and stevedores, who were predominantly black, had to be registered on a single list and were required to wear a copper bracelet engraved with their registry number.[20]

These and other acts suggest that by the 1830s in Brazil, the status of African and Afro-Brazilian slaves and *libertos* (freed slaves) held marginal distinctions, even though there were considerable social tensions between Brazilian and African-born slaves.[21] The free and the enslaved often worked side by side.[22] By this time, the Brazilian empire relied on the discourse of the social problem to refer to free and nonfree blacks as vagrants and idlers (*vadios e ociosos*) to avoid the complexities of distinguishing the *escravo* from the *liberto*.[23] As in the United States, blackness overrode the constitutional or legal mandate of citizenship for Afro-Brazilians. Republican institutions, despite their status as impartial purveyors of law and merit, actually institutionalized racist discourses and practices, and empowered many individuals who believed that African presences in Brazil doomed their nation to second-class status. Immigration laws and policies specifically prohibited nonwhite immigration to Brazil,[24] and there were congressional debates over the alleged racial inferiority of Africans, Chinese and Southern Europeans.[25] When coupled with the powerful albeit contradictory ideology of whitening which asserted that miscegenation would eventually eliminate people of African descent, Afro-Brazilians were remarginalized in the shift from slave to

19. Hendrik Kraay, "As Terrifying as Expected: The Bahian Sabinada, 1837–1838" *Hispanic American Historical Review* 72(4) (1992): 501–521.

20. João Reis, *Muslim Uprising of 1835 in Bahia* (Baltimore: Johns Hopkins University Press, 1993); Reis, *Slave Rebellion in Brazil* (Baltimore: Johns Hopkins University Press, 1993).

21. Richard Graham, "Free African Brazilians and the State in Slavery Times." Paper presented at the conference, Racial Politics in Contemporary Brazil, University of Texas, Austin, April 8–10, 1993.

22. Thomas Flory, "Race and Social Control in Independent Bahia." *Latin American Studies* 9 (2) (1977): 199–224.

23. Flory, "Race and Social Control": 199–224, esp. 203.

24. Michael Mitchell, "Racial Consciousness and the Political Attitudes and Behavior of Blacks in São Paulo, Brazil." Ph.D. diss. University of Michigan, 1977.

25. Mitchell, "Racial Consciousness."

wage-labor in a manner which suggested far more than a desire to exclude these people from choice labor markets.

The politics of racial exclusion was even more comprehensive. The uneven but continuous oppression and marginalization of Afro-Brazilians in the late-nineteenth and early-twentieth centuries was an effort by Brazilian elites to expunge Afro-Brazilians and their cultural practices from their portrait of modernity. Modernity, in short, did not include Afro-Brazilians. They were the antithesis of a modern nation. This effort contrasted with the efforts of Brazilian Modernists such as Mário and Oswaldo de Andrade, the anthropologist Gilberto Freyre and even some politicians, who sought to refute the Positivist legacy in Brazil by suggesting that African and indigenous elements in their nation were uniquely Brazilian. It also contrasted with Afro-Brazilian modernism in dance, religious practice, drama and the plastic arts. Yet the landholding elites, the Catholic Church and culturally conservative politicians carried the day, setting the tone for any future discussion of Afro-Brazilian and national identity.

The irony of such maneuvers, which took place well into the 1930s, was the proliferation and expansion of African cultural presences within modern Brazil, presences that were stronger than in any other nation-state in the New World. These presences, at once residual and dominant in the sense that Raymond Williams uses these terms, are evidenced by national, transracial participation in Afro-Brazilian religions like Candomblé and Umbanda; and the importance of an African-derived corporal esthetics for a national standard of beauty.[26] In popular culture Samba was appro-

26. See Williams's essay "Dominant, Residual and Emergent Cultures" in *Marxism and Literature* (London: Oxford University Press, 1977). It may seem contradictory to suggest that the presence of Afro-Brazilian cultural practices and productions is at once residual and dominant, but it is the closest I can come at the present time in characterizing the pervasiveness of the "Africanisms" in Brazilian daily life and the relative powerlessness of Afro-Brazilian religious, cultural and political institutions relative to both state and civic institutions of the Brazilian polity. They are residual in a more explicitly political sense. Afro-Brazilian cultural practices are considered *national* practices, and are manipulated for their symbolic resonance by Brazilian elites to display the heterogenic cohesiveness of Brazilians; they are dominant in the sense that they are suffused in an almost transracial way throughout the norms and values of civil society. An example of this in Brazil, and found in Latin nations like Cuba and Venezuela, is a corporeal aesthetic of the female body which emphasizes distinctly African considerations of physical attractiveness—large hips, buttocks and narrow waist, with little attention to breast size—as opposed to the more Western standards of feminine beauty which in the twentieth century favor narrow hips and waist, large breasts and thin

priated by the emergent middle classes in the 1940s. They were seeking a popular form of recreation, and selected Samba despite the disdain it evoked among elites who detected an expression of sensuality not found in the fox-trot or other European imports. By the 1940s, African elements of Brazilian culture were selectively integrated into the discourses of national identity. With the ascendance of the ideologies of racial democracy and whitening, Afro-Brazilians came to be considered part of the cultural economy, in which their women and men embodied sexual desire and lascivious pleasure. At the same time, Afro-Brazilians were denied access to virtually all institutions of civil society that would have given them equal footing with the middle classes of modernizing Brazil. Prestigious schools, neighborhoods, clubs and professions were closed off to Afro-Brazilians much in the way that they were to African-Americans in the United States, Afro-Cubans and other New World blacks during this period, only in more ambiguous, coded ways.[27] Thus in both eighteenth-century Europe and twentieth-century Latin America, the bourgeois public sphere was a contradictory, politically bifurcated domain, open to some groups and closed to others. The extent of marginality was, and is, determined by the degree and conditions of otherness on each continent.

Claims to citizenship and equality of opportunity in labor and ancillary markets could not be the hallmarks of Afro-Brazilians' modern identities. Instead the denial of participatory citizenship in the bourgeois public sphere for Afro-Brazilians marked their existence as subaltern elements of modern life. Yet they lived within this sphere nonetheless, so that any characterization of their lives as premodern or archaic[28] ignores the discontinuity of modern time and the multiplicity of spheres within bourgeois civil society.

A common characteristic that Afro-Brazilians shared with their counterparts of the African diaspora in the New World was the constant attacks

---

thighs. For a U.S. audience, or more broadly, those familiar with contemporary U.S. popular culture and rap music in particular, one would have to imagine Sir Mix-A-Lot's hit "Baby's Got Back" not merely as a popular song, but as an expression of a *national* disposition towards a particular standard of beauty, to appreciate the extent to which the fetishization of the *bunda* (buttocks) in Brazil is as much evidence of African presence as it is a specifically national cultural norm. The "Africanization" of the female bodily aesthetic (male gaze) is one of Brazil's distinctive features as a nation with the largest population of people of African descent outside of Nigeria.

27. Florestan Fernandes, *The Negro in Brazilian Society* (New York: Columbia University Press, 1969); Andrews, *Blacks and Whites*.

28. Fernandes, *The Negro*.

on their dignity. Charles Taylor identifies dignity as a key element in the constitution of the modern, individual self. It reflects "our power, our sense of dominating public space; or our invulnerability to power; or our self-sufficiency, our life having its own centre, or our being like and looked to by others, a centre of attention."[29] The keywords and phrases relevant to my critique of Taylor's passage are "public space," "invulnerability to power," "self-sufficiency" and "centre." Taylor appears to use the phrase "public space" in a manner indistinguishable from contemporary usage of "public sphere." This usage has come to be equated with civil society itself, in which a diverse array of interests, institutions and individuals are intertwined to constitute the modern moment. An important, if subtle, distinction could be made here that relates to a point I raised earlier about the totalizing quality implicit in the notion of the public sphere. This particular sphere could be a dimension of public space but not its totality, despite its representation as such. Yet, for Taylor, this form of dignity is seemingly universal and not limited to a particular sphere.

What happens to this notion of dignity when the role of racial or gendered inequality in Taylor's public space is viewed from theoretical and historical perspectives? In theoretical terms, it is possible for people who are denied the constitutional and normative rudiments of modern citizenship to operate in public space with such a *general* sense of dignity, a presumption of citizenship? Considering the previous discussion of Afro-Brazilians and the emergent public sphere in Brazil, would it not have been impossible for those porters and stevedores in Salvador, Bahia to have imagined that they could "dominate public space" even in the mild form that Taylor suggests? For Ana Flávia, the Governor's daughter, her inability to dominate public space as an individual stemmed from the lowly status accorded those who resemble her, regardless of their differences as individual, private citizens. Thus, the public and private distinctions so neatly laid out by Taylor collapse at the intersection of reason and coercion, power and powerlessness. Considering the legacy of the civil rights movement in the United States, the anti-apartheid movement in South Africa and other social movements engineered by people of African descent in distinct parts of the world, there clearly has not been "invulnerability to power" in public space for them in modern times.[30]

29. Charles Taylor, *Sources of the Self: The Making of Modern Identity* (Cambridge, MA: Harvard University Press, 1989), 15.

30. Unless of course, one considers Gandhi's or King's nonviolent resistances as movements which, given their appeals to a higher moral order, projected a sense of invulnerability to the power of the state, colonial authority or dominant ethnic group. Yet one is still struck by the reality of their respective struggles; they made

The sense of self-sufficiency, which Taylor defines as the ability to provide for oneself, one's family, and to command respect, is structurally inaccessible for African-American communities of the New World.

Despite Taylor's lofty standards and claims, his universalizing principles for the moral sources of dignity presuppose a subject who is male, property-owning, Western and white. His characterization is informed by what feminist psychoanalytic critics call the male gaze, a projection of his particular "subject position" onto the rest of the world, with the desire that others conform to the image he has of himself, and of others as a wished-for extension of himself.[31] In racial and gendered terms, being a "centre of attention" has distinct connotations for different racialized and gendered subjects.

As a communitarian Taylor could respond to this critique on theoretical and historical grounds. The claim might be made that the Brazilian polity is not the West that Taylor had in mind; this is a legitimate point since Brazilian society is pervaded by the confluence of feudalism and dependent capitalist culture. It could be further argued that both Habermas and Taylor have laid the economic, administrative and normative foundations for the public sphere/space and cannot be critiqued for the less-than-ideal functioning of these domains in the real world. After all, the histories of racial oppression shared among peoples of African descent in the West, which Habermas and Taylor briefly note and deplore, also disclose the malfunctioning of the public sphere according to its own principles. The eventual, if uneasy, inclusion of previously disenfranchised groups could be perceived as another triumph of reason and rationalization, a pit stop along the tortuous track toward liberal pluralism (Taylor) or democratic socialism (Habermas).

Such neat distinctions between Western and non-Western, ideal and practical public spheres have a flimsy ontological basis. They ignore the fact that the geographic distinctions of West and non-West are not only arbitrary but also neglectful of the role of Western *influences* globally, in hundreds of societies built upon variations of parliamentary, republican models. Moreover, such distinctions ignore the reaction within Western polities to the others, and the chasm between liberal theory and liberal history.[32] Recent events in both Western and Eastern Europe demonstrate

---

appeals based upon the moral authority of reason, and were answered with coercion, the highest form of unreason.

31. Laura Mulvey, *Visual and Other Pleasures* (Bloomington: Indiana University Press, 1989).

32. Uday S. Mehta, "Liberal Strategies of Exclusion." *Politics and Society* 18 (4) (1990): 427–454.

the intensity of reactions to otherness—anti-immigration violence, Neo-Nazism and other facist movements—and how intensely the public sphere is *racialized*. This refutes positions supporting notions of abstract, individual propriety in the public sphere, and emphasizes the ways that citizenship is differentially embodied by race and gender. Modernity requires some sense of the past in order to distinguish itself, and it uses people of African descent in predominantly white nation-states as contrasting symbols of noncitizenship in the public sphere, just as colonial rulers have used "Third World" peoples in the same manner.[33] Afro-Brazilians, like so many other people of African descent in the New World, are used for the same purpose.

Blackness Then and Now

It is not really race in a narrow, phenotypical sense that links Ana Flávia, the Governor's daughter, to the seemingly disparate incidents of the slave revolt in 1835 or the marginalization of Afro-Brazilians in the shift from slave to wage labor between 1880 and 1920. More precisely, the *meanings* attached to purported racial groups are markers that convey the alleged disparities in intellect, industriousness, wealth, beauty and aesthetics—as well as the capacity to alter them. As long as Brazilian society in general, whites and nonwhites alike, share a commonsense basis for negative stereotypes of blacks and positive stereotypes of whites, then the apparent fluidity historically associated with racial categorization in Brazil needs to be qualified. The preoccupation with color categories belies the other dimension of racial "common sense" in Brazil: the widespread belief held by many whites and nonwhites that Brazil is a racial democracy.

The equation of blackness with sloth, deceit, hypersexuality and waste of all kinds is confirmed by the relative infrequency in which the terms *preto* or *negro* (black) are used in daily life. Brazilians reluctantly use these terms in describing others; they rarely describe friends this way, for fear of insulting them.[34] This underscores the paradox of racial politics in Brazil and in much of the hemisphere. While racial identification is more contextual in Brazil than in other multi-racial polities certain limits also obtain. One person's mulatto is another's negro; yet negro remains a racial category many people do not want ascribed to them. If preto or negro only meant dark skin color, then why would the usage of these terms be any

33. Partha Chatterjee, *Nationalist Thought and the Colonial World* (London: Zed, 1986).

34. Yvonne Maggie, "O que se cala quando se fala do negro no Brazil" (Photocopy, 1988).

different from say, referring to someone as white? Part of the reason for a multiplicity of descriptions for nonwhite Brazilians, particularly for those whose African descent is visible in the texture of their hair, the shape of their nose or buttocks, is because such categorizations attempt to avoid the mark of blackness. Why is it more likely that a "colored" person would be described as "brown" or "mulatto" than as half-white, nearly or quasi-white? Focus on the numerous color categories in Brazilian racial politics can obscure the broader racialized social totality in which these categories operate and the racial meanings which *structure* social interactions and limit individuals' ability to simply choose their own racial category.

When considered comparatively these examples illustrate limits of blackness over historical/racial time. In the case of the 1835 revolt in Bahia, African-Brazilians responded to their mistreatment through revolt, regardless of occupational distinctions among them. The animosity between Brazilian-born slaves, mulattos and whites on the one hand, and African-Brazilians on the other suggests at the least that blackness, laden with negative connotations, pertained to African-Brazilians and not necessarily to those who looked black. Ana Flávia, the daughter of a black man and a white woman, could easily be considered a mulatta in both contemporary and historical Brazil. Her blackness in the eyes of her assailants implies a broadening of the category of negro/a in Brazil and more importantly, an increasing polarization of racial categories. Her beating may signal that the mark of blackness has come to include Brazilians who are perceived as people of African descent, whether from Brazil or not. Unlike the distinctions between African- and Brazilian-born slaves in the previous century, Africanness—the parent symbol for blackness—no longer marks a place; it now marks a people.

The seemingly arbitrary manner in which Ana Flávia the mulatta could become Ana Flávia the negra affirms the greater importance of the interpretive, as opposed to the phenotypical, criterion of racial differentiation. Like McCarthyism in the United States and the military dictatorship from 1964 to 1985 in Brazil, the enemy is continually invented. Thus in the absence of "real" blacks, Ana Flávia becomes black, much in the same way that liberals and other moderates were transformed into communists during the era of anti-communist hysteria. Once identified as the enemy, the actual ideological or racial position of the signified has secondary importance. The meaning of racial or ideological difference attached to the individual or group is paramount for understanding the politics of polarization, of distancing the marginal or soon-to-be marginal subject from the center of the body politic.

This gives credence to Thomas Skidmore's assertion that Brazil's racial politics are becoming more and more like the relatively dichotomous patterns of racial interaction in the United States.[35] With the emergence of groups calling themselves Skinheads and Black Muslims in São Paulo, the existence of organizations that reflect the most obvious forms of and responses to racial animus affirms racially discriminatory practices in Brazil that are long-standing and embedded in the ideology of racial democracy. As far as I know such organizations are new to Brazil, yet such sentiments must have been in place for some time in order for them to assume organizational, collective form.

The meanings attached to blackness, whiteness and positions in between constitute the public aspect of the racial dimension of public spheres: these meanings are located in specific social contexts. Habermas's etymological and genealogical considerations of the terms publicity and public opinion are relevant here. Tracing the meaning and conceptualization of these terms in philosophers as diverse as Locke, Rousseau, Kant and Hegel, Habermas notes how public opinion was often meant to infer a normative matrix of the good, right and just in emergent civil societies of the West. Though Hegel would disparage public opinion as unmediated mass knowledge, each aforementioned philosopher acknowledged public opinion's power to convey a popular authority, what Foucault refers to as a regime of truth. Racist ideologies are facets of publicity and public opinion, insofar as they mark bodies to inform others of the meanings of those bodies in racial terms.

It is not, therefore, only discursive formations, processes of reason and rationalization, that shape publicity and public opinion about race. *Nondiscursive* formations also define people's location and degrees of participation in public realms. In short, it is the *structures* of race, racial difference and racism, which often go unsaid that provide the parameters of racial dynamics and the range of possibilities of discourse itself. This is why the Brazilian historian João Reis suggests that the Bahia slave revolt of 1835 was not, as previous historical accounts imply, merely a Muslim revolt of a certain category of slaves. Both slaves and *libertos* participated in the revolt, along with a high percentage of non-Muslim Africans. Reis regards the revolt as principally the result of an "embryonic Pan-African identity," an emergent ethnic consciousness among liberto and escravo participants that was forged by the similarity of racial and economic exploitation.[36] Religious affiliation was the vehicle through which the

---

35. Thomas Skidmore, "Race Relations in Brazil." *Camões Center Quarterly* 4 (3–4) (1993): 49–61.

36. João Reis and Eduardo Silva, *Negociação e Conflitó: A Resisténcia Negra No Brasil Escravista* (São Paulo: Editora Schwarz, 1989), 109.

revolt's leadership emerged, but was certainly not the sole reason for the revolt itself.[37] Moreover, the distinctions between escravo and liberto were principally *occupational* distinctions, which by themselves tell us little about the respective treatment accorded individuals from either category in the public sphere. As noted earlier, libertos were not given the same status or rights of whites, and could only vote in primary elections. Therefore, while the degree of racial/civic exclusion might have been less for the liberto, the nature and kind of exclusion was more similar than dissimilar to that of the escravo. Reis and Silva described the broader context in which these occupational distinctions operated:

> If the freed black stopped being a slave, he did not exactly become a free man. He did not possess any political right and, even though considered a foreigner, was not granted the privileges of a citizen from another country. The stigma of slavery was irreducibly associated with the color of his skin and above all, his origin. The free Africans were treated by whites, blacks, browns and even by creoles as slaves. They were not second or third class citizens. They were simply not citizens.[38]

At the level of resistance, however, the 1835 revolt is an historical example of an activity which emerged from a micro-public sphere, one which operated outside the purview of the liberal-minded but ultimately oligarchic elite within the dominant public sphere. The participants in the revolt were mindful of the activities and crises of their masters and employers, and fashioned modes of racial and ethnic consciousness in response to them. The simultaneity of these two spheres suggests that an elite public sphere, such as in the case of nineteenth-century Brazil or eighteenth-century Europe, is also an essentially *privatized* domain. This privatization is also apparent in twentieth-century Brazil, as Ana Flávia was rudely reminded that public space is not necessarily a democratic space. It is not democratic precisely because of the manner in which it is privatized for members of a certain race and/or class. Thus, while the old Brazilian adage that "money whitens" is true in certain cases, it is equally true that blackness taints.

This leads us to another understanding of how the public sphere and public space is privatized by the manner in which its privileged subjects or citizens publicly discriminate against the less privileged. Even in circum-

---

37. Reis notes that the *malês* decided upon Ramadan as the moment for revolt because it is a time when Allah is said to "control malignant spirits and reorder the affairs of the world." See Reis and Silva, *Negociação e Conflitó*, 122.

38. Reis and Silva, *Negociação e Conflitó*, 106. The translation is mine.

stances where citizenship is a given, as in contemporary Brazil, some people are considered lesser citizens than others. Racial prejudice is not only privately held but invariably, publicly articulated and at some level sanctioned. Thus the liberal presumption of reason in Habermas's formulation is often rebuffed at the lived conjectures of white and black, as in the case of Ana Flávia. It was precisely at this moment that ideology and coercive power outstripped reason as the bordering, structuring parameters of the elite public sphere. Moreover, contrary to the liberal—and often communtarian—notion that citizens are abstract bearers of rights, black Cinderella highlights the need to conceive of citizenship as that which should inhere in concrete persons. Along with property, gender, age and reason, race and racial differences imbue individuals with their concreteness, a material and symbolic grounding of their existence.

Afro-Brazilian Culture and the Public Sphere

As Wade[39] has noted in his study of Afro-Colombians, one of the comparative peculiarities of Latin American racial politics has been its rhetorical collapse of racial difference under the banner of national identity. In Brazil, Mexico, Cuba, Venezuela, Colombia and other nations of the region, Afro-Latino Americans are supposedly without a racially specific identity, unlike their Afro-North American, Afro-European or English-speaking counterparts in the Caribbean. Some allege that this has been due to the absence of legislated racial discrimination and segregation. Such forms of racial apartheid have led to the development of parallel institutions in other multi-racial polities such as the United States. Thus, music, cuisine, dress and artifacts that would be representative of a particular racial, or more accurately, cultural group elsewhere appears as a national commodity in Latin American polities.[40]

Afro-Brazilian cultural production fit this model until the 1970s, when Afro-Brazilian cultural and political activists affiliated with the *movimento negro* began to explore symbolic linkages with other communities of the African diaspora. These explorations led to the formation of organizations and cultural expressions that were neither Brazilian nor national but Afro-diasporic. Ironically, racially specific Afro-Brazilian cultural practices, namely forms of expression produced and directed toward Afro-Brazilians, emerged during the height of the military dictatorship in Brazil. Black Soul, the dance hall phenomena of the 1970s that first emerged

---

39. Peter Wade, *Blackness and Race Mixture: The Dynamics of Racial Identity in Colombia* (Baltimore: The Johns Hopkins University Press, 1993).

40. Peter Fry, *Para ingles ver* (Rio de Janeiro: Zahar, 1983).

in Rio de Janeiro but later spread to other cities in the country, was the precursor to the African blocs (*blocos Afros*) such as Olodum and Illê-Aiyê. Such organizations have a specifically Afro-Brazilian leadership and constituency; they produce lyrics and musics that utilize Afro-Brazilian identity and racial discrimination as a principal theme.[41] These organizations are quite distinct from Samba schools, Candomblé, Umbanda and other Brazilian cultural artifacts that are perceived and manipulated as national symbols. In the realm of cultural and religious practice, *terreiros de candomblé*, samba schools, ethnic brotherhoods and the emergent *blocos Afros* like Agbara Dudu, Olodum and Illê-Aiyê represent the increasing racialization of Afro-Brazilian cultural practice. Afro-Brazilians increasingly recognize the need to use cultural practice and production as an organizing principle against racial oppression, and as tools for constructing and enacting Afro-Brazilian identities. In many instances these organizations are successful attempts at creating both spaces and values of Afro-Brazilian identity and community which are related to but distinct from the Catholic Church, mass culture and markets. The emphasis on space within the *terreiro* provides the articulation of an alternative public sphere.[42]

Organizations such as Olodum and Illê-Aiyê do not necessarily affirm an increasing polarization along clearly demarcated racial lines, but rather an increasing awareness among Afro-Brazilians and white Brazilians that Afro-Brazilians *can* use racial identity as a principle to organize collective action. It is not a sign of increasing racism among Afro-Brazilians, though at some level it is surely a response to racism in the land of racial democracy. The Afro-Brazilian public sphere shares a paradox with its white, more dominant counterpart: it is at once public and private.[43]

41. For more information on Afro-Brazilian cultural practices, especially Black Soul, see *Orpheus and Power* (Hanchard 1994), "Religion, Class and Context: Continuities and Discontinuities in Brazilian Umbanda" (Brown and Bick 1987), and "Black Soul: Aglutinação espontanea ou identidade etnica" (Rodrigues da Silva 1983).

42. Julio Braga, "Candomblé: Força e Resistência," *Afro-Asia* 15 (1992): 13–17; Juana Elbein dos Santos and Deoscoredes M. Dos Santos, "Religion and Black Culture." In *Africa in Latin America*, ed. Manuel Moreno Fraginals. (New York: Holmes and Meir, 1984).

43. The diaphanous nature of the barrier between black private and public spheres is also evident in other national contexts. Consider the following autobiographical observations of Wahneema Lubiano, a U.S. African-American theorist, on her childhood experiences as a preacher's daughter whose father's church was next door to a brothel. "Our church and our apartment were both private and public:

Brazilian national culture has always translated and transformed Afro-Brazilian culture practices into national cultural practices, thereby rendering them as commodities in popular culture to be consumed by all.[44] Thus, the question, just what is Afro-Brazilian culture? is much more complicated than in the United States, South Africa or Britain, where residential and other forms of racial segregation make distinct histories more obvious. It appears, however, that with the increasing racial polarization in Brazilian society, African blocs and other organizations are using music, dance and religion as explicit organizing principles to create schools, child care facilities, political and other organizations specifically for Afro-Brazilians. In turn, this increases tensions between a Brazilian elite that has historically claimed Afro-Brazilian cultural practices as simply Brazilian cultural practices, and Afro-Brazilian activists and intellectuals who seek to claim some form of autonomy within their own public sphere.

The struggles between dominant and subordinate racial groups, the politics of race, help constitute modernity and modernizing projects across the globe. It uses racial phenotypes to assess, categorize and judge persons as citizens and noncitizens. Racial politics operate not only in a polity's defining moments but in the ongoing process of its re-creation. It permeates the minutiae of daily life: nervous, furtive glances are exchanged in elevators, men and women are rendered suspects without ever having committed a crime; not yet socialized by racist practices, white children run gleefully into the arms of their parents' racial others as their parents watch nervously. This is racial politics between whites and blacks in the late-twentieth century, and Brazil is no exception. For Ana Flávia—the black Cinderella—the clock struck midnight the moment she was born.

---

the two constituted a space that described both the destitution and constellation of the neighborhood, and what black people in that neighborhood and town meant to themselves and to the larger social, economic and political space of the town. It marked us, we marked it." See Wahneema Lubiano, "If I Could Talk about It, This Is Not What I Would Say," *Assemblage* 20 (April 1993): 56.

44. Michael Hanchard, "Culturalism versus Cultural Politics: Movimento Negro in Rio de Janeiro and São Paulo, Brazil." In *The Violence Within*, edited by Kay B. Warren, 57–86 (Boulder, CO: Westview Press, 1993); Hanchard, *Orpheus and Power.*

18

Michael Omi and Howard Winant,
Racial Formation in the United States

Michael Omi is Professor of Ethnic Studies at the University of California, Berkeley. Howard Winant is Professor of Sociology at Temple University. His publications include Racial Conditions *(1993),* Racial Conditions: Politics, Theory, Comparisons *(1994), and numerous articles in journals. In this essay, the authors highlight the importance of racial classifications in everyday experience by drawing attention to the concept's social and political function.*

In 1982–83, Susie Guillor Phipps unsuccessfully sued the Louisiana Bureau of Vital Records to change her racial classification from black to white. The descendant of an 18th-century white planter and a black slave, Phipps was designated "black" in her birth certificate in accordance with a 1970 state law which declared anyone with at least 1/32nd "Negro Blood" to be black.

The Phipps case raised intriguing questions about the concept of race, its meaning in contemporary society, and its use (and abuse) in public policy. Assistant Attorney General Ron Davis defended the law by pointing out that some type of racial classification was necessary to comply with federal record-keeping requirements and to facilitate programs for the prevention of genetic diseases. Phipps's attorney, Brian Begue, argued that the assignment of racial categories on birth certificates was unconstitutional and that the 1/32nd designation was inaccurate. He called on a retired Tulane University professor who cited research indicating that most Louisiana whites have at least 1/20th "Negro" ancestry.

In the end, Phipps lost. The court upheld the state's right to classify and quantify racial identity.[1]

1. *San Francisco Chronicle,* 14 September 1982, 19 May 1983. Ironically, the 1970 Louisiana law was enacted to supersede an old Jim Crow statute which relied on the idea of "common report" in determining an infant's race. Following Phipps' unsuccessful attempt to change her classification and have the law declared unconstitutional, a legislative effort arose which culminated in the repeal of the law. See *San Francisco Chronicle,* 23 June 1983.

Phipps's problematic racial identity, and her effort to resolve it through state action, is in many ways a parable of America's unsolved racial dilemma. It illustrates the difficulties of defining race and assigning individuals or groups to racial categories. It shows how the racial legacies of the past—slavery and bigotry—continue to shape the present. It reveals both the deep involvement of the state in the organization and interpretation of race, and the inadequacy of state institutions to carry out these functions. It demonstrates how deeply Americans both as individuals and as a civilization are shaped, and indeed haunted, by race.

Having lived her whole life thinking that she was white, Phipps suddenly discovers that by legal definition she is not. In U.S. society, such an event is indeed catastrophic.[2] But if she is not white, of what race is she? The *state* claims that she is black, based on its rules of classification,[3] and another state agency, the court, upholds this judgment. But despite these classificatory standards which have imposed an either-or logic on racial identity, Phipps will not in fact "change color." Unlike what would have happened during slavery times if one's claim to whiteness was successfully challenged, we can assume that despite the outcome of her legal challenge, Phipps will remain in most of the social relationships she had occupied before the trial. Her socialization, her familial and friendship networks, her cultural orientation, will not change. She will simply have to wrestle with her newly acquired "hybridized" condition. She will have to confront the "Other" within.

The designation of racial categories and the determination of racial identity is no simple task. For centuries, this question has precipitated intense debates and conflicts, particularly in the U.S.—disputes over natural and legal rights, over the distribution of resources, and indeed, over who shall live and who shall die.

A crucial dimension of the Phipps case is that it illustrates the inadequacy of claims that race is a mere matter of variations in human physiognomy, that it is simply a matter of skin color. But if race cannot be understood in this manner, how *can* it be understood? We cannot fully

2. Compare the Phipps case to Andrew Hacker's well-known "parable" in which a white person is informed by a mysterious official that "the organization he represents has made a mistake" and that ". . . [a]ccording to their records . . . , you were to have been born black; to another set of parents, far from where you were raised." How much compensation, Hacker's official asks, would "you" require to undo the damage of this unfortunate error? See Hacker, *Two Nations: Black and White, Separate, Hostile, Unequal* (New York: Charles Scribner's Sons, 1992) pp. 31–32.

3. On the evolution of Louisiana's racial classification system, see Virginia Dominguez, *White by Definition: Social Classification in Creole Louisiana* (New Brunswick: Rutgers University Press, 1986).

hope to address this topic—no less than the meaning of race, its role in society, and the forces which shape it—in one chapter, nor indeed in one book. Our goal in this chapter, however, is far from modest: we wish to offer at least the outlines of a theory of race and racism.

What is Race?

There is a continuous temptation to think of race as an *essence*, as something fixed, concrete, and objective. And there is also an opposite temptation: to imagine race as a mere *illusion*, a purely ideological construct which some ideal non-racist social order would eliminate. It is necessary to challenge both these positions, to disrupt and reframe the rigid and bipolar manner in which they are posed and debated, and to transcend the presumably irreconcilable relationship between them.

The effort must be made to understand race as an unstable and "decentered" complex of social meanings constantly being transformed by political struggle. With this in mind, let us propose a definition: *race is a concept which signifies and symbolizes social conflicts and interests by referring to different types of human bodies.* Although the concept of race invokes biologically based human characteristics (so-called "phenotypes"), selection of these particular human features for purposes of racial signification is always and necessarily a social and historical process. In contrast to the other major distinction of this type, that of gender, there is no biological basis for distinguishing among human groups along the lines of race.[4] Indeed, the categories employed to differentiate among human groups along racial lines reveal themselves, upon serious examination, to be at best imprecise, and at worst completely arbitrary.

If the concept of race is so nebulous, can we not dispense with it? Can we not "do without" race, at least in the "enlightened" present? This question has been posed often, and with greater frequency in recent years.[5] An affirmative answer would of course present obvious practical

---

4. This is not to suggest that gender is a biological category while race is not. Gender, like race, is a social construct. However, the biological division of humans into sexes—two at least, and possibly intermediate ones as well—is not in dispute. This provides a basis for argument over gender divisions—how "natural," etc.— which does not exist with regard to race. To ground an argument for the "natural" existence of race, one must resort to philosophical anthropology.

5. "The truth is that there are no races, there is nothing in the world that can do all we ask race to do for us. . . . The evil that is done is done by the concept, and by easy—yet impossible—assumptions as to its application." (Kwame Anthony Appiah, *In My Father's House: Africa in the Philosophy of Culture* [New York: Oxford University Press, 1992].) Appiah's eloquent and learned book fails, in our view, to

difficulties: it is rather difficult to jettison widely held beliefs, beliefs which moreover are central to everyone's identity and understanding of the social world. So the attempt to banish the concept as an archaism is at best counterintuitive. But a deeper difficulty, we believe, is inherent in the very formulation of this schema, in its way of posing race as a *problem*, a misconception left over from the past, and suitable now only for the dustbin of history.

A more effective starting point is the recognition that despite its uncertainties and contradictions, the concept of race continues to play a fundamental role in structuring and representing the social world. The task for theory is to explain this situation. It is to avoid both the utopian framework which sees race as an illusion we can somehow "get beyond," and also the essentialist formulation which sees race as something objective and fixed, a biological datum.[6] Thus we should think of race as an element of social structure rather than as an irregularity within it; we should see race as a dimension of human representation rather than an illusion. These perspectives inform the theoretical approach we call racial formation.

Racial Formation

We define *racial formation* as the sociohistorical process by which racial categories are created, inhabited, transformed, and destroyed. Our attempt to elaborate a theory of racial formation will proceed in two steps. First, we argue that racial formation is a process of historically situated *projects* in which human bodies and social structures are represented and organized. Next we link racial formation to the evolution of hegemony, the way in which society is organized and ruled. Such an approach, we believe, can facilitate understanding of a whole range of contemporary controversies and dilemmas involving race, including the nature of racism, the relationship of race to other forms of differences, inequalities, and oppression such as sexism and nationalism, and the dilemmas of racial identity today.

---

dispense with the race concept, despite its anguished attempt to do so; this indeed is the source of its author's anguish. We agree with him as to the non-objective character of race, but fail to see how this recognition justifies its abandonment. This argument is developed below.

6. We understand essentialism as *belief in real, true human, essences, existing outside or impervious to social and historical context.* We draw this definition, with some small modifications, from Diana Fuss, *Essentially Speaking: Feminism, Nature, & Difference* (New York: Routledge, 1989) p. xi.

From a racial formation perspective, race is a matter of both social structure and cultural representation. Too often, the attempt is made to understand race simply or primarily in terms of only one of these two analytical dimensions.[7] For example, efforts to explain racial inequality as a purely social structural phenomenon are unable to account for the origins, patterning, and transformation of racial difference.

Conversely, many examinations of racial difference—understood as a matter of cultural attributes *à la* ethnicity theory, or as a society-wide signification system, *à la* some poststructuralist accounts—cannot comprehend such structural phenomena as racial stratification in the labor market or patterns of residential segregation.

An alternative approach is to think of racial formation processes as occurring through a linkage between structure and representation. Racial *projects* do the ideological "work" of making these links. *A racial project is simultaneously an interpretation, representation, or explanation of racial dynamics, and an effort to reorganize and redistribute resources along particular racial lines.* Racial projects connect what race *means* in a particular discursive practice and the ways in which both social structures and everyday experiences are racially *organized*, based upon that meaning. Let us consider this proposition, first in terms of large-scale or macro-level social processes, and then in terms of other dimensions of the racial formation process.

Racial Formation as a Macro-Level Social Process

To *interpret the meaning of race is to frame it social structurally.* Consider for example, this statement by Charles Murray on welfare reform:

> My proposal for dealing with the racial issue in social welfare is to repeal every bit of legislation and reverse every court decision that in any way requires, recommends, or awards differential treatment according to race, and thereby put us back onto the track that we left in 1965. We may argue about the appropriate limits of government intervention in trying to enforce the ideal, but at least it should be possible to identify the ideal: Race is not a morally admissible reason for treating one person differently from another. Period.[8]

7. Michael Omi and Howard Winant, "On the Theoretical Status of the Concept of Race" in Warren Crichlow and Cameron McCarthy, eds., *Race, Identity, and Representations in Education* (New York: Routledge, 1993).

8. Charles Murray, *Losing Ground: American Social Policy, 1950–1980* (New York: Basic Books, 1984) p. 223.

Here there is a partial but significant analysis of the meaning of race: it is not a morally valid basis upon which to treat people "differently from one another." We may notice someone's race, but we cannot act upon that awareness. We must act in a "color-blind" fashion. This analysis of the meaning of race is immediately linked to a specific conception of the role of race in the social structure: it can play no part in government action, save in "the enforcement of the ideal." No state policy can legitimately require, recommend, or award different status according to race. This example can be classified as a particular type of racial project in the present-day U.S.—a "neoconservative" one.

Conversely, *to recognize the racial dimension in social structure is to interpret the meaning of race.* Consider the following statement by the late Supreme Court Justice Thurgood Marshall on minority "set-aside" programs:

> A profound difference separates governmental actions that themselves are racist, and governmental actions that seek to remedy the effects of prior racism or to prevent neutral government activity from perpetuating the effects of such racism.[9]

Here the focus is on the racial dimensions of *social structure*—in this case of state activity and policy. The argument is that state actions in the past and present have treated people in very different ways according to their race, and thus the government cannot retreat from its policy responsibilities in this area. It cannot suddenly declare itself "color-blind" without in fact perpetuating the same type of differential, racist treatment.[10] Thus, race continues to signify difference and structure inequality. Here, racialized social structure is immediately linked to an interpretation of the meaning of race. This example too can be classified as a particular type of racial project in the present-day U.S.—a "liberal" one.

To be sure, such political labels as "neoconservative" or "liberal" can not fully capture the complexity of racial projects, for these are always multiply determined, politically contested, and deeply shaped by their

9. Justice Thurgood Marshall, dissenting in *City of Richmond v. J. A. Croson Co.*, 488 U.S. 469 (1989).

10. See, for example, Derrick Bell, "Remembrances of Racism Past: Getting Past the Civil Rights Decline." in Herbert Hill and James E. Jones, Jr., eds., *Race in America: The Struggle for Equality* (Madison: The University of Wisconsin Press, 1993) pp. 75–76; Gertrude Ezorsky, *Racism and Justice: The Case for Affirmative Action* (Ithaca: Cornell University Press, 1991) pp. 109–111; David Kairys, *With Liberty and Justice for Some: A Critique of the Conservative Supreme Court* (New York: The New Press, 1993) pp. 138–41.

historical context. Thus, encapsulated within the neoconservative example cited here are certain egalitarian commitments which derive from a previous historical context in which they played a very different role, and which are rearticulated in neoconservative racial discourse precisely to oppose a more open-ended, more capacious conception of the meaning of equality. Similarly, in the liberal example, Justice Marshall recognizes that the contemporary state, which was formerly the architect of segregation and the chief enforcer of racial difference, has a tendency to reproduce those patterns of inequality in a new guise. Thus he admonishes it (in dissent, significantly) to fulfill its responsibilities to uphold a robust conception of equality. These particular instances, then, demonstrate how racial projects are always concretely framed, and thus are always contested and unstable. The social structure they uphold or attack, and the representations of race they articulate, are never invented out of the air, but exist in a definite historical context, having descended from previous conflicts. This contestation appears to be permanent in respect to race.

These two examples of contemporary racial projects are drawn from mainstream political debate; they may be characterized as center-right and center-left expressions of contemporary racial politics.[11] We can, however, expand the discussion of racial formation processes far beyond these familiar examples. In fact, we can identify racial projects in at least three other analytical dimensions: first, the political spectrum can be broadened to include radical projects, on both the left and right, as well as along other political axes. Second, analysis of racial projects can take place not only at the macro-level of racial policy-making, state activity, and collective action, but also at the micro-level of everyday experience. Third, the concept of racial projects can be applied across historical time, to identify racial formation dynamics in the past. We shall now offer examples of each of these types of racial projects.

The Political Spectrum of Racial Formation

We have encountered examples of a neoconservative racial project, in which the significance of race is denied, leading to a "color-blind" racial politics and "hands off" policy orientation; and of a "liberal" racial project, in which the significance of race is affirmed, leading to an egalitarian and "activist" state policy. But these by no means exhaust the political

11. Howard Winant has developed a tentative "map" of the system of racial hegemony in the U.S. circa 1990, which focuses on the spectrum of racial projects running from the political right to the political left. See Winant, "Where Culture Meets Structure: Race in the 1990s," in idem, *Racial Conditions: Politics, Theory, Comparisons* (Minneapolis: University of Minnesota Press, 1994).

possibilities. Other racial projects can be readily identified on the contemporary U.S. scene. For example, "far right" projects, which uphold biologistic and racist views of difference, explicitly argue for white supremacist policies. "New right" projects overtly claim to hold "color-blind" views, but covertly manipulate racial fears in order to achieve political gains.[12] On the left, "radical democratic" projects invoke notions of racial "difference" in combination with egalitarian politics and policy.

Further variations can also be noted. For example, "nationalist" projects, both conservative and radical, stress the incompatibility of racially defined group identity with the legacy of white supremacy, and therefore advocate a social structural solution of separation, either complete or partial.[13] As we saw in Chapter 3, nationalist currents represent a profound legacy of the centuries of racial absolutism that initially defined the meaning of race in the U.S. Nationalist concerns continue to influence racial debate in the form of Afrocentrism and other expressions of identity politics.

Taking the range of politically organized racial projects as a whole, we can "map" the current pattern of racial formation at the level of the public sphere, the "macro-level" in which public debate and mobilization takes place.[14] But important as this is, the terrain on which racial formation occurs is broader yet.

Racial Formation as Everyday Experience

At the micro-social level, racial projects also link signification and structure, not so much as efforts to shape policy or define large-scale meaning, but as the applications of "common sense." To see racial projects operating at the level of everyday life, we have only to examine the many ways in which, often unconsciously, we "notice" race.

One of the first things we notice about people when we meet them (along with their sex) is their race. We utilize race to provide clues about

12. A familiar example is use of racial "code words." Recall George Bush's manipulations of racial fear in the 1988 "Willie Horton" ads, or Jesse Helms's use of the coded term "quota" in his 1990 campaign against Harvey Gants.

13. From this perspective, far right racial projects can also be interpreted as "nationalist." See Ronald Walters, "White Racial Nationalism in the United States," *Without Prejudice* Vol. I, no. 1 (Fall 1987).

14. To be sure, any effort to divide racial formation patterns according to social structural location—"macro" vs. "micro," for example—is necessarily an analytic device. In the concrete, there is no such dividing line. See Winant, "Where Culture Meets Structure."

who a person is. This fact is made painfully obvious when we encounter someone whom we cannot conveniently racially categorize—someone who is, for example, racially "mixed" or of an ethnic/racial group we are not familiar with. Such an encounter becomes a source of discomfort and momentarily a crisis of racial meaning.

Our ability to interpret racial meanings depends on preconceived notions of a racialized social structure. Comments such as, "Funny, you don't look black," betray an underlying image of what black should be. We expect people to act out their apparent racial identities; indeed we become disoriented when they do not. The black banker harassed by police while walking in casual clothes through his own well-off neighborhood, the Latino or white kid rapping in perfect Afro patois, the unending *faux pas* committed by whites who assume that the non-whites they encounter are servants or tradespeople, the belief that non-white colleagues are less qualified persons hired to fulfill affirmative action guidelines, indeed the whole gamut of racial stereotypes—that "white men can't jump," that Asians can't dance, etc., etc.—all testify to the way a racialized social structure shapes racial experience and conditions meaning. Analysis of such stereotypes reveals the always present, already active link between our view of the social structure—its demography, its laws, its customs, its threats—and our conception of what race means.

Conversely, our ongoing interpretation of our experience in racial terms shapes our relations to the institutions and organizations through which we are imbedded in social structure. Thus we expect differences in skin color, or other racially coded characteristics, to explain social differences. Temperament, sexuality, intelligence, athletic ability, aesthetic preferences, and so on are presumed to be fixed and discernible from the palpable mark of race. Such diverse questions as our confidence and trust in others (for example, clerks or salespeople, media figures, neighbors), our sexual preferences and romantic images, our tastes in music, films, dance, or sports, and our very ways of talking, walking, eating, and dreaming become racially coded simply because we live in a society where racial awareness is so pervasive. Thus in ways too comprehensive even to monitor consciously, and despite periodic calls—neoconservative and otherwise—for us to ignore race and adopt "color-blind" racial attitudes, skin color "differences" continue to rationalize distinct treatment of racially identified individuals and groups.

To summarize the argument so far: the theory of racial formation suggests that society is suffused with racial projects, large and small, to which all are subjected. This racial "subjection" is quintessentially ideological. Everybody learns some combination, some version, of the rules of racial classification, and of her own racial identity, often without obvious teaching or conscious inculcation. Thus we are inserted in a comprehensively racialized social structure. Race becomes "common sense"—a way of comprehending, explaining, and acting in the world. A vast web of racial projects mediates between the discursive or representational means in which race is identified and signified on the one hand, and the institutional and organizational forms in which it is routinized and standardized on the other. These projects are the heart of the racial formation process.

Under such circumstances, it is not possible to represent race discursively without simultaneously locating it, explicitly or implicitly, in a social structural (and historical) context. Nor is it possible to organize, maintain, or transform social structures without simultaneously engaging, once more either explicitly or implicitly, in racial signification. Racial formation, therefore, is a kind of synthesis, an outcome, of the interaction of racial projects on a society-wide level. These projects are, of course, vastly different in scope and effect. They include large-scale public action, state activities, and interpretations of racial conditions in artistic, journalistic, or academic fora,[15] as well as the seemingly infinite number of racial judgments and practices we carry out at the level of individual experience.

Since racial formation is always historically situated, our understanding of the significance of race, and of the way race structures society, has changed enormously over time. The processes of racial formation we encounter today, the racial projects large and small which structure U.S. society in so many ways, are merely the present-day outcomes of a complex historical evolution. The contemporary racial order remains transient. By knowing something of how it evolved, we can perhaps better discern where it is heading. We therefore turn next to a historical survey of the racial formation process, and the conflicts and debates it has engendered.

The Evolution of Modern Racial Awareness

The identification of distinctive human groups, and their association with differences in physical appearance, goes back to prehistory, and can be found in the earliest documents—in the Bible, for example, or in Herodotus. But the emergence of a modern conception of race does not occur until the rise of Europe and the arrival of Europeans in the Americas. Even the hostility and suspicion with which Christian Europe viewed its two significant non-Christian "Others"—The Muslims and the Jews—cannot be viewed as more than a rehearsal for racial formation,

15. We are not unaware, for example, that publishing this work is in itself a racial project.

since these antagonisms, for all their bloodletting and chauvinism, were always and everywhere religiously interpreted.[16]

It was only when European explorers reached the Western Hemisphere, when the oceanic seal separating the "old" and the "new" worlds was breached, that the distinctions and categorizations fundamental to a racialized social structure, and to a discourse of race, began to appear. The European explorers were the advance guard of merchant capitalism, which sought new openings for trade. What they found exceeded their wildest dreams, for never before and never again in human history has an opportunity for the appropriation of wealth remotely approached that presented by the "discovery."[17]

But the Europeans also "discovered" people, people who looked and acted differently. These "natives" challenged their "discoverers'" preexisting conceptions of the origins and possibilities of the human species.[18] The representation and interpretation of the meaning of the indigenous peoples' existence became a crucial matter, one which would affect the outcome of the enterprise of conquest. For the "discovery" raised disturbing questions as to whether *all* could be considered part of the same "family of man," and more practically, the extent to which native peoples could be exploited and enslaved. Thus religious debates flared over the attempt to reconcile the various Christian metaphysics with the existence of peoples who were more "different" than any whom Europe had previously known.[19]

16. Antisemitism only began to be racialized in the 18th century, as George L. Mosse clearly shows in his important *Toward the Final Solution: A History of European Racism* (New York: Howard Fertig, 1978)

17. As Marx put it:

The discovery of gold and silver in America, the extirpation, enslavement, and entombment in mines of the aboriginal population, the beginning of the conquest and looting of the East Indies, the turning of Africa into a warren for the commercial hunting of blackskins, signalized the rosy dawn of the era of capitalist production. These idyllic proceedings are the chief moments of primitive accumulation. (Karl Marx, *Capital*, Vol. 1 [New York: International Publishers, 1967] p. 751.)

David E. Stannard argues that the wholesale slaughter perpetrated upon the native peoples of the Western hemisphere is unequalled in history, even in our own bloody century. See his *American Holocaust: Columbus and the Conquest of the New World* (New York: Oxford University Press, 1992).

18. Winthrop Jordan provides a detailed account of the sources of European attitudes about color and race in *White Over Black: American Attitudes Toward the Negro, 1550–1812* (New York: Norton, 1977 [1968]) pp. 3–43.

19. In a famous instance, a 1550 debate in Valladolid pitted the philosopher and translator of Aristotle, Ginés de Sepúlveda, against the Dominican Bishop of the

In practice, of course, the seizure of territories and goods, the introduction of slavery through the *encomeienda* and other forms of coerced native labor, and then through the organization of the African slave trade—not to mention the practice of outright extermination—all presupposed a worldview which distinguished Europeans, as children of God, full-fledged human beings, etc., from "Others." Given the dimensions and the ineluctability of the European onslaught, given the conquerors' determination to appropriate both labor and goods, and given the presence of an axiomatic and unquestioned Christianity among them, the ferocious division of society into Europeans and "Others" soon coalesced. This was true despite the famous 16th-century theological and philosophical debates about the identity of indigenous peoples.[20]

Indeed debates about the nature of the "Others" reached their practical limits with a certain dispatch. Plainly they would never touch the essential: nothing, after all, would induce the Europeans to pack up and go home. We cannot examine here the early controversies over the status of American souls. We simply wish to emphasize that the "discovery" signalled a break from the previous proto-racial awareness by which Europe contemplated its "Others" in a relatively disorganized fashion. In other words, the "conquest of America" was not simply an epochal historical

---

Mexican state of Chiapas, Bartolomé de Las Casas. Discussing the native peoples, Sepúlveda argued that:

> In wisdom, skill, virtue and humanity, these people are as inferior to the Spaniards as children are to adults and women to men; there is as great a difference between them as there is between savagery and forbearance, between violence and moderation, almost—I am inclined to say, as between monkeys and men (Sepúlveda, *Democrates Alter,* quoted in Tsvetan Todorov, *The Conquest of America: The Question of the Other* [New York: Harper and Row, 1984], p. 153).

In contrast, Las Casas defended the humanity and equality of the native peoples, both in terms of their way of life—which he idealized as one of innocence, gentleness, and generosity—and in terms of their readiness for conversion to Catholicism, which for him as for Sepúlveda was the true and universal religion (Las Casas, "Letter to the Council of the Indies," quoted ibid., p. 163). William E. Connolly interrogates the linkages proposed by Todorov between early Spanish colonialism and contemporary conceptions of identity and difference in *Identity/Difference: Democratic Negotiations of Political Paradox* (Ithaca: Cornell University Press, 1991) pp. 40–48.

20. In Virginia, for example, it took about two decades after the establishment of European colonies to extirpate the indigenous people of the greater vicinity; fifty years after the establishment of the first colonies, the elaboration of slave codes establishing race as *prima facie* evidence for enslaved status was well under way. See Jordan, *White Over Black.*

event—however unparalleled in its importance. It was also the advent of a consolidated social structure of exploitation, appropriation, domination. Its representation, first in religious terms, but soon enough in scientific and political ones, initiated modern racial awareness.

The conquest, therefore, was the first—and given the dramatic nature of the case, perhaps the greatest—racial formation project. Its significance was by no means limited to the Western Hemisphere, for it began the work of constituting Europe as the metropole, the center, of a group of empires which could take, as Marx would later write, "the globe for a theater."[21] It represented this new imperial structure as a struggle between civilization and barbarism, and implicated in this representation all the great European philosophies, literary traditions, and social theories of the modern age.[22] In short, just as the noise of the "big bang" still resonates through the universe, so the overdetermined construction of world "civilization" as a product of the rise of Europe and the subjugation of the rest of us, still defines the race concept.

From Religion to Science

After the initial depredations of conquest, religious justifications for racial difference gradually gave way to scientific ones. By the time of the Enlightenment, a general awareness of race was pervasive, and most of the great philosophers of Europe, such as Hegel, Kant, Hume, and Locke, had issued virulently racist opinions.

The problem posed by race during the late 18th century was markedly different than it had been in the age of "discovery," expropriation, and slaughter. The social structures in which race operated were no longer primarily those of military conquest and plunder, nor of the establishment of thin beachheads of colonization on the edge of what had once seemed a limitless wilderness. Now the issues were much more complicated: nation-building, establishment of national economies in the world trading system, resistance to the arbitrary authority of monarchs, and the assertion of the "natural rights" of "man," including the right of revolution.[23] In such a situation, racially organized exploitation, in the form of slavery, the expansion of colonies, and the continuing expulsion of native peoples, was both necessary and newly difficult to justify.

21. Marx, *Capital,* p. 751.

22. Edward W. Said, *Culture and Imperialism* (New York: Alfred A. Knopf, 1993).

23. David Brion Davis, *The Problem of Slavery in the Age of Revolution* (Ithaca: Cornell University Press, 1975).

The invocation of scientific criteria to demonstrate the "natural" basis of racial hierarchy was both a logical consequence of the rise of this form of knowledge, and an attempt to provide a more subtle and nuanced account of human complexity in the new, "enlightened" age. Spurred on by the classificatory scheme of living organisms devised by Linnaeus in *Systema Naturae* (1735), many scholars in the 18th and 19th centuries dedicated themselves to the identification and ranking of variations in humankind. Race was conceived as a *biological* concept, a matter of species. Voltaire wrote that "the negro race is a species of men (sic) as different from ours . . . as the breed of spaniels is from that of greyhounds," and in a formulation echoing down from his century to our own, declared that

> If their understanding is not of a different nature from ours . . . , it is at least greatly inferior. They are not capable of any great application or association of ideas, and seem formed neither for the advantages nor the abuses of philosophy.[24]

Jefferson, the preeminent exponent of the Enlightenment doctrine of "the rights of man" on North American shores, echoed these sentiments:

> In general their existence appears to participate more of sensation than reflection. . . . [I]n memory they are equal to whites, in reason much inferior . . . [and] in imagination they are dull, tasteless, and anomalous. . . . I advance it therefore . . . that the blacks, whether originally a different race, or made distinct by time and circumstances, are inferior to the whites. . . . Will not a lover of natural history, then, one who views the gradations in all the animals with the eye of philosophy, excuse an effort to keep those in the department of Man (sic) as distinct as nature has formed them?[25]

Such claims of species distinctiveness among humans justified the inequitable allocation of political and social rights, while still upholding the doctrine of "the rights of man." The quest to obtain a precise scientific definition of race sustained debates which continue to rage today. Yet despite efforts ranging from Dr. Samuel Morton's studies of cranial

24. Quoted in Thomas F. Gossett, *Race: The History of an Idea in America* (New York: Schocken Books, 1965) p. 45.

25. *Thomas Jefferson, Notes on Virginia* [1787], Merrill D. Peterson, *Writings of Thomas Jefferson* (New York: The Library of America, 1984) pp. 264–66, 270. Thanks to Kimberly Benston for drawing our attention to this passage.

capacity[26] to contemporary attempts to base racial classification on shared gene pools,[27] the concept of race has defied biological definition.

In the 19th century, Count Joseph Arthur de Gobineau drew upon the most respected scientific studies of his day to compose his four-volume *Essay on the Inequality of Races* (1853–1855).[28] He not only greatly influenced the racial thinking of the period, but his themes would be echoed in the racist ideologies of the next one hundred years: beliefs that superior races produced superior cultures and that racial intermixtures resulted in the degradation of the superior racial stock. These ideas found expression, for instance, in the eugenics movement launched by Darwin's cousin, Francis Galton, which had an immense impact on scientific and sociopolitical thought in Europe and the U.S.[29] In the wake of civil war and emancipation, and with immigration from southern and Eastern Europe as well as East Asia running high, the U.S. was particularly fertile ground for notions such as social darwinism and eugenics.

Attempts to discern the *scientific meaning* of race continue to the present

26. Proslavery physician Samuel George Morton (1799–1851) compiled a collection of 800 crania from all parts of the world which formed the sample for his studies of race. Assuming that the larger the size of the cranium translated into greater intelligence, Morton established a relationship between race and skull capacity. Gossett reports that "In 1849, one of his studies included the following results: the English skulls in his collection proved to be the largest, with an average cranial capacity of 96 cubic inches. The Americans and Germans were rather poor seconds, both with cranial capacities of 90 cubic inches. At the bottom of the list were the Negroes with 83 cubic inches, the Chinese with 82, and the Indians with 79." Gossett, *Race,* p. 74. More recently, Steven Jay Gould has reexamined Morton's data, and shown that his research data were deeply, though unconsciously, manipulated to agree with his "a priori conviction about racial ranking" (Gould, *The Mismeasure of Man* (New York: W. W. Norton, 1981) pp. 50–69).

27. Definitions of race founded upon a common pool of genes have not held up when confronted by scientific research which suggests that the differences *within* a given human population are every bit as great as those *between* populations. See L. L. Cavali-Sforza, "The Genetics of Human Populations," *Scientific American* (September 1974) pp. 81–89.

28. A fascinating summary critique of Gobineau is provided in Tsvetan Todorov, *On Human Diversity: Nationalism, Racism, and Exoticism in French Thought,* trans. Catherine Porter (Cambridge, MA: Harvard University Press, 1993), esp. pp. 129–40.

29. Two recent histories of eugenics are Allen Chase, *The Legacy of Malthus* (New York: Knopf, 1977); Daniel J. Kevles, *In the Name of Eugenics: Genetics and the Uses of Human Heredity* (New York: Knopf, 1985).

day. For instance, an essay by Arthur Jensen which argued that hereditary factors shape intelligence not only revived the "nature or nurture" controversy, but also raised highly volatile questions about racial equality itself.[30] All such attempts seek to remove the concept of race from the historical context in which it arose and developed. They employ an *essentialist* approach which suggests instead that the truth of race is a matter of innate characteristics, of which skin color and other physical attributes provide only the most obvious, and in some respects most superficial, indicators.

From Science to Politics

It has taken scholars more than a century to reject biologistic notions of race in favor of an approach which regards race as a *social* concept. This trend has been slow and uneven, and even today remains somewhat embattled, but its overall direction seems clear. At the turn of the century Max Weber discounted biological explanations for racial conflict and instead highlighted the social and political factors which engendered such conflict.[31] W. E. B. Du Bois argued for a sociopolitical definition of race by identifying "the color line" as "the problem of the 20th century."[32] Pioneering cultural anthropologist Franz Boas rejected attempts to link racial identifications and cultural traits, labelling as pseudoscientific any assumption of a continuum of "higher" and "lower" cultural groups.[33]

30. Arthur Jensen, "How Much Can We Boost IQ and Scholastic Achievement?" *Harvard Educational Review* 39 (1969) pp. 1–123.

31. See Weber, *Economy and Society*, Vol. I (Berkeley: University of California Press, 1978), pp. 385–87; Ernst Moritz Manasse, "Max Weber on Race," *Social Research*, Vol. 14 (1947) pp. 191–221.

32. Du Bois, *The Souls of Black Folk* (New York: Penguin, 1989 [1903]), p. 13. Du Bois himself wrestled heavily with the conflict between a fully sociohistorical conception of race, and the more essentialized and deterministic vision he encountered as a student in Berlin. In "The Conservation of Races" (1897) we can see his first mature effort to resolve this conflict in a vision which combined racial solidarity and a commitment to social equality. See Du Bois, "The Conservation of Races," in Dan S. Green and Edwin D. Driver, eds., *W. E. B. Du Bois on Sociology and the Black Community* (Chicago: University of Chicago Press, 1978) pp. 238–49; Manning Marable, *W. E. B. Du Bois: Black Radical Democrat* (Boston: Twayne, 1986) pp. 35–38. For a contrary, and we believe incorrect reading, see Appiah, *In My Father's House*, pp. 28–46.

33. A good collection of Boas's work is George W. Stocking, ed., *The Shaping of American Anthropology, 1883–1911: A Franz Boas Reader* (Chicago: University of Chicago Press, 1974).

Other early exponents of social, as opposed to biological, views of race included Robert E. Park, founder of the "Chicago school" of sociology, and Alain Leroy Locke, philosopher and theorist of the Harlem Renaissance.[34]

Perhaps more important than these and subsequent intellectual efforts, however, were the political struggles of racially defined groups themselves. Waged all around the globe under a variety of banners such as anti-colonialism and civil rights, these battles to challenge various structural and cultural racisms have been a major feature of 20th-century politics. The racial horrors of the 20th century—colonial slaughter and apartheid, the genocide of the holocaust, and the massive bloodlettings required to end these evils—have also indelibly marked the theme of race as a political issue *par excellence.*

As a result of prior efforts and struggles, we have now reached the point of fairly general agreement that race is not a biologically given but rather a socially constructed way of differentiating human beings. While a tremendous achievement, the transcendence of biologistic conceptions of race does not provide any reprieve from the dilemmas of racial injustice and conflict, nor from controversies over the significance of race in the present. Views of race as socially constructed simply recognize the fact that these conflicts and controversies are now more properly framed on the terrain of politics. By privileging politics in the analysis which follows we do not mean to suggest that race has been displaced as a concern of scientific inquiry, or that struggles over cultural representation are no longer important. We do argue, however, that race is now a preeminently political phenomenon. Such an assertion invites examination of the evolving role of racial politics in the U.S. This is the subject to which we now turn.

Dictatorship, Democracy, Hegemony

For most of its existence both as European colony and as an independent nation, the U.S. was a *racial dictatorship.* From 1607 to 1865—258 years—most non-whites were firmly eliminated from the sphere of poli-

---

34. Robert E. Park's *Race and Culture* (Glencoe, IL: Free Press, 1950) can still provide insight; see also Stanford H. Lyman, *Militarism, Imperialism, and Racial Accommodation: An Analysis and Interpretation of the Early Writings of Robert E. Park* (Fayetteville: University of Arkansas Press, 1992); Locke's views are concisely expressed in Alain Leroy Locke, *Race Contacts and Interracial Relations,* ed. Jeffrey C. Stewart (Washington, DC: Howard University Press, 1992), originally a series of lectures given at Howard University.

tics.[35] After the Civil War there was the brief egalitarian experiment of Reconstruction which terminated ignominiously in 1877. In its wake followed almost a century of legally sanctioned segregation and denial of the vote, nearly absolute in the South and much of the Southwest, less effective in the North and far West, but formidable in any case.[36] These barriers fell only in the mid-1960s, a mere quarter-century ago. Nor did the successes of the black movement and its allies mean that all obstacles to their political participation had now been abolished. Patterns of racial inequality have proven, unfortunately, to be quite stubborn and persistent.

It is important, therefore, to recognize that in many respects, racial dictatorship is the norm against which all U.S. politics must be measured. The centuries of racial dictatorship have had three very large consequences: first, they defined "American" identity as white, as the negation of racialized "otherness"—at first largely African and indigenous, later Latin American and Asian as well.[37] This negation took shape in both law and custom, in public institutions and in forms of cultural representation. It became the archetype of hegemonic rule in the U.S. It was the successor to the conquest as the "master" racial project.

Second, racial dictatorship organized (albeit sometimes in an incoherent and contradictory fashion) the "color line" rendering it the fundamental division in U.S. society. The dictatorship elaborated, articulated, and drove racial divisions not only through institutions, but also through psyches, extending up to our own time the racial obsessions of the conquest and slavery periods.

Third, racial dictatorship consolidated the oppositional racial consciousness and organization originally framed by marronage[38] and slave revolts, by indigenous resistance, and by nationalisms of various sorts. Just

---

35. Japanese, for example, could not become naturalized citizens until passage of the 1952 McCarran-Walter Act. It took over 160 years, since the passage of the Law of 1790, to allow all "races" to be eligible for naturalization.

36. Especially when we recall that until around 1960, the majority of blacks, the largest racially defined minority group, lived in the South.

37. Toni Morrison, *Playing in the Dark: Whiteness and the Literary Imagination* (Cambridge, MA: Harvard University Press, 1992); Richard Drinnon, *Facing West: The Metaphysics of Indian-Hating and Empire-Building* (Minneapolis: University of Minnesota Press, 1980; Michael Paul Rogin, *Fathers and Children: Andrew Jackson and the Subjugation of the American Indian* (New York: Knopf, 1975).

38. This term refers to the practice, widespread throughout the Americas, whereby runaway slaves formed communities in remote areas, such as swamps, mountains, or forests, often in alliance with dispossessed indigenous peoples.

as the conquest created the "native" where once there had been Pequot, Iroquois, or Tutelo, so too it created the "black" where once there had been Asante or Ovimbundu, Yoruba or Bakongo.

The transition from a racial dictatorship to a racial democracy has been a slow, painful, and contentious one; it remains far from complete. A recognition of the abiding presence of racial dictatorship, we contend, is crucial for the development of a theory of racial formation in the U.S. It is also crucial to the task of relating racial formation to the broader context of political practice, organization, and change.

In this context, a key question arises: in what way is racial formation related to politics as a whole? How, for example, does race articulate with other axes of oppression and difference—most importantly class and gender—along which politics is organized today?

The answer, we believe, lies in the concept of *hegemony*. Antonio Gramsci—the Italian communist who placed this concept at the center of his life's work—understood it as the conditions necessary, in a given society, for the achievement and consolidation of rule. He argued that hegemony was always constituted by a combination of coercion and consent. Although rule can be obtained by force, it cannot be secured and maintained, especially in modern society, without the element of consent. Gramsci conceived of consent as far more than merely the legitimation of authority. In his view, consent extended to the incorporation by the ruling group of many of the key interests of subordinated groups, often to the explicit disadvantage of the rulers themselves.[39] Gramsci's treatment of hegemony went even farther: he argued that in order to consolidate their hegemony, ruling groups must elaborate and maintain a popular system of ideas and practices—through education, the media, religion, folk wisdom, etc.—which he called "common sense." It is through its production and its adherence to this "common sense," this ideology (in the broadest sense of the term), that a society gives its consent to the way in which it is ruled.[40]

These provocative concepts can be extended and applied to an understanding of racial rule. In the Americas, the conquest represented the violent introduction of a new form of rule whose relationship with those it subjugated was almost entirely coercive. In the U.S., the origins of racial

39. Antonio Gramsci, *Selections from the Prison Notebooks*, edited and translated by Quintin Hoare and Geoffrey Nowell Smith (New York: International Publishers, 1971) p. 182.

40. Anne Showstack Sassoon, *Gramsci's Politics*, 2nd ed. (London: Hutchinson, 1987); Sue Golding, *Gramsci's Democratic Theory: Contributions to Post-Liberal Democracy* (Toronto: University of Toronto Press, 1992).

division, and of racial signification and identity formation, lie in a system of rule which was extremely dictatorial. The mass murders and expulsions of indigenous people, and the enslavement of Africans, surely evoked and inspired little consent in their founding moments.

Over time, however, the balance of coercion and consent began to change. It is possible to locate the origins of hegemony right within the heart of racial dictatorship, for the effort to possess the oppressor's tools— religion and philosophy in this case—was crucial to emancipation (the effort to possess oneself). As Ralph Ellison reminds us, "The slaves often took the essence of the aristocratic ideal (as they took Christianity) with far more seriousness than their masters."[41] In their language, in their religion with its focus on the Exodus theme and on Jesus's tribulations, in their music with its figuring of suffering, resistance, perseverance, and transcendence, in their interrogation of a political philosophy which sought perpetually to rationalize their bondage in a supposedly "free" society, the slaves incorporated elements of racial rule into their thought and practice, turning them against their original bearers.

Racial rule can be understood as a slow and uneven historical process which has moved from dictatorship to democracy, from domination to hegemony. In this transition, hegemonic forms of racial rule—those based on consent—eventually came to supplant those based on coercion. Of course, before this assertion can be accepted, it must be qualified in important ways. By no means has the U.S. established racial democracy at the end of the century, and by no means is coercion a thing of the past. But the sheer complexity of the racial questions U.S. society confronts today, the welter of competing racial projects and contradictory racial experiences which Americans undergo, suggests that hegemony is a useful and appropriate term with which to characterize contemporary racial rule.

Our key theoretical notion of racial projects helps to extend and broaden the question of rule. Projects are the building blocks not just of racial formation, but of hegemony in general. Hegemony operates by simultaneously structuring and signifying. As in the case of racial opposition, gender- or class-based conflict today links structural inequity and injustice on the one hand, and identifies and represents its subjects on the other. The success of modern-day feminism, for example, has depended on its ability to reinterpret gender as a matter of both injustice and identity/difference.

Today, political opposition necessarily takes shape on the terrain of hegemony. Far from ruling principally through exclusion and coercion

41. Ralph Ellison, *Shadow and Act* (New York: New American Library, 1966) p. xiv.

(though again, these are hardly absent) hegemony operates by including its subjects, incorporating its opposition. *Pace* both Marxists and liberals, there is no longer any universal or privileged region of political action or discourse.[42] Race, class, and gender all represent potential antagonisms whose significance is no longer given, if it ever was.

Thus race, class, and gender (as well as sexual orientation) constitute "regions" of hegemony, areas in which certain political projects can take shape. They share certain obvious attributes in that they are all "socially constructed," and they all consist of a field of projects whose common feature is their linkage of social structure and signification.

Going beyond this, it is crucial to emphasize that race, class, and gender, are not fixed and discrete categories, and that such "regions" are by no means autonomous. They overlap, intersect, and fuse with each other in countless ways. Such mutual determinations have been illustrated by Patricia Hill Collins's survey and theoretical synthesis of the themes and issues of black feminist thought.[43] They are also evident in Evelyn Nakano Glenn's work on the historical and contemporary racialization of domestic and service work.[44] In many respects, race is gendered and gender is racialized. In institutional and everyday life, any clear demarcation of specific forms of oppression and difference is constantly being disrupted.

There are no clear boundaries between these "regions" of hegemony, so political conflicts will often invoke some or all these themes simultaneously. Hegemony is tentative, incomplete, and "messy." For example, the 1991 Hill-Thomas hearings, with their intertwined themes of race and gender inequality, and their frequent genuflections before the altar of hard work and upward mobility, managed to synthesize various race, gender, and class projects in a particularly explosive combination.[45]

What distinguishes political opposition today—racial or otherwise—is its insistence on identifying itself and speaking for itself, its determined

42. Chantal Mouffe makes a related argument in "Radical Democracy: Modern or Postmodern?" in Andrew Ross, ed., *Universal Abandon: The Politics of Postmodernism* (Minneapolis: University of Minnesota Press, 1988).

43. Patricia Hill Collins, *Black Feminist Thought: Knowledge, Consciousness, and the Politics of Empowerment* (New York and London: Routledge, 1991).

44. Evelyn Nakano Glenn, "From Servitude to Service Work: Historical Continuities in the Racial Division of Paid Reproductive Labor," *Signs: Journal of Women in Culture & Society*, Vol. 18, no. 1 (Autumn 1992).

45. Toni Morrison, ed., *Race-ing Justice, En-gendering Power: Essays on Anita Hill, Clarence Thomas, and the Construction of Social Reality* (New York: Pantheon, 1992).

demand for the transformation of the social structure, its refusal of the "common sense" understandings which the hegemonic order imposes. Nowhere is this refusal of "common sense" more needed, or more imperilled, than in our understanding of racism.

What Is Racism?

Since the ambiguous triumph of the civil rights movement in the mid-1960s, clarity about what racism means has been eroding. The concept entered the lexicon of "common sense" only in the 1960s. Before that, although the term had surfaced occasionally,[46] the problem of racial injustice and inequality was generally understood in a more limited fashion, as a matter of prejudiced attitudes or bigotry on the one hand,[47] and discriminatory practices on the other.[48] Solutions, it was believed, would therefore involve the overcoming of such attitudes, the achievement of tolerance, the acceptance of "brotherhood," etc., and the passage of laws which prohibited discrimination with respect to access to public accommodations, jobs, education, etc. The early civil rights movement explicitly reflected such views. In its espousal of integration and its quest for a "beloved community" it sought to overcome racial prejudice. In its litigation activities and agitation for civil rights legislation it sought to challenge discriminatory practices.

The later 1960s, however, signalled a sharp break with this vision. The emergence of the slogan "black power" (and soon after, of "brown power," "red power," and "yellow power"), the wave of riots that swept the urban ghettos from 1964 to 1968, and the founding of radical movement organizations of nationalist and Marxist orientation, coincided with the recognition that racial inequality and injustice had much deeper roots. They were

46. For example, in Magnus Hirschfeld's prescient book, *Racism* (London: Victor Gollancz, 1938).

47. This was the framework, employed in the crucial study of Myrdal and his associates; see Gunnar Myrdal, *An American Dilemma: The Negro Problem and Modern Democracy*, 20th Anniversary Edition (New York: Harper and Row, 1962 [1944]). See also the articles by Thomas F. Pettigrew and George Fredrickson in Pettigrew et al., *Prejudice: Selections from The Harvard Encyclopedia of American Ethnic Groups* (Cambridge, MA: The Belknap Press of Harvard University, 1982).

48. On discrimination, see Frederickson in ibid. In an early essay which explicitly sought to modify the framework of the Myrdal study, Robert K. Merton recognized that prejudice and discrimination need not coincide, and indeed could combine in a variety of ways. See Merton, "Discrimination and the American Creed," in R. M. McIver, ed., *Discrimination and National Welfare* (New York: Harper and Row, 1949).

not simply the product of prejudice, nor was discrimination only a matter of intentionally informed action. Rather, prejudice was an almost unavoidable outcome of patterns of socialization which were "bred in the bone," affecting not only whites but even minorities themselves.[49] Discrimination, far from manifesting itself only (or even principally) through individual actions or conscious policies, was a structural feature of U.S. society, the product of centuries of systematic exclusion, exploitation, and disregard of racially defined minorities.[50] It was this combination of relationships—prejudice, discrimination, and institutional inequality— which defined the concept of racism at the end of the 1960s.

Such a synthesis was better able to confront the political realities of the period. Its emphasis on the structural dimensions of racism allowed it to address the intransigence which racial injustice and inequality continued to exhibit, even after discrimination had supposedly been outlawed[51] and

49. Gordon W. Allport, *The Nature of Prejudice* (Cambridge, MA: Addison-Wesley, 1954) remains a classic work in the field; see also Philomena Essed, *Understanding Everyday Racism: An Interdisciplinary Theory* (Newbury Park, CA: Sage, 1991). A good overview of black attitudes toward black identities is provided in William E. Cross, Jr., *Shades of Black: Diversity in African-American Identity* (Philadelphia: Temple University Press, 1991).

50. Stokely Carmichael and Charles V. Hamilton first popularized the notion of "institutional" forms of discrimination in *Black Power: The Politics of Liberation in America* (New York: Vintage, 1967), although the basic concept certainly predated that work. Indeed, President Lyndon Johnson made a similar argument in his 1965 speech at Howard University:

But freedom is not enough. You do not wipe away the scars of centuries by saying: Now you are free to go where you want, do as you desire, and choose the leaders you please.

You do not take a person who, for years, has been hobbled by chains and liberate him (sic), bring him up to the starting line of a race and then say, "You are free to compete with all the others," and still justly believe that you have been completely fair.

Thus it is not enough just to open the gates of opportunity. All our citizens must have the opportunity to walk through those gates.

This is the next and more profound stage of the battle for civil rights. We seek not just freedom but opportunity—not just legal equity but human ability—not just equality as a right but equality as a fact and as a result. (Lyndon B. Johnson, "To Fulfill These Rights," reprinted in Lee Rainwater and William L. Yance, *The Moynihan Report and the Politics of Controversy* [Cambridge, MA: MIT Press, 1967, p. 125]).

This speech, delivered at Howard University on June 4, 1965, was written in part by Daniel Patrick Moynihan. A more systematic treatment of the institutional racism approach is David T. Wellman, *Portraits of White Racism* (New York: Cambridge University Press, 1977).

51. From the vantage point of the 1990s, it is possible to question whether discrimination was ever effectively outlawed. The federal retreat from the agenda of integration began almost immediately after the passage of civil rights legislation,

bigoted expression stigmatized. But such an approach also had clear limitations. As Robert Miles has argued, it tended to "inflate" the concept of racism to a point at which it lost precision.[52] If the "institutional" component of racism were so pervasive and deeply rooted, it became difficult to see how the democratization of U.S. society could be achieved, and difficult to explain what progress had been made. The result was a levelling critique which denied any distinction between the Jim Crow era (or even the whole *longue durée* of racial dictatorship since the conquest) and the present. Similarly, if the prejudice component of racism were so deeply inbred, it became difficult to account for the evident hybridity and interpenetration that characterizes civil society in the U.S., as evidenced by the shaping of popular culture, language, and style, for example. The result of the "inflation" of the concept of racism was thus a deep pessimism about any efforts to overcome racial barriers, in the workplace, the community, or any other sphere of lived experience. An overly comprehensive view of racism, then, potentially served as a self-fulfilling prophecy.

Yet the alternative view—which surfaced with a vengeance in the 1970s—urging a return to the conception of racism held before the movement's "radical turn," was equally inadequate. This was the neoconservative perspective, which deliberately restricted its attention to injury done to the individual as opposed to the group, and to advocacy of a color-blind racial policy.[53] Such an approach reduced race to ethnicity,[54] and almost entirely neglected the continuing organization of social inequality and oppression along racial lines. Worse yet, it tended to rationalize racial injustice as a supposedly natural outcome of group attributes in competition.[55]

---

and has culminated today in a series of Supreme Court decisions making violation of these laws almost impossible to prove. See Ezorsky, *Racism and Justice;* Kairys, *With Liberty and Justice for Some.* As we write, the Supreme Court has further restricted antidiscrimination laws in the case of *St. Mary's Honor Center v. Hicks.* See Linda Greenhouse, "Justices Increase Workers' Burden in Job-Bias Cases," *The New York Times,* 26 June 1993, p. 1.

52. Robert Miles, *Racism* (New York and London: Routledge, 1989), esp. chap. 2.

53. The *locus classicus* of this position is Nathan Glazer, *Affirmative Discrimination: Ethnic Inequality and Public Policy,* 2nd ed. (New York: Basic Books, 1978); for more recent formulations, see Murray, *Losing Ground;* Arthur M. Schlesinger, *The Disuniting of America: Reflections on a Multicultural Society* (New York: W. W. Norton, 1992).

54. See Chapter 1.

55. Thomas Sowell, for example, has argued that one's "human capital" is to a

The distinct, and contested, meanings of racism which have been advanced over the past three decades have contributed to an overall crisis of meaning for the concept today. Today, the absence of a clear "common sense" understanding of what racism means has become a significant obstacle to efforts aimed at challenging it. Bob Blauner has noted that in classroom discussions of racism, white and non-white students tend to talk past one another. Whites tend to locate racism in color consciousness and find its absence color-blindness. In so doing, they see the affirmation of difference and racial identity among racially defined minority students as racist. Non-white students, by contrast, see racism as a system of power, and correspondingly argue that blacks, for example, cannot be racist because they lack power. Blauner concludes that there are two "languages" of race, one in which members of racial minorities, especially blacks, see the centrality of race in history and everyday experience, and another in which whites see race as "a peripheral, nonessential reality."[56]

Given this crisis of meaning, and in the absence of any "common sense" understanding, does the concept of racism retain any validity? If so, what view of racism should we adopt? Is a more coherent theoretical approach possible? We believe it is.

We employ racial formation theory to reformulate the concept of racism. Our approach recognizes that racism, like race, has changed over time. It is obvious that the attitudes, practices, and institutions of the epochs of slavery, say, or of Jim Crow, no longer exist today. Employing a similar logic, it is reasonable to question whether concepts of racism which developed in the early days of the post–civil rights era, when the limitations of both moderate reform and militant racial radicalism of various types had not yet been encountered, remain adequate to explain circumstances and conflicts a quarter-century later.

Racial formation theory allows us to differentiate between race and racism. The two concepts should not be used interchangeably. We have argued that race has no fixed meaning, but is constructed and transformed

---

large extent culturally determined. Therefore the state cannot create a false equality which runs counter to the magnitude and persistence of cultural differences. Such attempts at social engineering are likely to produce negative and unintended results: "If social processes are transmitting real differences—in productivity, reliability, cleanliness, sobriety, peacefulness (!)—then attempts to impose politically a very different set of beliefs will necessarily backfire. . . ." (Thomas Sowell, *The Economics and Politics of Race: An International Perspective* (New York: Quill, 1983) p. 252).

56. Bob Blauner, "Racism, Race, and Ethnicity: Some Reflections on the Language of Race" (unpublished manuscript, 1991).

sociohistorically through competing political projects, through the necessary and ineluctable link between the structural and cultural dimensions
of race in the U.S. This emphasis on projects allows us to refocus our
understanding of racism as well, for racism can now be seen as characterizing some, but not all, racial projects.

A racial project can be defined as *racist* if and only if it *creates or
reproduces structures of domination based on essentialist*[57] *categories of race.*
Such a definition recognizes the importance of locating racism within a
fluid and contested history of racially based social structures and
discourses. Thus there can be no timeless and absolute standard for what
constitutes racism, for social structures change and discourses are subject
to rearticulation. Our definition therefore focuses instead on the "work"
essentialism does for domination, and the "need" domination displays to
essentialize the subordinated.

Further, it is important to distinguish racial awareness from racial
essentialism. To attribute merits, allocate values or resources to, and/or
represent individuals or groups on the basis of racial identity should not
be considered racist in and of itself. Such projects may in fact be quite
benign.

Consider the following examples: first, the statement, "Many Asian
Americans are highly entrepreneurial"; second, the organization of an
association of, say, black accountants.

The first racial project, in our view, signifies or represents a racial
category ("Asian Americans") and locates that representation within the
social structure of the contemporary U.S. (in regard to business, class
issues, socialization, etc.). The second racial project is organizational or
social structural, and therefore must engage in racial signification. Black
accountants, the organizers might maintain, have certain common experiences, can offer each other certain support, etc. Neither of these racial
projects is essentialist, and neither can fairly be labelled racist. Of course,
racial representations may be biased or misinterpret their subjects, just as
racially based organizational efforts may be unfair or unjustifiably exclusive. If such were the case, if for instance in our first example the statement
in question were "Asian Americans are naturally entrepreneurial," this
would by our criterion be racist. Similarly, if the effort to organize black
accountants had as its rationale the raiding of clients from white accountants, it would by our criterion be racist as well.

Similarly, to allocate values or resources—let us say, academic
scholarships—on the basis of racial categories is not racist. Scholarships

---

57. Essentialism, it will be recalled, is understood as belief in real, true human
essences, existing outside or impervious to social and historical context.

are awarded on a preferential basis to Rotarians, children of insurance company employees, and residents of the Pittsburgh metropolitan area. Why then should they not also be offered, in particular cases, to Chicanos or Native Americans?

In order to identify a social project as racist, one must in our view demonstrate a link between essentialist representations of race and social structures of domination. Such a link might be revealed in efforts to protect dominant interests, framed in racial terms, from democratizing racial initiatives.[58] But it might also consist of efforts simply to reverse the roles of racially dominant and racially subordinate.[59] There is nothing inherently white about racism.[60]

Obviously a key problem with essentialism is its denial, or flattening, of differences within a particular racially defined group. Members of subordinate racial groups, when faced with racist practices such as exclusion or discrimination, are frequently forced to band together in order to defend their interests (if not, in some instances, their very lives). Such "strategic essentialism" should not, however, be simply equated with the essentialism practiced by dominant groups, nor should it prevent the interrogation of internal group differences.[61]

58. An example would be the "singling out" of members of racially defined minority groups for harsh treatment by authorities, as when police harass and beat randomly chosen ghetto youth, a practice they do not pursue with white suburban youth.

59. For example, the biologistic theories found in Michael Anderson Bradley, *The Iceman Inheritance: Prehistoric Sources of Western Man's Racism, Sexism and Aggression* (Toronto: Dorset, 1978), and in Frances Cress Welsing, *The Isis (Yssis) Papers* (Chicago: Third World Press, 1991).

60. "These remarks should not be interpreted as simply an effort to move the gaze of African-American studies to a different site. I do not want to alter one hierarchy in order to institute another. It is true that I do not want to encourage those totalizing approaches to African-American scholarship which have no drive other than the exchange of dominations—dominant Eurocentric scholarship replaced by dominant Afrocentric scholarship. More interesting is what makes intellectual domination possible; how knowledge is transformed from invasion and conquest to revelation and choice; what ignites and informs the literary imagination, and what forces help establish the parameters of criticism." (Toni Morrison, *Playing in the Dark*, p. 8; emphasis original.)

61. Lisa Lowe states: "The concept of 'strategic essentialism' suggests that it is possible to utilize specific signifiers of ethnic identity, such as Asian American, for the purpose of contesting and disrupting the discourses that exclude Asian Americans, while simultaneously revealing the internal contradictions and slippages of Asian Americans so as to insure that such essentialisms will not be reproduced and

Without question, any abstract concept of racism is severely put to the test by the untidy world of reality. To illustrate our discussion, we analyze the following examples, chosen from current racial issues because of their complexity and the rancorous debates they have engendered:

- Is the allocation of employment opportunities through programs restricted to racially defined minorities, so-called "preferential treatment" or affirmative action policies, racist? Do such policies practice "racism in reverse"? We think not, with certain qualifications. Although such programs necessarily employ racial criteria in assessing eligibility, they do not generally essentialize race, because they seek to overcome specific socially and historically constructed inequalities.[62] Criteria of effectiveness and feasibility, therefore, must be considered in evaluating such programs. They must balance egalitarian and context-specific objectives, such as academic potential or job-related qualifications. It should be acknowledged that such programs often do have deleterious consequences for whites who are not personally the source of the discriminatory practices the programs seek to overcome. In this case, compensatory measures should be enacted to vitiate the charge of "reverse discrimination."[63]
- Is all racism the same, or is there a distinction between white and non-white versions of racism? We have little patience with the argument that racism is solely a white problem, or even a "white disease."[64] The idea that non-whites cannot act in a racist manner, since they do not possess "power," is another variant of this formulation.[65]

---

proliferated by the very apparatuses we seek to disempower." Lisa Lowe, "Heterogeneity, Hybridity, Multiplicity: Marketing Asian American Differences," *Diaspora*, Vol. 1, no. 1 (Spring 1991) p. 39.

62. This view supports Supreme Court decisions taken in the late 1960s and early 1970s, for example in *Griggs v. Duke Power*, 401 U.S. 424 (1971). We agree with Kairys that only ". . . [F]or that brief period in our history, it could accurately be said that governmental discrimination was prohibited by law" (Kairys, *With Liberty and Justice for Some*, p. 144).

63. This analysis draws on Ezorsky, *Racism and Justice*.

64. See for example, Judy H. Katz, *White Awareness: Handbook for Anti-Racism Training* (Norman: University of Oklahoma Press, 1978).

65. The formula "racism equals prejudice plus power" is frequently invoked by our students to argue that only whites can be racist. We have been able to uncover little written analysis to support this view (apart from Katz, ibid., p. 20), but consider that it is itself an example of the essentializing approach we have identi-

For many years now, racism has operated in a more complex fashion than this, sometimes taking such forms as self-hatred or self-aggrandizement at the expense of more vulnerable members of racially subordinate groups.[66] Whites can at times be the victims of racism—by other whites or non-whites—as in the case with anti-Jewish and anti-Arab prejudice. Furthermore, unless one is prepared to argue that there has been no transformation of the U.S. racial order over the years, and that racism consequently has remained unchanged—an essentialist position *par excellence*—it is difficult to contend that racially defined minorities have attained no power or influence, especially in recent years.

Having said this, we still do not consider that all racism is the same. This is because of the crucial importance we place in situating various "racisms" within the dominant hegemonic discourse about race. We have little doubt that the rantings of a Louis Farrakhan or Leonard Jeffries—to pick two currently demonized black ideologues—meet the criteria we have set out for judging a discourse to be racist. But if we compare Jeffries, for example, with a white racist such as Tom Metzger of the White Aryan Resistance, we find the latter's racial project to be far more menacing than the former's. Metzger's views are far more easily associated with an essentializing (and once very powerful) legacy: that of white supremacy and racial dictatorship in the U.S., and fascism in the world at large. Jeffries's project has far fewer examples with which to associate: no more than some ancient African empires and the (usually far less bigoted) radical phase of the black power movement.[67] Thus black supremacy may be an instance of racism, just as its advocacy may be offensive, but it can hardly constitute the threat that white supremacy has represented in the U.S., nor can it be so easily absorbed and rearticulated in the dominant hegemonic discourse on race as white su-

---

fied as central to racism. In the modern world, "power" cannot be reified as a thing which some possess and others don't, but instead constitutes a relational field. The minority student who boldly asserts in class that minorities cannot be racist is surely not entirely powerless. In all but the most absolutist of regimes, resistance to rule itself implies power.

66. To pick but one example among many: writing before the successes of the civil rights movement, E. Franklin Frazier bitterly castigated the collaboration of black elites with white supremacy. See Frazier, *Black Bourgeoisie: The Rise of a New Middle Class in the United States* (New York: The Free Press, 1957).

67. Interestingly, what they share most centrally seems to be their antisemitism.

premacy can. All racisms, all racist political projects, are not the same.

* Is the redrawing—or gerrymandering—of adjacent electoral districts to incorporate large numbers of racially defined minority voters in one, and largely white voters in the other, racist? Do such policies amount to "segregation" of the electorate? Certainly this alternative is preferable to the pre–Voting Rights Act practice of simply denying racial minorities the franchise. But does it achieve the Act's purpose of fostering electoral equality across and within racial lines? In our view such practices, in which the post–1990 redistricting process engaged rather widely—are vulnerable to charges of essentialism. They often operate through "racial lumping," tend to freeze rather than overcome racial inequalities, and frequently subvert or defuse political processes through which racially defined groups could otherwise negotiate their differences and interests. They worsen rather than ameliorate the denial of effective representation to those whom they could not effectively redistrict—since no redrawing of electoral boundaries is perfect, those who get stuck on the "wrong side" of the line are particularly disempowered. Thus we think such policies merit the designation of "tokenism"—a relatively mild form of racism—which they have received.[68]

Parallel to the debates on the concept of race, recent academic and political controversies about the nature of racism have centered on whether it is primarily an ideological or structural phenomenon. Proponents of the former position argue that racism is first and foremost a matter of beliefs and attitudes, doctrines and discourse, which only then give rise to unequal and unjust practices and structures.[69] Advocates of the latter view see racism as primarily a matter of economic stratification, residential segregation, and other institutionalized forms of inequality which then give rise to ideologies of privilege.[70]

68. Having made a similar argument, Lani Guinier, Clinton's nominee to head the Justice Department's Civil Rights Division, was savagely attacked and her nomination ultimately blocked. See Guinier, "The Triumph of Tokenism: The Voting Rights Act and the Theory of Black Electoral Success," *Michigan Law Review* (March 1991).

69. See Miles, *Racism*, p. 77. Much of the current debate over the advisability and legality of banning racist hate speech seems to us to adopt the dubious position that racism is primarily an ideological phenomenon. See Mari J. Matsuda et al., *Words That Wound: Critical Race Theory, Assaultive Speech, and the First Amendment* (Boulder, CO: Westview Press, 1993).

70. Or ideologies which mask privilege by falsely claiming that inequality and injustice have been eliminated. See Wellman, *Portraits of White Racism*.

From the standpoint of racial formation, these debates are fundamentally misguided. They frame the problem of racism in a rigid "either-or" manner. We believe it is crucial to disrupt the fixity of these positions by simultaneously arguing that ideological beliefs have structural consequences, and that social structures give rise to beliefs. Racial ideology and social structure, therefore, mutually shape the nature of racism in a complex, dialectical, and overdetermined manner.

Even those racist projects which at first glance appear chiefly ideological turn out upon closer examination to have significant institutional and social structural dimensions. For example, what we have called "far right" projects appear at first glance to be centrally ideological. They are rooted in biologistic doctrine, after all. The same seems to hold for certain conservative black nationalist projects which have deep commitments to biologism.[71] But the unending stream of racist assaults initiated by the far right, the apparently increasing presence of skinheads in high schools, the proliferation of neo-Nazi computer bulletin boards, and the appearance of racist talk shows on cable access channels, all suggest that the organizational manifestations of the far right racial projects exist and will endure.[72] Perhaps less threatening but still quite worrisome is the diffusion of doctrines of black superiority through some (though by no means all) university-based African American Studies departments and student organizations, surely a serious institutional or structural development.

By contrasts, even those racisms which at first glance appear to be chiefly structural upon closer examination reveal a deeply ideological component. For example, since the racial right abandoned its explicit advocacy of segregation, it has not seemed to uphold—in the main—an ideologically racist project, but more primarily a structurally racist one. Yet this very transformation required tremendous efforts of ideological production. It demanded the rearticulation of civil rights doctrines of equality in suitably conservative form, and indeed the defense of continuing large-scale racial inequality as an outcome preferable to (what its advocates have seen as) the threat to democracy that affirmative action, busing, and large-scale "race-specific" social spending would entail.[73] Even more tellingly, this project took shape through a deeply manipulative coding of subtextual appeals to white racism, notably in a series of political

71. Racial teachings of the Nation of Islam, for example, maintain that whites are the product of a failed experiment by a mad scientist.

72. Elinor Langer, "The American Neo-Nazi Movement Today," *The Nation*, July 16/23, 1990.

73. Such arguments can be found in Nathan Glazer, *Affirmative Discrimination*, Charles Murray, *Losing Ground*, and Arthur M. Schlesinger, Jr., *The Disuniting of America*, among others.

campaigns for high office which have occurred over recent decades. The retreat of social policy from any practical commitment to racial injustice, and the relentless reproduction and divulgation of this theme at the level of everyday life—where whites are now "fed up" with all the "special treatment" received by non-whites, etc.—constitutes the hegemonic racial project at this time. It therefore exhibits an unabashed structural racism all the more brazen because on the ideological or signification level, it adheres to a principle of "treating everyone alike."

In summary, the racism of today is no longer a virtual monolith, as was the racism of yore. Today, racial hegemony is "messy." The complexity of the present situation is the product of a vast historical legacy of structural inequality and invidious racial representation, which has been confronted during the post–World War II period with an opposition more serious and effective than any it had faced before. As we will survey in the chapters to follow, the result is a deeply ambiguous and contradictory spectrum of racial projects, unremittingly conflictual racial politics, and confused and ambivalent racial identities of all sorts. We begin this discussion by addressing racial politics and the state.

Further Reading

Anderson, Margaret, and Patricia Hill Collins, eds. *Race, Class, and Gender: An Anthology.* Belmont, Calif.: Wadsworth, 1992.

Appiah, K. Anthony, and Amy Gutmann. *Color Conscious.* Princeton: Princeton University Press, 1996.

Appiah, Kwame Anthony. *In my Father's House.* Oxford: Oxford University Press, 1992.

Augstein, Hannah F., ed. *Race: The Origins of an Idea, 1760–1850.* Bristol: Thoemmes Press, 1996.

Banton, Michael. *Racial Theories.* Cambridge: Cambridge University Press, 1987.

Bernasconi, Robert, ed. *Race.* Oxford: Blackwell, 2000.

Collins, Patricia Hill. *Black Feminist Thought: Knowledge, Consciousness, and the Politics of Empowerment.* New York: Routledge, 1991.

Count, Earl W., ed. *This Is Race.* New York: Henry Schuman, 1950.

Delgado, Richard, ed. *Critical Race Theory.* Philadelphia: Temple University Press, 1995.

Eze, Emmanuel, ed. *Race and the Enlightenment.* Oxford: Blackwell, 1997.

Fanon, Frantz. *Black Skin, White Masks.* New York: Grove Weidenfeld, 1967.

Goldberg, David T. *Racist Culture.* Oxford: Blackwell, 1993.

Haney López, Ian F. *White by Law: The Legal Construction of Race.* New York: New York University Press, 1996.

Hannaford, Ivan. *Race: The History of an Idea in the West.* Washington, D.C.: Woodrow Wilson Center Press, 1996.

hooks, bell. *Yearning, Race, Gender, and Cultural Politics,* Boston: South End Press, 1996.

Jacobson, Matthew Frye. *Whiteness of a Different Color.* Cambridge, Mass.: Harvard University Press, 1998.

Jordan, Winthrop D. *White over Black: American Attitudes Toward the Negro, 1550–1812.* Chapel Hill: University of North Carolina Press, 1968.

Locke, Alain L. *Race Contacts and Interracial Relations.* Jeffrey C. Stewart, ed. Washington, D.C.: Howard University Press, 1992.

Mills, Charles. *The Racial Contract.* Ithaca: Cornell University Press, 1997.

Outlaw, Lucius. *On Race and Philosophy.* New York: Routledge, 1996.

Poliakov, Leon. *The Aryan Myth.* New York: Basic Books, 1971.

Popkin, Richard H. *Isaac La Peyrère (1596–1676): His Life, Work, and Influence.* Leiden: E. J. Brill, 1987.

Young, Robert J. C. *Colonial Desire: Hybridity in Theory, Culture and Race.* New York: Routledge, 1995.

Zack, Naomi, ed. *Race/Sex.* New York: Routledge, 1997.